THE

SECOND NUCLEAR AGE

THE

SECOND NUCLEAR AGE

Colin S. Gray

LYNNE
RIENNER
PUBLISHERS

BOULDER
LONDON

Published in the United States of America in 1999 by
Lynne Rienner Publishers, Inc.
1800 30th Street, Boulder, Colorado 80301

and in the United Kingdom by
Lynne Rienner Publishers, Inc.
3 Henrietta Street, Covent Garden, London WC2E 8LU

Library of Congress Cataloging-in-Publication Data
Gray, Colin S.
  The second nuclear age / by Colin S. Gray.
    p.   cm.
  Includes bibliographical references and index.
  ISBN 1-55587-331-6 (hc : alk. paper)
  1. Nuclear weapons. 2. Weapons of mass destruction. 3. Security,
International. 4. World politics—1989–   I. Title.
U264.G734   1999
327.1'747—dc21   99-35633
                                                          CIP

British Cataloguing in Publication Data
A Cataloguing in Publication record for this book
is available from the British Library.

Printed and bound in the United States of America

        The paper used in this publication meets the requirements
 ∞ of the American National Standard for Permanence of
        Paper for Printed Library Materials Z39.48-1984.

        5 4 3 2 1

Contents

Foreword, Keith B. Payne   vii
Preface   xi

1   Nuclear Problem, Nuclear Condition   1

2   The Second Nuclear Age:
    The Hunt for Political Context   17

3   Beyond the Fuel Cycle:
    Strategy and the Proliferation Puzzle   47

4   To Confuse Ourselves: Nuclear Fallacies   79

5   Nuclear Strategy   115

6   Coping with a Nuclear Future   153

Bibliography   171
Index   187
About the Book   193

Foreword

Keith B. Payne

The Second Nuclear Age is the most recent of Colin Gray's already prodigious roster of published works. His writings, now familiar in expert defense circles from Washington to Tokyo and all stops in between, span more than two and a half decades. In toto, they earn him the status of one of the West's preeminent civilian strategists. Whenever Professor Gray pens a new title, expectations are high and note must be taken; when that title proclaims the arrival of a "new nuclear age," particular attention is warranted.

The analytic goals identified for *The Second Nuclear Age* are not modest. They are, first, to understand the strategic threats posed by nuclear, chemical, and biological weapons in a dramatically unfamiliar international political context (until now described only by what it is not, i.e., the "post–Cold War period"); and, second, to identify those measures most useful to the West in addressing those threats, including discerning what is and is not worth retaining from Cold War security policies. The enormity of this analytic task is daunting, calling for Gray's obvious mastery of military history, Cold War strategic policies both East and West, the direction of current threats and policies, and a keen insight as to the significance of emerging features of international politics.

Gray's starting point is to observe that Cold War thinking and policy concerning nuclear weapons were shaped decisively by the context of East-West enmity and competition. With the collapse of the Soviet Union and the Warsaw Pact, that context was so altered as to call into question established wisdom and policy involving nuclear weapons. Nevertheless, the security age now dawning remains dominated by the existence of nuclear weapons (with biological weapons emerging as a particularly salient factor). In short, the Eastern bloc's political upheaval of the early 1990s gave birth to a dramatically different security context, albeit one that continues to be shaped decisively by nuclear weapons—hence a "second nuclear age."

Gray's conclusion about the continuing significance of nuclear weapons does not reflect any harkening back to the comfort of long-familiar approaches to strategy and policy; far from it. He poses and addresses without flinching the fundamental questions of the emerging security environment that still only rarely surface in Washington's corridors of power: Western Cold War strategic theory and nuclear policies were creatures of the then-existing bipolar divide. What of that body of thought and policy, if any, is likely to retain integrity in the very different unfolding political conditions, and what new directions may be most useful?

As in the past, Gray is masterful at dissecting and dismantling the illusions du jour that pass for sophistication concerning nuclear weapons and nonproliferation. For example, progressive circles in Washington place enormous significance on the international "nuclear taboo" and the emerging global "norm" against nuclear weapons. These, they confidently claim, have created a solid basis for the West to aim its sights at nuclear abolition. Gray subjects all such views to empirical scrutiny without sentiment and concludes that Washington's obvious longing to move away from nuclear weapons is not shared in key regional capitals. He reminds us that although a "nuclear taboo" shapes much Western thinking, we dare not confuse with reality Washington's vision of a world in its own image. He does not claim that all future ages must be nuclear, but that until the current ratio of vision-to-evidence is reversed, "movement for nuclear abolition is as hopeless as it is well-intentioned."

Indeed, Gray makes the devastating point that a goal underlying at least some of Washington's promotion of the "nuclear taboo" is a security environment wherein the United States' overwhelming conventional force cannot be trumped by regional nuclear powers. Denying the U.S. such an advantage is ample reason alone for some to seek security in nuclear weapons and the threat of escalation. Washington's self-serving, nonproliferation goal carries the seeds of its own demise. Why expect "rogues" to eschew a nuclear security path that NATO trod for decades in response to the Warsaw Pact's conventional force advantages?

In *The Second Nuclear Age,* Gray sets his analytic sights on the strategic meaning of the recent international political upheaval and emerging threats. The topic could not be more significant nor the author more qualified. The result is a text that is original and brilliant, and in classic Gray style, one that does not shy from boldly identifying intellectual chaff. Gray's work is disciplined by his multiple roles: he is both a rigorous academic and an adviser heeded by serious power. *The Second Nuclear Age* is what all too few works can be: it is both scholarly and pertinent, academic without being ponderous. If we are fortunate, as has happened in the past, much of what Gray presents in these pages will initially raise considerable ire, then be repeated by others as their own, and ultimately become the basis for actual policy.

Keith B. Payne is chairman of the National Institute for Public Policy, Fairfax, Virginia, and adjunct professor at Georgetown University.

Preface

A t the close of the twentieth century, Western governments and
peoples do not want to think strategically about nuclear
weapons and do not know how to think strategically about biological and chemical arms. *The Second Nuclear Age* is designed to help
correct those deficiencies.

The drive behind this book is the conviction that Western defense communities are doing everything about what have come to
be termed weapons of mass destruction (WMD)—except take
them seriously as a source of major menace. By way of terse explanation, I cite a few examples: in 1997, the United States accepted new, indeed the first ever, formal constraints on theater
missile defense (no space-based interceptors), even though the
Soviet/Russian-U.S. ABM Treaty of 1972 has no strategic relevance
for a world bereft of a Russian-U.S. strategic balance; impracticable measures of arms control are lauded for biological, toxin, and
chemical arms even though they are systemically incapable of
helping to alleviate security problems; much confidence continues
to be reposed in mechanisms of deterrence, despite plausible arguments that advise to the contrary; many Western experts believe
that there is extant a "nuclear taboo" against the use of nuclear
arms; and Western governments and publics are setting themselves up to be shocked by WMD events early in the next century.

Although I feel strongly about the subject of this book, as the
paragraph immediately above attests, I have chosen to write a
scholarly and balanced review of the WMD—though especially the
nuclear—dimension to our future insecurity. Although the text is
scholarly in attitude and approach, I have striven to keep the lan-
guage lively and the footnoting minimal. Furthermore, although

the argument is balanced, it is not balanced between truth and error to the point where error is honored beyond its station.

Rightly or wrongly, I strive here to play the ball rather than the ballplayer. This intention can have the effect of depersonalizing the argument to the point where I may appear evasive, or where I may risk offering a caricature of positions that I oppose. On balance, I choose to risk appearing guilty of confronting unnamed persons rather than drag the debate into the zone of personalities.

The text cites and explores much evidence of intellectual laziness, imprudence in policy, and plain old misunderstanding; I therefore confine my observations here to four claims that contain both good and bad news. First, notwithstanding the arguable arrival of an information-led revolution in military affairs (RMA), we continue to live in a nuclear era, and this nuclear era has distinctive nuclear "ages." Second, we should not be lulled by five-plus decades of nuclear peace into the complacent belief that some happy mixture of deterrence, arms control, political evolution, and military-technical progress has banished the specter of nuclear war. Third, WMD are likely to be used for biological, toxin, and chemical—as well as nuclear—war; and such war easily could generate casualty lists for which Western governments and publics are wholly unprepared. Fourth, and finally, we are far from helpless: the real reason this book was worth writing is because there are measures that states can take, especially with respect to the provision of robustly layered offensive and defensive counterforce capabilities, that would help us to cope well enough (if not really well) with the perils posed by WMD. Otherwise we are reduced to a condition wherein our security must reside in faith, hope, and UN weapons inspectors.

Some readers will not like this book because it speaks of matters that make people, and governments, uncomfortable. The nonmarginal prospect of a "small" nuclear war in, say, South Asia, or the menace of biological or toxin agents in the hands of terrorists, does not make for comfortable reading. Scarcely less comfortable is the implication that if the argument about threats presented in this book is judged plausible—perhaps not implausible—then money and political courage are required if policy is to be prudent.

The Second Nuclear Age is a work that stands alone; it does, however, necessarily share arguments with a previous book of mine, *House of Cards: Why Arms Control Must Fail* (1992), and it benefits from my broader study, *Modern Strategy* (1999). During the course of researching and writing *The Second Nuclear Age,* I benefited greatly from the excellent cognate study, by my longtime friend and colleague Keith B. Payne of the National Institute for Public Policy, *Deterrence in the Second Nuclear Age* (1996). I could not be more pleased that he has contributed the Foreword to this book.

One of the great pleasures of academic life is having a colleague who disapproves thoroughly of your argument but whose points in detail put you on your mettle. I am hugely indebted to Eric Herring of the University of Bristol for demonstrating error to me so plausibly.

I am grateful to my students and colleagues at the University of Hull for their generally empathetic forbearance while I committed my thoughts on the second nuclear age to paper. I am even more grateful to my family, who have endured my lengthy obsession with the thoroughly unpleasant subjects of nuclear, biological, and chemical warfare.

Colin S. Gray

1

Nuclear Problem, Nuclear Condition

This is a second nuclear age. The good news is that the first nuclear age that was defined and driven by Soviet-U.S. superpower antagonism definitively is dead. The less good news is that a nuclear quality to world politics persists beyond the erstwhile great East-West Cold War. The prospectively even less good news is that a third nuclear age probably lurks in the wings and could see the return of a single dominant political axis of nuclear-armed hostility.

This book is about our future with nuclear weapons and with other so-called weapons of mass destruction (WMD): biological, toxin, chemical, and radiological. It is tempting to frame the argument explicitly with truly long-term suggestions about a likely succession of nuclear ages, but the hypothesis of a second nuclear age is sufficiently novel to dampen incentives to more heroic theoretical outreach. A professional person is always most vulnerable at the level of assumptions. I am acutely aware of the need to bed my argument within a well-built house of plausible propositions about the workings of world politics.

The Second Nuclear Age is about the meaning of nuclear weapons for national and international security today and tomorrow. Beyond that magisterial and rather daunting description lies a host of more modest ambitions. The subject here is both the character of an emerging era and a requirement to define how particular kinds of menaces can be defeated, otherwise neutralized, or simply endured on tolerable terms. The problem is how to cope well enough with a persistently, albeit evolving, nuclear (and biological and chemical) future.

Because propositions drive analysis and shape conclusions, it is important to be aware of their presence, identity, and influence. This

1

book explores the twin views, first, that nuclear weapons are an important subject for security and, second, that they will continue indefinitely to be such. The former view is not particularly controversial. A fair-sized legion of security theorists, conservative and liberal alike, endorses this first view so strongly that in some cases they hope by their educational efforts to be able to deny validity to the second view.[1] As the exceptionally bloody twentieth century moves to its close, the sentiment and principled determination to marginalize and then effectively, if not necessarily quite literally, to abolish nuclear arms is very much in the political and ethical ascendant.

In my view, the movement for nuclear abolition is as hopeless of achievement as it is frequently well intentioned. As the title of this chapter suggests, nuclear weapons provide a particular character of condition as well as constituting a problem. Since strategy by definition is a practical subject[2]—it is about bridging what can be a yawning gap between political purpose and military (and other grand-strategic) means—it is foolish, because impractical, to treat what we will show is a permanent nuclear condition as if it were a problem that could be resolved and thereby expunged. To risk overemphasis of claim, nuclear weapons are not akin to the horse cavalry and mounted infantry of yore, albeit quite recent yore. The future, we can hope, is a long time—asteroids and other (e.g., geophysical, pandemic) hazards permitting. The future cannot be foreseen in detail, but for both good and ill one can foresee a long-term role for nuclear weapons and other WMD. In principle, and one day for near certain, nuclear weapons might be superseded by functionally superior substitutes; indeed, for some purposes and for some countries—one in particular, the United States—such substitution already is far advanced.[3] Nonetheless, the nuclear era endures.

Another view that is significant for the plot of the analysis—this time at a much higher level than weaponry—is that the nature of world politics will not so alter in the twenty-first century that security demand for the several strategic services that can be provided by nuclear arms will evaporate. It is most plausible to argue that the nature and purpose of war and strategy are eternal in their essentials but that their character is ever changing. One might well endorse the proposition that, at most, nuclear weapons were a vital part of yesterday's answers to yesterday's security and strategic questions. Then one might seek logically to outflank the potential provision of strategic effect by nuclear armament with the claim that those weapons are no longer relevant to the questions that security communities ask.

By way of a partial analogy, one can suggest that a possible reason Carl von Clausewitz's master work *On War* has had no worthy successors in the field of the theory of war and strategy is that the dominant question in need of answer has changed in the course of this century. Whereas Clausewitz delved straight into "war proper,"[4] without diversion into either the causes of war or even into how real war for limited political goals might influence the course of military operations, many people since 1918 have been apt to see war itself as the question in need of answer. As a person of his time, place, and therefore culture, Clausewitz did not romanticize war and generalship, but neither did he question their necessity.

The challenge to nuclear weapons appears at several levels. Three ascending altitudes must be noted. First, one can argue that the military, strategic, and hence even political effect that once could flow only from nuclear capabilities in the future will be provided by non-nuclear military means. Precise "conventional" destruction or disablement will, indeed already can, replace some of the desired effects of nuclear use and in forms that are more user-friendly for appropriately fearful, not to say ethically aware, policymakers.

Second, one can argue that the future of warfare will not register conflicts of kinds to which nuclear (or other) weapons of mass destruction will be militarily relevant. On this claim, the great wars of the twenty-first century will see widespread and hugely savage combat, but that combat will occur at very close quarters in ever more urban geography.[5] The future of warfare, in this view, though savage indeed, is unlikely to have the character of the great struggles of the Westphalian period of modern history, which is to say of state against state.

Third, and finally, the approach of the millennium encourages a millennial optimism that is as well meant as it is imprudent. One could argue that the competition for security (and other goals and values) is a condition of anarchy that describes the essentials of the political world of Homer's graphically violent *Iliad,* just as it describes at least the core character of world politics in the twentieth century,[6] but that that condition is now in process of radical change. Chris Brown, a leading British academic theorist of international relations, tells us that today "we may not have world government, but we do have 'global governance.'"[7] Brown is correct in pointing to the fact that world politics today is not in a Hobbesian condition of anarchy, but, one should add, it never really was in such a state. One can note the complex interdependencies among polities, societies, economies, and cultures yet still harbor dark suspicions to the effect that the chameleon-like social institution that is war will be adapted to changing times more successfully than it will be tackled by abolitionist impulses. Readers may care to recall that, since the 1850s, what Michael Walzer terms "the war convention" has aggregated an ever larger and more rigorously demanding body of norms and regulations for the control of beastliness in war.[8] Nonetheless, as the famous book title of 1948 expressed the matter, this century has seen an "advance to barbarism" awesome in its actual, and even more in its officially licensed potential, record of violence.[9] The 1990s registered the commission in Europe and Africa of war crimes that are at least in junior league with the Holocaust of the early 1940s, and as recently as the late 1980s, two super states had in place contingency war plans for nuclear use on a scale that easily could have produced an immediate and delayed death toll in the tens, or even hundreds, of millions. All of this may argue the necessity for radical benign change in the condition of world politics, but, alas, it does not argue conclusively, or even persuasively on the evidence available, a sufficiency of pressure for such change.

The attitude that informs this book is that although anything is possible in security affairs—the Holocaust in the heart of "civilized" Europe has settled that matter[10]—we have seen at least the structure of the most relevant future because we have good enough access to much of our past. This attitude, perspective perhaps, is of course controversial. I believe it to be well founded, but I do not claim it as a Great Truth. It is neither atavistic nor unimaginative to argue that "strategy will, *or should,* rule" in the next century, as it has in this one.[11] This is not to claim any dominance for distinctively strategic competence, only an enduring relevance of the strategic function for security communities.

* * *

This book aspires to explain the structure of the problem of a persistently *nuclear* security and insecurity condition so that appropriate classes of measures can be readily identified and eventually win political acceptance. The ambition to recommend how we can survive more securely by coping as effectively as possible with the characteristics of this second nuclear age constitutes journey's end in Chapter 6. En route to Chapter 6, the analytical narrative trajectory proceeds by explaining the concept and "working" of the second nuclear age (Chapter 2) and takes a fresh look at the somewhat overstudied subject of nuclear proliferation, this time with a view to uncover some of the more unhelpful of the fallacies that impede clear thought and (what I regard as) prudent policy (Chapters 3 and 4). Next, the analysis visits the intellectual and policy terrain of nuclear strategy to see what remains useful from the glory decades of the Cold War in the different security conditions of this second nuclear age (Chapter 5). The concluding chapter (Chapter 6) considers the ways in which we can cope tolerably well with our nuclear, biological, and chemical weapons future.

OF "AGES" AND REVOLUTIONS IN MILITARY AFFAIRS _____

To call a book *The Second Nuclear Age* is to register a conceptual claim before the evidence is presented. Historical periodization can be apparently arbitrary, is often contestable even on its own leading criterion, and is neither right nor wrong. In common with definitions, periodization is either more or less useful and, on the evidence available, more or less plausible. Letters of fire in the sky did not proclaim on 6 August 1945 that the (first) atomic, or nuclear, age had dawned. Similarly, on 22 December 1989—the day that the Berlin Wall began to be dismantled—no unarguably authoritative source insisted that a second nuclear age was dawning. Although the concepts of first and second nuclear ages are intellectual constructs, these concepts are both massively supportable empirically and, above all else, they are useful.

There is a paradoxical quality about the hypothesis of a second nuclear age. On the one hand, it proclaims a major change in nuclear security context. On the other hand, this central hypothesis—that we are in a second nuclear age—intentionally amd inherently devalues the significance of that major change. If it is claimed that a first nuclear age is being displaced by a second, it should follow that a third nuclear age could succeed this second one, then a fourth, and so on. A sense of serialization is exactly what is intended. The suggestion is not that just because there have been clearly distinctive first and second nuclear ages, future strategic history has to witness a series of distinguishable nuclear ages. It is possible that nuclear weapons might lose all attractiveness for potential owners. It is more probable that nuclear weapons, like gunpowder arms, effectively have entered human arsenals forever; but that has to be a matter strictly for speculation.

The first contribution to the paradox cited above is the claim that the years 1945–1989 (arguably 1947–1991) constituted a first nuclear age, an age organized and dominated by the rivalry between two superpowers. Of course, the USSR was never quite a superpower in the same category of global excellence as was the United States—a geopolitical and geostrategic fact of some historical significance (ask Fidel Castro).[12] I claim further that the fall of the Berlin Wall and of the Soviet imperium in East-Central Europe, and then the demise of the USSR itself, so altered the political context that provides the structure for nuclear-related matters of international security that it is plausible, and useful, to hypothesize the arrival of a second nuclear age.

This book proclaims that nuclear (and biological and chemical) menace remains important—both negatively and, more contentiously, positively—for our security but that the character of that menace changed almost beyond recognition from, say, the mid-1980s to the late 1990s. *The Second Nuclear Age* is about the problems of coping with the largely unfamiliar challenges of a different—hence "second"—nuclear security environment from that in which today's policymakers were educated strategically. Also, the book is about the process of trying to cope with a new nuclear age when the conceptual, and much of the material, "toolkit" derives from a previous period.

Narrative history may be old-fashioned, but it corresponds quite well to the physical laws of space and time. The course of historical events proceeds consequentially from causes to outcomes, none of which can be final. Several aspects of the hypothesized "second nuclear age" are eminently contestable. Nonetheless, proclamation of "second" suggests both distinctive differences from "first" and the possibility of "third" and beyond.

Scholars of nuclear security issues have neither been particularly well integrated in their analyses with military security debate as a whole, nor been well integrated into broad arguments about the course of world politics. The hypothesis upon which this book rests simply is that there was a first nuclear age coterminous with the Cold War, and now there is a second nuclear age that has important implications for the global security condition after the Cold War. Whether or not a "third," "fourth," or "fifth" nuclear age beckons in our security future is irrelevant to the argument.

Readers are requested to be strategically bifocal. Above all else, this book is about coping well enough with the second nuclear age that now is dawning. Of less immediate moment is the strategic historical probability that the nuclear connected facts of today are building the conditions that will emerge one day as a third nuclear age. On current form in world politics, though not yet quite predictably, a putative third nuclear age is most likely to be organized by the return of a single central axis of antagonism in world politics. Over the next fifty years or so, there are very few even semiplausible worthy competitors to a United States that geopolitically has to constitute one side of the axis in question. The short list of possible candidates for status of "principal *and worthy* foe" (or foes) of the United States includes Russia, the European Union, Japan, China, and—to be fanciful—Brazil and an Islamic state or coalition.

None of the candidate-worthy foes identified above are plausibly truly peer competitors; that is, none of the polities either cited or hypothesized appears to have the multidimensional strength to develop into a globally hegemonic superstate. But each of the possible foes mentioned either is or could be strategically competitive in at least one or two regions and in one or more varieties of conflict. One might recall that because of the rich multidimensionality of war and strategy, as well as of belligerents, North Vietnam—the Prussia of Southeast Asia—was entirely strategically competitive in the 1960s with a hugely self-confident (at least initially) United States.[13] It is probable that in neither a second nor possibly even a third nuclear age will the United States be obliged to cope with a nuclear-armed antagonist fully in the same league of capabilities as itself (recall that during the Cold War the USSR was never really a first-class superpower). But that thought implies less good news for the United States than one might expect.

By far the most probable future central axis of antagonism in world politics is one between the United States and China.[14] The possibility, or probability, has to be mentioned at this early juncture, because the reemergence of Sino-U.S. antagonism is a trend that could carry the political traffic necessary to incubate and deliver a third nuclear age. Such an age is incubating today, much as the seeds, roots, or origins of conflicts grow during postwar, interwar, and then prewar years. There is no certainty about the general character, let alone the detail, of the age after the current one, but much of the material from which that future age will be fashioned is around us now.

Every conflict is distinctive. I do not confuse the China of, say, 2020 with the USSR of 1980, or with Nazi Germany. Furthermore, I do not confuse nuclear armament with any "last move" in weaponry, nor do I suggest that the key algorithm for periodization in strategic history has to be geopolitical change rather than technical development or ideological revolution (a new religion, for example, or revival of old ones). It just so happens that the dominant differences between the first and the second nuclear ages were wholly political, as the USSR foundered and the great Cold War died a strategically natural and unpredictably peaceful death. The argument that the contemporary, which is to say "second," nuclear age eventually will give way to a third nuclear age is not seriously troubled by the recent excitement over an information-led revolution in military affairs (RMA).[15] A third nuclear age, which I judge—or guess—will likely be triggered by intense Sino-U.S. antagonism, will thus be the product principally of geopolitical and geostrategic calculation. In the twenty-first century, the United States and China are likely to define each other as the preponderant menace to their vital interests.

The idea of a second nuclear age is under heavy conceptual and empirical challenge from what might be termed the forces of RMA. One might suggest that the admitted novelty of the current nuclear context in practice is overshadowed by a contemporary RMA geared to the exploitation of cyberspace or, more radically, that the new age that is dawning is not a second nuclear age but rather an information age. The several meanings of the information-led candidate RMA—especially, on one hand, the more precise delivery of bombs and bullets and, on the other hand, information power in cyberspace—and their implications are discussed as appropriate throughout this text.

Both nuclear ages and RMAs are eminently contestable concepts of convenience. However, the case for claiming that today we live in a nuclear age radically different from the nuclear age of the Cold War decades is empirically clearer and more plausible than is the claim for arrival of an information-led RMA. Notwithstanding my conviction that nuclear weapons will remain significant as instruments variably of security and insecurity, I cannot simply dismiss out of hand the theory that information technologies will transform war—that is, the "grammar" of strategy,[16] not the nature of war—and in the process condemn nuclear armaments to the garbage heap of strategic history. In historical practice, quite often RMAs—and RMA remains a slippery grand idea—can appear other than strictly and neatly seriatim.[17] Moreover, the several fruits of RMAs can persist, even when those "revolutions" appear on the stage successively; the stage may just become more crowded. Eschewing arid definitional discussion of RMA, one needs to understand that the political, social, and military domain of purportedly revolutionary change is apt in practice to be limited. If nuclear weapons heralded a true revolution, an RMA on anybody's terms, what was it that they revolutionized? The practicability of great war between nuclear-armed states perhaps; but large-scale conventional warfare certainly has not been abandoned, even though fears of uncontrollable escalation have discouraged nuclear powers from fighting each other.[18] No matter how genuinely revolutionary one judges the nuclear revolution to have been, the fact remains that almost the full panoply of late pre–nuclear weapon types remain in the arsenals of many countries. The nuclear era, in its two ages, has proved compatible with (non-nuclear-armed) aircraft, armored fighting vehicles of all kinds, surface ships and submarines, and all manner of personal and crew-served firearms. This does not amount to an eccentric claim that there has been no nuclear RMA, but it does constitute a warning about the practicably restricted domain even of apparently the most unarguably revolutionary of RMAs.

Although the contemporary armies of nuclear-armed states bear more than a slight similarity to the most effective armies of 1918,[19] one should be prepared for the strong possibility, probability even, that a mature information-led RMA will prove entirely compatible with a persistently nuclear context. Not only can RMAs appear in tandem or more, they can also persist in authority—albeit bounded authority—as they are adapted to changing conditions. This is precisely what *The Second Nuclear Age* is about. The nuclear RMA has transmuted significantly as its political context has been revolutionized.

PRINCIPAL THEMES

This book most directly is about nuclear weapons and nuclear strategy in strategic history, but the analysis also bears upon some enduring and universal themes in relation to which nuclear matters can be viewed as a case study. Both singly and in shifting coalition, seven themes weave in and out of this text.

My first theme is the prospective permanence of the nuclear fact for strategy. In its more inclusive form, this theme amounts to the claim that strategic history is more cumulative than serial. No matter what governments and others may decide about nuclear arsenals, the clock of strategic history cannot be wound back to an era of pre-nuclear innocence. Much as people have children whether or not they are ready to be parents, and newborn polities were declared independent from colonial rule whether or not they were technically and ethically fit for self-government, so in the 1940s humankind acquired through military atomic knowledge the ability to make unprecedented hell on earth, even though the structures and attitudes of world politics were not radically reformed. The nuclear fact

was layered both on top of and in some competition with more traditional grand-strategic and military-strategic instruments of statecraft. The nuclear era with its several "ages" may prove to be a pass-
ing phase in strategic history, but it is a phase with no terminal point
plausibly predictable from today.

Second, the nuclear challenge to our security does not reduce to
a simple menace, even though the eventual emergence of a third
nuclear age characterized by a dominant axis of nuclear-armed
antagonism is likely. In more general terms, this theme is a reminder
that strategic peril is wont to come in multiple forms. As the discussion in Chapters 3 and 4 demonstrates plainly, the interests and
motives behind and the character of the nuclear challenges in this
new nuclear age require a complementary layering of policy initiatives if the requisite flexibility to cope with nuclear danger is to be
achieved. In the near future, nuclear peril can take the form of an
intended counterdeterrent to a U.S. regional protection role (for
example, over the Republic of China on Taiwan); of an attempt at
commercially minded criminal extortion (history at last would catch
up with fiction); of an emphatic political statement by one of world
history's "loser" causes; or of an initially small nuclear war waged by
regional rivals. And this is to cite but a few among the appalling possibilities. One should not exaggerate nuclear danger. Kenneth Waltz,
for example, no matter how persuasive one finds his central thesis
that nuclear-armed neighborhoods tend to be polite neighborhoods,
has performed a most valuable service with his powerfully argued
deflation of some of the overexpanded balloons of nuclear menace
that have been floated in recent years.[20] Nonetheless, one should not
discount nuclear threats. Indeed, it is the unique potency of nuclear
threats upon which Waltz's thesis leans most essentially.

My third general theme is a troubling addendum to the second
theme. We will have occasion to treat more than casually the other
(than nuclear) WMD (i.e., biological, toxin, and chemical weapons),
which pose a growing array of threats that are in part at least distinctive in profile from nuclear menaces. Scientifically speaking, biotechnology is probably the most dynamic of the sciences today and—
notwithstanding the public and official fascination with information
technologies—bears truly awesome menace for international security. Compared with nuclear weapons, biological and toxin weapons
are relatively cheap to produce, conceal, and deliver. As Martin
Shubik has argued persuasively, global security conditions change
when a small group of terrorists, criminals, patriots, freedom fight-
ers, or whatever quite reliably by their own unaided effort can kill

millions of people.[21] Welcome to the biotechnological age of warfare in the twenty-first century. This is not, at least not quite, to suggest that this current, "second" nuclear age will be succeeded by a biotoxin/chemical age of war whose lethal instruments will comprise stocks of weapons that would spread botulism, bubonic plague, typhoid, and anthrax or would deliver hydrogen cyanide or VX nerve gas. But, readers are alerted to the fact that throughout this book, even when it is apparent that the text deals explicitly with nuclear problems, biological, toxin, and chemical menaces are always on the author's mind. When necessary, the discussion treats those extranuclear WMD as separately as strategically they require to be treated.

Just as the acronym WMD conflates large and potentially strategically significant differences among broad categories of weapons, the acronyms BCW (biological and chemical weapons) and BTCW (biological, toxin, and chemical weapons) similarly conflate major technical distinctions that have strategic significance.[22] With reference to the essential nature of each category of weapon: biological weapons are infectious microorganisms that reproduce within the human target-victim host and cause an incapacitating or fatal illness; toxin weapons are poisonous chemicals that are produced by living organisms and have some features common to both chemical and biological agents; and chemical weapons consist of artificial, nonliving poisons. Fortunately, perhaps, biological weaponry, which is by far the most potent category of menace among this hellish brew, is also the most difficult to weaponize for reliable, temporally useful military and strategic effect. Whereas chemical weapons (CW) and toxin weapons (TW) produce lethal or incapacitating effects within minutes, and certainly in hours, biological weapons (BW)—needing time to reproduce within human hosts—have incubation periods in the range of twenty-four hours to six weeks. To take an extreme example, it would have to be an unusually long-term strategic planner who would target an enemy society with the AIDS virus, given that that virus has a mean incubation period of close to ten years. Apart from the operational problem that BW weapons really are only weapons for truly strategic assault, one needs to bear in mind the caveat that employment, or misemployment, of BW weaponry could give the concept of fratricide a whole new scale of meaning.

For obvious convenience, the discussion in this book employs the synonymous acronyms WMD and NBC (nuclear, biological, and chemical weapons); and when considering non-nuclear WMD, it refers to BC (biological and chemical, with the toxins category left silent but understood as included).

The twins of "change and continuity" are the fourth theme of this text. RMAs happen; at least great changes in the character of war keep recurring. But the irregular recurrence of such change in the grammar of war and strategy does not alter the nature and purpose of those phenomena. This book provides both broad conceptual and some narrowly detailed examination of a very great change indeed in the character of world politics, which is to say the historic transition from a first nuclear age to a second. Furthermore, the book must deal speculatively with the strong possibility, even probability, of yet another historic transition—in this case from a second to a third nuclear age. In addition, the discussion here of WMD is conducted against the backdrop of the implications of the major cumulative changes for security and strategy that currently are being effected by the arrival of new information technologies. This theme may appear so familiar as to warrant dismissal as a cliché. How many tedious reports, articles, and speeches have carried the deadly twin ideas of change and continuity? I risk the charge of purveying a truism by arguing that change and continuity is a compound theme that typically is not handled well by strategic theorists; whether this book can be an exception only time will tell. It is no mean feat to sort out, as scholars should, what is wont to change and what is not and—above all else—why that should be so.

Fifth, deterrence is unreliable;[23] there are inherent, structural problems with the reliability of deterrence, even of nuclear deterrence. This theme is not intended to convey the message that deterrence does not work, and neither is it chosen to imply that deterrence should not be attempted. The point rather is that defense professionals are wont to forget that (nuclear) deterrence is an effect in a mixed coercive and cooperative relationship. To attempt to deter is to offer the intended deterree the choice either to cooperate or not to cooperate. The elegance and sophistication of the theory of deterrence, especially of nuclear deterrence, stand in sharp contrast with the difficulties that can impede the successful practice of deterrence.

Sixth among the themes explored in this work is the persistence of the distortion that the lenses of both political and strategic culture and national but parochial interest can wreak upon strategic policy.[24] Rephrased, local culture and interest fuel self-delusion. Candidate cases of this self-delusion especially relevant for this book include the propositions that the international community can be divided into responsible, as contrasted with "rogue," states (or groups) and that the dawn of the proclaimed information age will promote the conduct of cleaner, more "surgical," information-led military campaigns.

Precise delivery of ordnance from unmanned, standoff arsenal platforms (floating, flying, or orbiting) allegedly will remove much of
the pain, and blame (for unwanted collateral damage), from war
because it will be waged by the United States' information warriors.[25]
An underrecognized, albeit obvious, dimension of war and strategy
is the adversarial relationship between belligerents. Forms of conflict
that we deem most attractive, which is to say forms that play overwhelmingly to our comparative strategic advantage, are unlikely to
appeal to our foes.[26] That logic may or may not matter very much,
depending upon the practicable choices open to the enemy.
Nonetheless, this theme of the self-deluding potential of local culture and interest bears a notable promise to distort defense policy
over the next several decades. It can be easy to forget that the character of this second nuclear age is not shaped solely by the negative
attitudes toward nuclear armament dominant in an ever more I-war-
minded U.S. defense community. Indeed, the less strategically
attractive nuclear weapons appear to the United States, the greater
the attraction of those weapons and other WMD to possible foes and
other "rogues."

There is, and can be, no objective definition of rogue states.
Were the idea of a rogue state not in widespread usage today, certainly I would be delighted not to promote it further. However, this
particular pejorative term-of-art does enjoy both wide currency and
tolerably plain meaning. A rogue state is a polity judged by us to be
committed to overturn a settled framework of order that we regard
as legitimate (at least, legitimate enough). The principal problem
with the concept is that its rather casual deployment can encourage
an unhelpful disdain for the rationality, and indeed the sincerity, of
the policymaking of the "rogue."

Finally, the seventh theme is the Clausewitzian revelation that
friction can rule.[27] Scholars, including myself, no less than public
officials, are tempted to draw neat and orderly pictures of the future.
Understandably, if unfortunately, scholars and officials are massively
liable to seduction by the structure of their distinctive responsibili-
ties. It is the duty of the strategic scholar to explain the structure of
those future problems that he or she anticipates. Logically, and
sometimes with a perilous hubris, the scholar proceeds to explain
that *if*, as predicted, this or that were to prove a serious danger, *then*
this or that should provide the strategic effect necessary to defeat
that danger. Unsurprisingly, we scholars are liable to design appropriate solutions to the problems that we also have designed. Similarly,
though with greater excuse because of the pressures of immediate

public accountability, officials are all but required to appear to believe that what they propose must be uniquely the correct response to anticipated perils. Because the process of defense planning cannot yield definitely correct answers—so many divisions, squadrons, and the like—definite scenarios are likely either to drive force planning or at least to dignify force plans developed according to other, less reputable criteria. Given that this book is a policy-scientific study of the problem of coping with a persistently nuclear future,[28] the theme of friction, chance, uncertainty, and risk asserts that the future course of strategic history is certain to contain surprises, some of them major and some of them significant in their potentially negative effect upon our security. Even if friction does not rule, it can stage a coup attempt at any time with consequences that must challenge the prudence in statecraft, strategy, and defense planning. To cite but one basket of perils, nuclear accidents of several kinds can happen and have happened. Recent scholarship is particularly eloquent on the statistically cumulative dangers that attend the nuclear era of whatever "age."[29]

SO WHAT?

Nuclear security problems have not gone away and are unlikely to vanish over the next several decades. The subject of *The Second Nuclear Age* is a set of WMD perils that, in a later "age" born out of this second age, will most probably return as the dominant danger embedded in the return of a great balance-of-power struggle. For the nearer term, in the second nuclear age (of uncertain duration) there are numerous local, regional, and criminal perils to international security that challenge our ability to adapt and to empathize with cultures different from our own.

Now that the great Cold War is history and new RMAs are being touted by theorists and salespeople, the time is ripe for reconsideration in detail of our strategic knowledge of nuclear affairs. Most of that knowledge was discovered, or created, to meet the immediate needs of the Cold War. With the Cold War definitively interred, and with even the post–Cold War period disappearing into history, how much of that nuclear knowledge from the decades structured preeminently by the bilateral Soviet-U.S. rivalry retains its integrity? What need is there for nuclear *strategy* today? If strategy bridges the gap between military means and political ends, what ends can, and should, nuclear military means now serve?

For a disturbing thought with which to conclude this opening chapter, is it even sound to argue that we can interrogate the nuclear "knowledge" inherited from the decades of Cold War in order to find the nuggets of theory and practice that can continue to serve us well? What if our problem is not only one of adapting past nuclear wisdom to the new conditions of a second nuclear age, but also is one of possible base metal in what long has been believed to be gold? What should we endorse from the theories and practice of nuclear security of Cold War vintage when we suspect that our physical and political survival may have been achieved despite, rather than because of, some of those theories and practices?

NOTES

1. Close approximations to this position may be located in Canberra Commission, *Report;* and National Academy of Sciences, *Future of U.S. Nuclear Weapons Policy.*

2. Brodie, *War and Politics,* pp. 652–653.

3. Blaker, *Understanding the Revolution in Military Affairs.*

4. Clausewitz, *On War,* p. 131.

5. Peters, "Our Soldiers, Their Cities."

6. Bull, *Anarchical Society;* Waltz, *Theory of International Politics.*

7. Chris Brown, *Understanding International Relations,* p. 121.

8. Walzer, *Just and Unjust Wars,* p. 44.

9. Jurist, *Advance to Barbarism.*

10. On "civilization," see Gong, *Standard of "Civilization."*

11. For detailed justification of this argument, see Gray, "RMAs and the Dimensions of Strategy."

12. The Cuban perspective is well, indeed possibly unduly well, treated in Fursenko and Naftali, *"One Hell of a Gamble."*

13. This is not to deny that pessimistic military prognoses of the scope and scale of the U.S. mission were not in short supply in the early 1960s. See Buzzanco, *Masters of War.* The telling point is that the U.S. government proceeded in Vietnam even though it was the beneficiary of much unwelcome news about the difficulty of the task.

14. The strongest statement to date of this possibility is Bernstein and Munro, *Coming Conflict with China.* Also see Shambaugh, "Chinese Hegemony"; and Nye, "China's Re-emergence."

15. See Krepinevich, "Cavalry to Computer"; Blaker, *Understanding the Revolution in Military Affairs;* Gray, *American Revolution in Military Affairs;* Murray, "Thinking About Revolutions in Military Affairs"; Arquilla and Ronfeldt, *Athena's Camp;* and Freedman, *Revolution in Strategic Affairs.*

16. Clausewitz, *On War,* p. 605.

17. Murray, "Thinking About Revolutions in Military Affairs."

18. Jervis, *Meaning of the Nuclear Revolution.*

19. See Jonathan Bailey, *First World War.*

20. Waltz, *Spread of Nuclear Weapons;* Sagan and Waltz, *Spread of Nuclear Weapons,* chs. 1, 3.

21. U.S. Congress, *Technologies Underlying Weapons of Mass Destruction,* chs. 2, 3; Dando, *Biological Warfare in the 21st Century;* Shubik, "Terrorism, Technology, and the Socioeconomics of Death"; Betts, "New Threat of Mass Destruction"; Cole, *Eleventh Plague.*

22. In this paragraph, as generally elsewhere in the text on the technical "basics" of biological, toxin, and chemical agency, I rely heavily upon U.S. Congress, *Technologies Underlying Weapons of Mass Destruction.* This excellent report warrants description as a manual for would-be proliferants.

23. For a previous venture into this analytical area, see Gray, *Explorations in Strategy,* ch. 3.

24. Booth, *Strategy and Ethnocentrism;* Bathurst, *Intelligence and the Mirror.*

25. Luttwak, "Toward Post-Heroic Warfare"; Friedman and Friedman, *Future of War.*

26. See Freedman, *Revolution in Strategic Affairs,* pp. 38–41; and Matthews, *Challenging the United States.*

27. Clausewitz, *On War,* pp. 119–121.

28. Lasswell, "The Policy Orientation"; Dror, *Design for Policy Science.*

29. Feaver, *Guarding the Guardians;* Blair, *Logic of Accidental Nuclear War;* Scott Sagan, *Limits of Safety;* Thayer, "Risk of Nuclear Inadvertence," and responses by Blair, Feaver, and Sagan (pp. 494–520); Pry, *War Scare.*

2

The Second Nuclear Age: The Hunt for Political Context

To adapt a familiar aphorism, "They cannot know nuclear matters, who only nuclear matters know."[1] Of the four chapters that compose the main body of this book, no fewer than three are devoted quite narrowly to questions of nuclear (and other WMD) policy (Chapters 3–5). It is all the more essential, therefore, that the political context for nuclear matters be explored early; hence this hunt for political context. To what character of world politics, to which era in those politics does the subsequent analysis pertain? At the very least, it is convenient to treat the question of political meaning here in a way that allows easy reference in the chapters to come without requiring later diversion from the analytical trajectory.

The discussion opens with consideration of the hypothesis of a second nuclear age and with a critical review of questions of evidence. We proceed next with thoughts on historical continuity and discontinuity. The principal section of the chapter offers full-frontal description of the most significant descriptors of this second nuclear age.

HYPOTHESIS, EVIDENCE, AND ARGUMENT

Students of nuclear security are scarcely more reliably knowledgeable about their subject than are the historians who contrive to write detailed accounts of Byzantine history in the seventh and eighth centuries. In the latter case there are next to no good sources remaining,[2] whereas in the former case there is a plethora of sources but a comprehensive absence of compelling evidence.

Allegedly definitive accounts of the Cuban missile crisis of October 1962 keep appearing.[3] That apparently most perilous "strategic moment" of the great Cold War now suffers the not uncommon modern distinction of yielding both too much and too little evidence for our understanding.

Because data, information, knowledge, understanding, and wisdom are distinguishable, it is not entirely self-evident that more scholarship necessarily must yield superior, let alone definitive, understanding of what happened. It can be a revelation to appreciate that historians of World War I—a subject of which we now know virtually everything that we can know—and future-oriented strategists, writing about a subject on which zero reliable knowledge is possible, share a like quality of artistry. A historian's speculation is just that, speculation. Because history is played only once, who can say (let alone prove) that Austria-Hungary bears the heaviest burden of guilt for the course of events in 1914?[4] Similarly, the strategic theorist as futurist writes wholly in the realm of "perhaps." The historian can amass a mountain of facts and probable facts to support the plausibility of his or her argument. The strategist as futurist has no facts or probable facts to deploy—beyond current trends, that is, which may count as semifacts for the future—so he or she too lives in a zone judged by plausibility.

These thoughts suggest, subversively, that much of what we think we know about today, and especially about yesterday, may be wrong. An unfortunate paradox lurks to ambush the seekers after strategic truth for the purpose of improving public policy: the more important the question—for example, why did nuclear combat not terminate the Cold War?—the less useful the historical evidence. Lurking beneath these thoughts is the proposition that we may know less about nuclear-era history to date than we think we do. For example, we are almost overinformed by scholars on the eminently researchable topic of the (domestic) politics of Minuteman (ICBM) vulnerability.[5] But until quite recently we knew (really knew, that is) painfully little about the domestic politics of Soviet weapons programs. Our knowledge of, as contrasted with speculative opinion concerning, the strategic history of the Cold War remains critically fragile. Moreover, even when historians of the first nuclear age uncover all that can be uncovered from archival, literary, and oral sources, the larger issues of peace and war, decline and political defeat are apt to remain definitively unanswerable. Such great questions as why was war avoided in October 1962, or why did the USSR decline and fall, and decline and fall peacefully—a quiet expiration as after a long illness—in the 1980s, will be debatable forever. Such questions require answers that transcend strictly factual evidence, or more information.

This is not to suggest that we should be reticent on grounds of absent evidence in our efforts to theorize from the hypothesis that a second nuclear age is under way, even though the facts are far from in on where the new security environment is tending. The point is that although the first nuclear age has passed, many of the more important facts about that now historical age are both missing today and prospectively will be missing in perpetuity. This is not to succumb to the fallacy of believing that because we do not understand everything about our nuclear history we do not know anything. Furthermore, I am not arguing that enquiry is futile just because authoritative answers to central questions must ever prove elusive.

Existentially, the most important aspect of the idea of a nuclear weapon is the demonstrated fact that the weapon works in practice (which is not to claim that every nuclear weapon in every country's arsenal actually would "work" to deliver close to the expected yield). In human, cultural, and several other terms, by far the most important aspect to the nuclear history of the Cold War is the unanswerable fact that it was neither terminated nor punctuated by nuclear combat. Today we know with absolute certainty that every actor who behaved to some strategic effect in the East-West Cold War behaved in ways consistent with the avoidance of general war, nuclear and otherwise. Apart from being massively important in itself, that fact of nonwar should be helpful to us as we consider how to cope with the problem of nuclear security today and tomorrow—but is it helpful?

Did an East-West nuclear war not occur because of our, and their, policies, strategies, and prudent activities in the category of behavior labeled by Clausewitz "preparations for war"?[6] Or did such a war not occur despite our policies, strategies, and relevant activities? Should we be self-congratulatory over the fact that war did not explode out of the Cuban imbroglio of October 1962, or appalled at how close to war we may well have been? Similarly, are we impressed by the fact that none of the nuclear accidents suffered by East or West produced a military outcome of strategic note? Or, again, are we chastened by the growing body of evidence now available on the apparent, if arguable, breadth and number of nuclear-related accidents? What matters here primarily is the avoidance of false conclusions, not the picking of the winner among necessarily subjective characterizations of the past.

We cannot know why there was no nuclear war from 1947 until the formal demise of the USSR in 1991. What is avoidable, however, is the drawing of unwarranted conclusions from essentially contestable, or absent, evidence. We know a great deal about both the first and even the new, second nuclear age. We know that the nuclear relevant structure of international and national security has been transformed by the change from a bipolar international political system to something else. Since the argument here ultimately is empirical rather than conceptual, meaning that my hypothesis is testable according to the relaxed standards of assay of qualitative social science, it is especially important that fact should be distinguished from judgment. The hypothesis and argument advanced here is that:

1. The period 1989–present constitutes a second nuclear age shaped principally, though not exclusively, by the new post–Cold War distribution of power.
2. Policy for and thoughts about nuclear weapons (and other WMD) in the second nuclear age are significantly at risk to beliefs that may rest upon a misreading of the ambiguous record of these weapons in strategic history to date.[7]
3. It is not self-evident what the more obvious differences between the first and second nuclear ages—preeminently the presence or absence of a dominant strategic balance—imply for prudent policy and strategy.
4. If we are unduly casual about our nuclear past—for example, if we assume that nuclear deterrence is reliable because nuclear war did not occur—we risk inflicting gratuitous damage upon our ability to cope with a nuclear future.
5. Scholarship that is careful about the "facts" may miss the point that in this second nuclear age, defense against some forms of delivery of WMD has become as necessary and feasible as generally it was only desirable in a first nuclear age, when deterrence alone proved to be good enough.

CONTINUITY AND DISCONTINUITY

When policy-oriented scholars look back into strategic history for educational assistance with contemporary challenges,[8] they are liable to discover that what they think they know about the past perhaps they do not really know. A hypothesis keyed to periodization has bias toward encouraging the theorist to seek discontinuity rather than continuity. But because this book has a transformation in the character, not nature, of the nuclear era as its central conceptual pillar, I have no compunction identifying continuities as well as changes. Nonlinear change in the political, and hence military, architecture of international security was effected between 1989 and 1991. Nonetheless, much of importance to security did not change, any more than the dramatic arrival of the first nuclear age in 1945 revolutionized all rules and conditions of world politics. Much of what this book suggests to be unsound attitudes toward nuclear weapons derives from a poor grasp of the vital distinction between the enduring dimensions of security, the persisting nature and purpose of statecraft and strategy, and the ever changing character of security conditions, statecraft, and strategy.[9]

Artful theorists of world politics, after the manner of "magic geography" perpetuated by cartographically gifted geopoliticians,[10] can so organize historical periodization as to tell a wide range of stories. Choice of organizing principle translates as choice of message. What is modern strategic history all about? The grand theorist can select a defining characteristic for periodization keyed to one or more of many candidates.

1. Scale of war: the age of total war, the age of limited war
2. Ideology: the age of faith, the age of absolutism, the democratic era
3. International system: the balance-of-power era, the Concert era
4. Economic engine: the age of agriculture, the age of industry, the information age
5. Military technologies, weapons, RMAs: the castle era, the gunpowder age, the nuclear revolution
6. Great people: the Stalin era, the Gorbachev era, the Reagan era
7. Dynamic sciences: the chemist's war, the physicist's and engineer's war, the biologist's war

Every exercise in periodization pays a price for the clarity of its central argument. That price includes the risk of exaggeration of quantity and quality of change and hence of undervaluation of elements of continuity. There will be cases when claims for status of "defining characteristic" are easily sustainable. For an obvious example, in any history of the Jewish people, assertion of the era of the Holocaust of 1941–1945, including its immediate antecedents and consequences, is not simply a historian's convenience.

Similarly, though admittedly in lesser key, to label 1945–1989 the first age of the nuclear era is more prosaic than fanciful. Much of world politics was not troubled by nuclear menace in those years, but the dominant architecture of the balance of power was supported critically by a web of contingent nuclear promises that just might have eventuated in a general cataclysm. Nonetheless, important questions remain to be answered, in some cases even addressed, about how nuclear the nuclear era really has been.

Periodization both emphasizes a claim for change rather than continuity and—since there has to be some chosen organizing principle(s) or defining characteristic(s)—promotes one dimension, element, or factor above others. To label the Cold War era "the first nuclear age" is to assert a defining strategic historical significance to nuclear weapons for those years. There is the existential difficulty that there were no operational nuclear events in action during the Cold War; indeed, for most people on both sides of the Cold War divide, the (first) nuclear age was distinctly a virtual reality. Of course, the same kind of point could be registered with reference to various ages of religious faith.

The concept of a second nuclear age plainly distinguishable from a first such age is keyed simply, perhaps too simply, to a single defining characteristic, albeit one that can have a dominant significance for security. Specifically, this book claims a second nuclear age distinctive from a first on the basis of a radically changed, indeed transformed, political architecture of threat. There has been a discontinuity in the Soviet/Russian polity, no less than at least a temporary loss of imperium, empire, and ideological rationale for rule. The U.S. end of the balance of power discovered abruptly that it was balancing nothing.

The world political events of 1989–1991 were on a scale, of a kind, and with consequences that modern history otherwise has recorded only in the aftermath of great (anti)hegemonic wars. For strict intensity of merited odium, the German Third Reich has set a standard for all time. Nonetheless, for sheer scope of domestic and international incivility, the USSR was a historical player of extraordinary note. That granted, the facts remain that the discontinuities claimed between both a nuclear and a prenuclear era, and between a first and a second nuclear age, can hardly help but risk misleading readers over the enduring nature, though changing character, of the general warp and woof of security affairs.

There can be no denying worth in the claim for a nuclear revolution in the mid-1940s. It is true that the U.S. nuclear arsenal contained zero ready atomic bombs in the fall of 1945, but still the potential for a revolutionary relationship between offense and defense plainly was evident: atomic power could be considered an absolute rather than a militarily relative weapon.[11] The next several decades demonstrated that this was by no means self-evidently the case, but for now it can stand as a robust basis for asserting a revolutionary character to the nuclear event.

General theorists among scholars of world politics are ever willing to pass beyond Clausewitz's "culminating point of victory."[12] It is a paradoxical empirical truth that although every bold thesis of purported long, or short, cycles in world politics typically meets with a skeptical yawn, a simple reminder of the radical change in security conditions between, say, 1909 and 1919, 1919 and 1929, 1929 and 1939, and so on, meets with no consumer resistance. It is more controversial to postulate a second nuclear age than it is to note the fact of a post–Cold War world. The latter means nothing at all other than that we now live in a period after the great Cold War. The public and policymakers do not need scholars to tell them that.

The thesis of a second nuclear age expresses continuity and discontinuity in strategic history. In and of itself, though, the thesis implies nothing in particular about the character of the age in question other than that it is a nuclear one. To proceed further and claim that nuclear weapons continue to be important as sources of security and insecurity, however, is by no means beyond argument. Indeed, one might try to argue that at the end of the twentieth century, nuclear weapons are all but irrelevant to global security problems yet are sufficiently menacing as to be worthy of abolition. If such an apparent contradiction can be explained to be more sensible than it sounds, one needs to argue that nuclear weapons contribute more notably to insecurity than they do to security, so that they are part of the problem rather than the solution. It is not obvious that this is true, as later discussion shows.

To assert a second nuclear age is not necessarily to make a judgment about the significance of nuclear weapons. Thus far this text has argued only that there are noteworthy differences between the roles and the probable strategic effect[13] of nuclear weapons today as contrasted with their roles and strategic effect during the Cold War. I am not arguing that the current period warrants labeling as a second nuclear age in preference to other candidate labels. This happens to be an information age; also, it is the age of nationalism, yet again. Much as an individual can have a strategic culture that contains an only possibly harmonious mixture of influences deriving from civilization (e.g., broadly Western or Oriental),[14] nation, region, ethnicity, individual armed service, branch of service, and personal experience,[15] so an age can be characterized variously. The challenge accepted here is to understand the multifaceted nuclear dimension to this age. The task mandates that the whole security context be explored.

Some readers may be uncomfortable with a decision rule for distinguishing between nuclear ages that rests overwhelmingly upon political criteria and that makes scant direct reference to trends in nuclear arsenals, in pressures for adherence to nonproliferation norms, and in reduced (U.S.-NATO) reliance upon nuclear deterrence for security. For the record, it is probably important for me to acknowledge readily the very large reductions achieved already in strategic nuclear warheads and delivery vehicles.[16] In addition, there is no doubting the fact of huge cuts in deployed nonstrategic nuclear weapons. Indefinite renewal of the Nuclear Nonproliferation Treaty (NPT) shows the general health of antinuclear sentiment, globally, whereas the information-led RMA is reinforcing the effect of an absent superpower foe in relegating nuclear deterrence very much to residual, backup status. Unfortunately, these large changes in nuclear matters are much less significant than they can appear.

In the first place, the changes in nuclear arsenals just cited substantially are the result of prior political changes, not vice versa. Second, as the analysis in Chapter 5 shows, even very large-scale reductions in U.S. and Russian nuclear arsenals are not strategically significant. Third, India and Pakistan have demonstrated the truth in the principle that negotiated measures of arms control, in any shape or form and on any subject, cannot handle the hard cases that matter most. Finally, although it is certainly true that nuclear deterrence has moved very much backstage for the United States since the demise of the USSR, even backstage roles can be vitally important (see Chapter 5), and those polities who find themselves distinctly RMA-challenged will be likely to discern more than residual duties for their nuclear WMD.

THE NEW SECURITY ENVIRONMENT

The term "new security environment," like "post–Cold War world," is essentially vacuous; it does, however, have the merit of pointing to nonlinearity in strategic history.[17] To mix chemistry with politics, the Soviet crisis of empire required in the 1980s a change of state. But just as the water that becomes steam when heated can condense back into liquid form, so the change of state from USSR to Russia barely conceals important constituent continuities. When world politics abruptly is disorganized, if not reorganized, theorists rush to their word processors to speculate on what it all means. Lest there be any misunderstanding, I admit to a preference for a minimalist theory of world politics. It is true that in some important senses in world politics "ideas rule," even "theory rules," but much of the scholarship classified as theory on international relations—the scholarly discipline—has painfully little to say of great interest, or perhaps does not say it in ways interesting, to the practical world of international relations.[18] This is both my personal opinion and is a generalization that rests on the evidence of my experience over nearly thirty years with the response of policymakers to much of academic international relations.

This book is only a minimalist exercise in the theory of international relations. The argument here is keyed to the presence or absence of a globally dominant political rivalry, which is an empirical matter. The first nuclear age that was the Cold War largely was organized by the bipolar rivalry between the U.S. and Soviet superpowers. The second nuclear age is a period defined—one can hardly say organized—by the absence of a dominant political rivalry (bipolar or otherwise). A third nuclear age is likely to be a return to a dominant political rivalry preeminently bipolar in organization and operation, if not quite in composition of balancing agents. It is possible that far from a third nuclear age comprising "bipolarity redux"—or "the Cold War rides again" minus much of the ideological baggage—such an age will be born out of and be shaped by an immensely awful, if probably regionally confined, nuclear event. This "sidebar" to the main line of argument requires careful attention at the right juncture.[19]

A leading problem with much of the academic theorizing about international relations is that such theorizing multiplies the factor of pretension, by the value of abstraction, to the power of fashion. The products are abstruse and arcane sets of propositions that are so "high concept" and "big picture," and so geared to demonstrate what the theorist began by believing, as to be substantively all but worthless. None of us can help but be the result of our time, place, and culture, but we can strive to control for some obvious potential biases. To note accurately what is happening today, a fleeting moment, is not to be seduced by fashion—unless one erects some edifice of theory on the basis of the unsound proposition that what one sees today is eternal truth. Ken Booth is right when he accuses "realist" theorists of international politics (including myself) of singing the same old songs, commenting on the same old games, and generally repeating what he regards as yesterday's errors in new guises.[20] We "realists," certainly we neo-classical realists, are confident that the game of security politics remains the same, even though the years after 1991 warrant categorization as a different season (or age).

I recognize that many scholars of international relations have responded to the challenge posed by the collapse of the USSR, the end of the Cold War, and the demise of the international system organized by Cold War security architecture by rushing to judgment with sundry grand theories. Once cast adrift from the solid anchor of bipolar superpower competition, how does one explain the organization and working of world politics? U.S. strategic theorists and defense analysts have been accused plausibly of attempting to function beyond a political context.[21] During the Cold War years, a small cottage industry developed wherein British professors lectured their U.S. colleagues on the perils of a technological reductionism (the illusion of the quest after a "technical peace"). I find myself guilty of perpetuating this somewhat prideful tradition of finger-wagging, in my case over the more enthusiastic strains of U.S. theorizing about the strategic promise in the contemporary information-led RMA.[22] Because innovation in strategic theory typically is triggered by pressing demands from national security policy,[23] the halls of strategy are rather quiet at present. Not so, however, the halls of theory on the emerging international political context. People and organizations have difficulty thinking strategically in close to a political void. To write strategy without a dominant strategic mission is an art in short supply. No less to the point, the energy expended in the generally healthy confusion that abounds today over what is, or might be, the international political context of security is largely unconnected to disciplined thought on grand, or military, strategy. We need to consider critically both what high theory is trying to persuade us and what it might be that our favored high theory or theories appear to imply by way of strategic questions in general and nuclear (and other WMD) matters for strategy in particular.

FOR THOSE ADRIFT IN STRATEGIC HISTORY _____

The second nuclear age is a hypothesis for analytical utility, not in some sense a hypothesis that can be tested for its quotient of truth. In my mind, of course, the second nuclear age is both more than a hypothesis yet less than critically important. After all, here we are only in the realm of names. What is going on in global security affairs is going on regardless of what we elect to call it. A reader could find the hypothesis of a second nuclear age analytically uninteresting yet still discern important merit in the arguments developed below about arms control and strategy.

The case for the hypothesis of a second nuclear age is strong but not overwhelmingly so. Stated more exactly, the case for the concept of a second nuclear age is a strong one, but there is so much continuity from Cold War practices (see Chapter 5) that it is easy to see why one might be accused of rerunning some nuclear first-age principles in different packaging for a claimed second age. There are times for subtlety, nuance, and even intended ambiguities, but this juncture in the book is not one of them. The analytical utility of the concept of a second nuclear age has the following justifications:

1. This is a book about nuclear weapons (and other WMD) in national and international security. All serious alternatives to "the second nuclear age" either miss the point—that nuclear weapons remain important—or simply are distinctions without meritworthy difference (e.g., the second coming of the nuclear age,[24] and so forth).

2. The hypothesis of a second nuclear age alerts us usefully to the possibility/probability of significant changes in matters of nuclear (and other WMD) security.

3. The hypothesis, though specifying only one element in the military equation, has the virtue of pointing to the (WMD) element most likely to trump all the others.[25]

4. The current period lends itself to several characterizations—the information age, the age of globalization, and so forth—but the second nuclear age, though unfashionable, points to the segment of the military dimension to security that has the potential to overshadow and even negate everything else.

Having defended the hypothesis of a second nuclear age, I must note that the argument here would not change even were I to scrap my preferred concept in favor of some alternative. All scholars, myself included, are apt to seduction by their favorite ideas. The second nuclear age is useful in pointing generically to some broad differences from the first age but in and of itself is non-specific. We academics should wear our favored concepts and verbal formulas lightly. Concepts and verbal formulas are important as levers to help make sense of the world, but they are not the world; they are but tools. There is a danger that some scholarly reviewers of this book may "lose the plot" by indulging in unduly rigorous examination of the hypothesis that this is a second nuclear age. A parallel phenomenon is scholastic scrutiny of the claims for an RMA. Is information-led warfare an RMA, a military-technological revolution (MTR), a military revolution (MR), a revolution in strategic affairs, and so forth? Sometimes, there are issues important for understanding lurking in the wings of such arcane discussion, but sometimes there are not. As Richard Betts has observed, even in strategic studies—a multidiscipline that tends to err on the side of a pragmatic approach to truth—the necessary process of theory construction all too often strays into the barren zone of theory for theory's sake. "One sure sign of intellectual degeneration in a field is when the logical relationship between generalization and specification is inverted, theories threaten to outnumber their applications, and the shelf life of theoretical work turns out to be hardly longer than that of policy analysis."[26]

The argument for the concept, or hypothesis, of a second nuclear age is good enough. Suggestions that this is not a second nuclear age but rather is some other character of age readily can descend into the murky reaches of academic trivial pursuit. My conceptual claim is less than imperial and should be treated as such. The claim would be vulnerable were one able to show plausibly that nuclear weapons have become irrelevant, at least unimportant, for national and international security. The entire text of this work can be read as being intended to take issue with such a view.[27]

U.S. merchants of high concepts and grand theories recently have risked overperformance. From a Cold War condition of notable, if understandable, underachievement, the scholarly authors of large organizing ideas have been working overtime since the USSR closed for business at the end of 1991. The problem is that from a condition in the 1980s wherein there was too little competitive theorizing of a basic kind about alternative political contexts, today we probably have too much of such theory. Albeit with a broader domain, the grand theorists of the 1990s have exhibited some of the less attractive traits of the theorists on nuclear strategy in the late 1950s and the 1960s. Specifically, concepts and theories are sprouting and gelling into scholarly thoughts, "discrete images, models, or paradigms,"[28] at a pace dictated more by energy in intellect than by well-refereed thought. It must be emphasized that the postulate of a second nuclear age as the leading organizing idea for this analysis truly rests upon only one principle, among several possible, of discrimination. That principle is the presence or absence of a dominant political-strategic rivalry. Such rivalry would not be inconsistent with more evidence of genuine multipolarity than generally was the case between 1945 and 1989—thinking especially of China—but it would have to be of a kind that had bipolar magnetic attraction. The idea is that if, as was suggested in Chapter 1, we drift from this second nuclear age toward a third such age, a key "sign of the times" that that process of drift was well under way would be the phenomenon of more and more polities taking careful account of the meaning for them of an emerging central rivalry in international security affairs. Not everyone would be obliged to join one or the other of two great "teams," but most polities would find that that bipolar rivalry was exercising more and more organizing power over world affairs.

The political context for the second nuclear age has six principal defining features.

First, we have a new global security environment and a new world order characterized by many features of a U.S. hegemony. Much as the Soviet-U.S. rivalry arose all but inevitably out of the destruction of the intra-European balance of power in two world wars, so the contemporary U.S. hegemony is the result of one of the erstwhile near-first-class teams abruptly vacating the field of play. "The American Century" continues, or so a theory—with which I agree—insists.[29] As recently as the mid to late 1980s, it was fashionable to proclaim the demise of the American *half*-century. It was no accident, as Marxist theorists used to say, that Paul Kennedy's Spengleresque morality tale, *The Rise and Fall of the Great Powers*—and especially the United States—hit the best-sellers lists in 1987–1988.[30] It is ironic that the spectacular popularity of that scholarly book was matched only by its spectacular degree of error concerning the United States. As Kennedy was proclaiming the fall of the U.S. imperium because of imperial overstretch, so the United States' superpower foe was moving into position to effect a bungee jump of desperate reform measures relying on a hugely rotten rope.

If the popular declinism of 1987–1988 was overadvertised, so its direct opposite—assertion of an unassailable unipolar primacy—has been equally overstated a decade later. The image of a hegemonic United States presiding over its "unipolar moment" does provide an essential contribution to the definition of this second nuclear age, a definition that emphasizes the singular power and influence of the United States.[31] This paradigm is not wrong, but neither is it wholly correct. Indeed, the world today truly is unipolar with a privileged United States, as modern social scientific jargon would express the matter. But just what does that mean? Self-evidently, the international political system at the close of the twentieth century is in some senses unipolar American. But what does that claim mean for the course of strategic history?

1. The United States is the only *complete* super/great power; it is formidable *on any standard* measure of material power as well as on almost any standard of soft, cultural power and influence.[32]
2. The United States is not only outstandingly strong today, but it also has the cultural and social assets that all but guarantee enduring strength. U.S. society is diverse yet tolerably coherent and is adaptable to changing conditions.
3. The United States is the only global military power, a power able to threaten to wage war successfully at any level anywhere on earth (or in space).[33]
4. The United States is not only the militarily dominant polity today but also the polity best equipped (with electronic prowess, economic strength, entrepreneurial skill, and political and economic stability) to dominate tomorrow.

The United States' "unipolar moment," let alone "the American Century," is one of those many cases in strategy and statecraft wherein a popular idea can mislead the unwary. The United States today is the sole global superpower. That truth, however, does not suppress entirely a need to pose the classic strategy question, So what? Recall that this text locates the most defining characteristic for a second nuclear age in the absence of dominant great power rivalry, not in the presence of U.S. unipolarity. Even if the United States showed more talent for imperial governance and had more stomach for the costs of hegemony than appears to be the case, still there are severe limits upon U.S. ability both to police the present and to shape the future. Moreover, those severe limits upon U.S. influence have a significant nuclear dimension.

There is some truth in Joseph Joffe's clever argument that contemporary U.S. policy, whether by purposeful grand design or benign accident, functionally approximates that of Bismarck's Germany rather than, say, Disraeli's Britain.[34] The United States today, as with Germany in the 1880s, has made itself so essential a security partner to potential rivals that an international effort to balance U.S. power and influence is difficult, if not impossible, to organize. One might venture further and suggest that much as Bismarck sought to keep France isolated by cunningly co-opting France's potential allies, so the United States tomorrow might keep China isolated be denying it a Japanese, Russian, or (German-led) European alliance.

Whatever one believes about the prospects for its longevity, there is no doubt that U.S. hegemony is a notable factor of this second nuclear age. But if one also claims that that hegemony is *the* defining paradigm for this new age, then one has a troubling empirical difficulty with the facts of the evident limits on U.S. power and influence. In principle, the lack of a countervailing state or coalition leaves the United States substantially unconstrained. In practice, however, the absence of a great rival hugely reduces the United States' will to act on behalf of its vision of world order. Ever fewer of the burgeoning conflicts that scar world politics today self-evidently engage U.S. major, vital (let alone survival) interests. America's well-advertised (indeed probably over-advertised) casualty shyness is not unconnected to the absence of perception of high stakes for the country in overseas quarrels today. Nevertheless, it is hard for a country to be, or look like, the unipolar hegemon when it demonstrates to the world that it is not prepared to accept casualties among its professional soldiers and that it is even squeamish about hurting foes.

The United States is the most important power in Europe and Asia, even though it is not a European or an Asian power. In some contrast to security conditions in the late 1940s at the beginning of the first nuclear age, the United States today is a superpower, indeed *the* superpower, more despite than because of nuclear facts.[35] Nuclear strength is important, nay vital, as we shall see; but it is an unfortunate and increasingly ill-understood necessity rather than the leading edge of national strategic prowess. On balance, but only on balance, the nuclear facts of this second nuclear age serve to restrict the will and capability of the United States to act on behalf of international order. As a general rule, nuclear menace today has the consequence of discouraging an activist policy by a U.S. polity superior to any political foe or group of foes in almost all categories of grand-strategic instruments. Nuclear and BC facts reduce U.S. power and influence in the world. For today, that claim is a slight exaggeration. For many years to come, however, the claim will point to a truly potent source of systemic weakness in the U.S. world role. The risks that attach to playing coach and quarterback for world order will be seriously out of step with popularly understood appreciation of the benefits.

One should not paint a picture of the United States as a helpless giant, as a muscle-bound but hog-tied Gulliver in Lilliput. But one must point out that even though the United States is today undoubtedly the most influential player in European and East Asian security, and even though it could impose its will upon most roguish or otherwise recalcitrant regional or local powers, its practical ability to shape the course of strategic history is modest. At some small risk of appearing deterministic, I believe that still there is a commonsense logic of geopolitics and geostrategy that already today is shaping the probability of the emergence of a major, possibly era-defining, rivalry between the United States and China. U.S. high policy choices toward security in East Asia are closely constrained, notwithstanding the supposed strategic blessings of a unipolar moment. Imperium can endure, but U.S. sway as the strategically dominant force in East Asian security must erode as, perhaps if, China both modernizes and brings to full maturity a strategic design that allows no positive role for U.S. influence in the region.[36]

U.S. hegemony, which does help define the second nuclear age, contains the seeds of its own demise—at least erosion—in that its regional manifestations around the world are not acceptable to rising regional powers who see little advantage in tolerating what amounts to U.S. organization of their regional security. The demise, or fencing-in, of the implications of the United States' unipolar moment must have a significant nuclear aspect to it. "Old-fashioned" nuclear weapons, as well as other old-fashioned WMD and some new BC options, have to be strategically attractive to East Asian, South Asian, and other polities, including the new Russia, who have a problem deterring a United States supreme in digitized, conventional military prowess.

Second, this period marries naturally a U.S. hegemony with an absence of the kind of great power rivalry, or rivalries, that can shape and direct much of the action in world affairs. Politicians and scholars do not know what to call the current era. "Post–Cold War World" is more than a little tired, not to say empty of positive connotation. Much of the architecture of international security of Cold War vintage remains in place—NATO preeminently—and for excellent reasons; but its roles are uncertain as officials and soldiers are cast adrift from the strategic historical course that they understood, or thought they understood. For Europe today it is not unfair to pose the matter thus: If NATO is the answer, what is the question?[37] For East Asia a parallel point can be made: If the U.S.-Japanese Mutual Security Treaty (1951) is the answer, what is the question?[38] One can try to argue slickly that defense planning today is risk-pulled rather than threat-pushed, but such a formula cannot obscure the fact that decisions are required on endorsement of the scale and character of those risks and on the priorities imposed among them.

In effect, this second nuclear age can be seen as a period of interregnum between irregular cyclical surges in the kind of great power rivalry that organizes many strands in the course of strategic history. There is a sense in which each of the leading players in world politics is adrift without a compass in strategic history, to press a favored metaphor. No ideological commandment, even for Beijing, requires particular nexuses of hostility today between pairs of "greater powers," but that benign cultural fact offers only limited comfort.

Each of the "greater powers" knows well enough where serious security trouble is likely to develop. The United States, informally as yet, has identified China as the leading potential "organizing threat" of tomorrow; that tentative identification encourages an already extant disinclination to credit the new Russia with the will and the capability to provide a "pole" of power. China is in no doubt whatsoever that if it has to contest regional hegemony for East Asia, by far the most plausible rival is the United States playing an extended protectionist role. Russia certainly is irritated by NATO's enlargement and by its belligerent peacemaking initiatives in the Balkans, but recognizes that irritation and genuine cause for alarm are different matters. Russia's alarm, as contrasted with irritation, can be predicted to focus eastward and southeastward rather than westward. Moreover, as the golden rule affirms, the enemy of my enemy is my friend. A Russia sharing northern and central Asia with China probably is going to be a Russia in need of friends and allies. Japan has no explicit foes, let alone a major foe in a single dominant rivalry. But Japan knows that there is only one plausible source of serious menace to its security—broadly defined—and that is the potential influence over its trading

policy and practices that might be achieved by a would-be regionally hegemonic China. Japan's (long-standing) difficulties with the
United States, genuine though they are, pale into near insignificance when compared with the problems that Japan could face
were it obliged to seek to accommodate, which is to say appease,
a risen China.[39]

The case of EU-Europe is more complex, because the demise
of the Soviet threat liberates Europe from the need for U.S. protection. Of all the major players—the "greater powers"—EU-
Europe, notwithstanding the solid-seeming security architecture of
NATO, actually is liable to be the most "adrift." If Russia comes to
focus its security gaze upon east and central Asia, a geopolitical
consequence is almost certain to be a loosening of the transatlantic bonds of security cooperation. If anything, there will be
some danger that an EU-Europe, out of the front line of international antagonisms, could be tempted to play Britain's nineteenth-
century role as "balancer" between more settled protagonists.[40]

For the time being, however, all of this speculation remains
strictly speculation. None of the greater powers can be certain
that a central and, as it were, system-organizing rivalry between
the United States and China actually will mature. Beyond U.S.
hegemony, at present there is no central organizing structure to
international security. In such a condition of uncertainty, the leading players are unsure as to the identity of their major and vital interests and are apt to be confused over what roles they should assume and play.

Third, there is some limited merit in the proposition that this
second nuclear age is set in an ever more globalized political context. Information technologies allow, indeed mandate, that events
that once would have been of local significance can now have
rapid global meaning. "Globalization" is not the issue; the issue,
rather, is whether there are processes of globalization at work that
carry some plausible promise of rewriting the script for world security politics. I am not convinced that globalization means a safer
world. This topic is discussed in the next few paragraphs, but really the whole of this book must stand as a challenge to those who
argue that globalization will translate as enhanced security.

Although some of the theorists of the postulated "American"
revolution in military affairs keyed to (1) intelligence, surveil-
lance, and reconnaissance (ISR), (2) command, control, communications, and computing (C4), and (3) precision strike are thinking in terms of uniquely national U.S. advantage,[41] there is a school

of thought, as just noted, that reads the meaning of the information age rather differently. The theory is that even though states continue to reign, only decreasingly do they rule. A range of possible futures can attend this theory, but the central logic is generally uncontroversial among adherents to the broad proposition. Specifically, a process of globalization allegedly is well advanced that is transforming old-fashioned international politics into world politics, preferably global politics. Problems of contemporary security, so the theory proceeds, embrace factors other than the military and indeed frequently relegate military security to the file of atavistic concerns. Political, economic, societal/cultural, and environmental factors are apt to be treated as pointing as much to core security concerns as do military questions.[42]

Globalization is a very big and amorphous idea. As a "sign of the times," it is worth noticing that a recent textbook, published by Britain's leading scholarly publisher and edited by scholars from the largest, oldest, and best-established of the British nurseries for production of theory on international relations, is entitled *The Globalization of World Politics*. In their introductory essay, the editors, with admirable evenhandedness, specify the arguments both supportive and critical of the thesis of globalization.[43] Among the supporting arguments they cite are pace of economic transformation away from states' ability to control their economies; global electronic (inter alia) communications; development of global culture (with electronic mass media as the midwife); growing homogeneity of peoples; the collapse of time and space as new information technologies defeat geography and chronology; an emerging global polity, with transference of identity and loyalty from the state to other bodies; cosmopolitan culture, or consciousness—growth of a global mind-set as a basis for local action; and appreciation that the risks to security that matter most are truly global in character and cannot be addressed by nation states. Needless to say, perhaps, a counterpoint or two (or three, or four) is possible to each of the arguments just suggested. There are both factual and normative objections to every one of these arguments.

Even if one rejects the bolder of the theories, as I do, plainly there exist processes of globalization that are helping to shape the context of security, including nuclear security. What one finds is that global trends and state-centric security foci are functioning synergistically. There is a global financial market, a global market for military-technical skills of all kinds, and a global market for scarce raw materials and finished products with military applications. In short, in very modern times—early modern and medieval Europe is another matter entirely—never have military goods and services been so mobile; never has military supply and demand been so well organized, expedited, and lubricated. If "global village" means global security community in key security senses, then the relative ease of trafficking in lethal items would matter little. If demand is slight, abundant supply can scarcely signify. The problem is that the current cascade of theory about the several forms of globalization is plausible *up to a point*. That cascade does rest upon evidence of actual, and expanding, global traffic flows that are real enough (even if much of it is only "virtual"). But the global political peace that may lurk somewhere down the pathway of globalization has yet to assume plausibly authentic forms. The argument that globalization correlates with a sharp reduction in the incidence of interstate war, let alone major interstate war, is interesting and worthy of careful consideration; but it ultimately fails to convince. States, and nations that wish to acquire states, continue to command the kind of loyalty necessary for war. Moreover, endangered species of beast or not, even only a very low incidence of interstate war can be sufficient to blight a whole era. One might argue that the twentieth century was ravaged by "only" two major interstate conflicts. Or one might assert that "only" one such conflict was practical in the decades from the 1940s to the 1980s.

The empirical, if not the more normative, theorists of globalization undoubtedly are on to something real and probably important. But just how important global processes are, as contrasted with old-fashioned national, subnational, and regional factors, remains to be seen. The elements of chaos in the structure, or lack of structure—even with U.S. hegemony—of international security referred to above is more than matched (indeed its effects are multiplied) by a globalization that mocks laws and frontiers. In a world abundantly endowed with fissile material and the cultures, precursor materials, and compounds for biological, toxin, and chemical weapons, and the relevant skills for weaponization, the emergence of a global market threatens to help define this second nuclear age. The traditional constraints upon individual initiative for private profit that flow from geopolitics, ideology, state controls, and—broadly—culture are much diminished at this millennium. Globalization means a global village more as a market for the skills, materials, and products for death than as a community wherein the demand for lethal instruments is absent.

Fourth, Samuel P. Huntington's theory of a "clash of civilizations" overreaches,[44] but it does point to an important strategic facet of this second nuclear age. As noted above, most of the world's conflicts are not between states and necessarily not about competition between the interests of states. To admit as much is not, however, to endorse some grand theory of inevitable war among civilizations. Many conflicts are really about political, social, and cultural identity and the rights that such assertion of multidimensional identity should be accorded.[45] Intercommunal violence, though, has only limited explanatory power for the course of world politics. It is true both that interstate war has become rare and that it has been delegitimized. Unfortunately, rare does not mean extinct, and delegitimization does not mean impossibility. More to the point, we have no good reason to believe that such extinction and impossibility are probable conditions for the next century. The current context, which is dominated by intrastate and transnational conflicts, may or may not prove to be a trend with longevity. Whatever one decides to conclude about the declining legitimacy and incidence of interstate conflict, however, cannot plausibly dominate the argument here. Readers might care to recall that major war was deeply unpopular across Europe in the 1930s, but war occurred anyway. Millennium optimism should be noted but rejected. It would have to err only in a tiny fraction of possible cases to be wrong catastrophically (after the fashion of a nuclear deterrence that "works" wonderfully well 99 percent of the time but not for the 1 percent of the time when we really need it).

The second nuclear age is defined most critically by U.S. hegemony and the absence of a dominant rivalry. Moving on, a third nuclear age is likely to be defined by the reassertion of an organizing bipolar competition for power. None of those most critically defining conditions have anything to do with clashing civilizations. The "clash of civilizations" may tell us a lot about the motives behind sundry "Islamic bombs" and assuredly alerts us to the malign impact of intercultural antagonisms; but it scarcely qualifies as a player when competing with the opposed interests of states as expressed in the practice of geopolitics.

Fifth, the United States' unipolar strategic moment of hegemony is as uncontestable as it is ambiguous in its implications. The victorious superpower in the great Cold War should be able to organize security structures in the postwar period. We know that the USSR lost the Cold War; it is less certain that the United

States won. Much of the challenge of the second nuclear age lies precisely in the inability, or political unwillingness, of the United States to play the heavy-handed policeman. The United States may have won the Cold War, but it has not obviously ruled in the years that have followed.

Unsurprisingly, U.S. politicians and officials have not known how to behave in this second nuclear age. In the absence of an "organizing" superstate foe, what is the role of U.S. hegemonic superpower? If, by geopolitical default, the United States is the polity most responsible for international security, what are the rights that balance and facilitate performance of that duty?

A hegemony flowing from unipolarity implies that extraordinary duties are laid uniquely at the door of the hegemonic power. "The imperial temptation," in current U.S. reality, is a chimera.[46] The temptation to U.S. statecraft today is to attempt too little, not too much. The core of the problem is the very character of this age. A period whose most defining characteristic is the absence of a dominant great power rivalry leaves the sole superstate desperately short of reliable navigation aids for policy guidance. The vague vision of a United States doing good in the world through a policy of "engagement" is no more helpful than is the idea of trying to prevent the emergence of regional hegemonic challenges to the United States' somewhat inchoate role as global guardian. Does an activist style of engagement in regional security discourage or, inadvertently perversely, encourage the emergence of regional would-be hegemons? For example, does the upgrading of potential military cooperation as specified under modernization of the terms of the U.S.-Japan Mutual Security Treaty make it less or more probable that China will need to be contained actively?[47] Or, for another example, on balance does the modest but significant enlargement to the east of the U.S. protection system that is NATO encourage or discourage Russian willingness to play the role of responsible Eurasian power?

Policymakers do not have confident answers to these all-too-real regional questions, but neither do scholars. The theory of international politics, after the fashion of Clausewitz's theory of war and strategy, should be able to help educate the mind of the statesperson or soldier, even though it does not yield reliable advice on policy action. U.S. hegemony is a fact, but it is both a fact of less than self-evident meaning and, for some people, a theory of long-term benign imperium. As with power, unipolarity or hegemony is both fact and value. A unipolar and hegemonic, if less than imperial, United States needs not only to understand the structure and "working" of this second nuclear age, but also to decide how best to act in order to shape the future.[48]

There is no very powerful argument to be made suggesting that we are witnessing today in the United States' reluctant hegemonism some fundamental shift in the terms and functioning of world politics. When the course of strategic history renders a polity hegemonic, let alone truly unipolar, the behavior of that polity must be shaped by its domestic character and strategic culture. Strategic history can have no truck with the follies of neorealist theory that would "black-box" disparate societies and states.[49] The modern scholarship that would pose even the possibility of a sharp distinction between culturalist and realist explanations of strategic behavior is fundamentally in error.[50] When policymakers act for their polities, they apply classically realist standards as shaped and fine-tuned by their cultural context.

The sixth defining feature of this current and second nuclear age is its residual, indeed probable, character as nursery of a succeeding bipolar era. One might well hesitate to conclude a chapter on the second nuclear age with presentation of a descriptor of the (nuclear) age most likely to follow. Nonetheless, anticipation of the probable consequences of contemporary trends must help shape nuclear policy decisions now. Recent debates in the United States on nuclear fundamentals—for example, should U.S. policy push for the total elimination of nuclear weapons?—relate directly both to views of the future course of strategic history and to assumptions about the way that world politics works. No matter what impression to the contrary may be given by studies on the details of nuclear matters, nuclear policy and nuclear strategy are subjects first and foremost driven by their political context.

There is no iron law of world politics that requires the effectively bipolar balance of power of 1945–1989 to be functionally replicated in the twenty-first century. The claim that most likely there will be a third nuclear age characterized by a return to approximate political bipolarity rests upon my classically realist appreciation of how world politics works. That appreciation finds leading concrete focus in the structure of Sino-U.S. strategic relations. China is a power that has the potential capability to play an extraordinarily influential role at least in Asia and that appears to be bound, for traditional geopolitical reasons, upon a collision path with the United States. Of course, twenty-first-century China may cease to be a significant player in regional security because of domestic trouble. That caveat granted, the scholar of nuclear (and other WMD) issues today has to develop analysis with a mind to

the strong possibility that world politics two to three decades
hence will be increasingly organized around the rival poles of U.S.
and Chinese power.

This thesis expresses the core of the structure of the future security condition in what would be a third nuclear age. Fortunately,
it does not much matter whether this belief is found to be persuasive or not. The theory cannot be proved, but neither can it be
disproved. What matters is only that the moderate to strong possibility, if not probability, of a future bipolar condition should be
recognized. Indeed, for the partial comfort of readers who
strongly dislike this thesis, one could suggest that the argument
has the potential to work in a way that would be self-negating.
Much as the successful conduct of deterrence paradoxically tends
retrospectively to undermine confidence in the need for, or actual
operation of, that deterrence, so energetic pursuit by the United
States of a neo-Bismarckian statecraft of hegemonic co-option
might postpone the evil day a truly peer competitor appears.

The second nuclear age, even now, is forging a third such age.
There is a sense in which the claim is true even if the United
States works effectively over the next several decades successfully
to discourage the emergence of a superstate rival. Most probably,
a conscious U.S. attempt to play co-optively at being Bismarck's
Germany reborn will prove futile. No matter how powerful the
U.S. military or how wonderfully and uniquely multidimensional
the U.S. ascendancy, primacy is a wasting condition. The American Century will not, at least need not, be terminated determinis-
tically by the reappearance of bipolar rivalry—any more than it
was by the appearance of such rivalry after World War II—but it
can hardly help but fuel the competition that must undermine it.
It is possible that China in the next century will discern more
value in cooperation than in competition with the security system
in East Asia preferred by the United States, just as it is possible
that a recovering Russia will choose to "join Europe" on whatever
terms NATO and the European Union elect to offer. But such possibilities should not be permitted to dominate thought about the
future. Modern strategic history already has registered quite sufficient cases wherein hope has triumphed over experience.

Although all the leading predictions are fraught with deep uncertainty, there are stronger grounds for predicting a return to
bipolar rivalry in Sino-U.S. form than any other pairing.

Consider why the proposition of a return to bipolarity is important for nuclear issues. First, this discussion bears directly on
the question of whether or not *military* security will figure very

significantly in U.S. national security policy over the coming decades.[51] Second, judgment about the political context bears explicitly on the issue of scale and quality of menace to U.S. interests. Third, more detailed consideration of the probable identity of a national rival or rivals leads immediately into scenario-specific structures in strategic relationships. It should be recalled that geopolitics drove geostrategy, which in turn drove choices in U.S. and NATO nuclear strategy, for the four decades of the Cold War.[52] A peer-competitor China would menace Japan—Japanese trade, at least, which would be the same thing—Russia in Asia, and ASEAN in Southeast Asia. A peer-competitor "returning" Russia most immediately would threaten independent Ukraine, the Baltics, all of the Eastern March of the new NATO, and the new EU-Europe. Geostrategically, China is a different rival to the United States than is Russia, and the difference matters.

It is no exaggeration to say that today there is profound uncertainty in the United States—and in NATO-Europe—over the future of the U.S. nuclear arsenal and nuclear strategy. Has nuclear strategy in some vital sense "gone away" because there is no longer in this second nuclear age a foe worthy of a Single Integrated Operational Plan (SIOP)?[53] Alternatively, perhaps, has nuclear strategy "gone away" because for the United States it has been banished into military-operational *and even deterrent* irrelevance by the several variants of the contemporary information-dependent RMA? Or, has nuclear strategy only appeared to go away, or allowed itself to be redefined almost wholly into the channel of disarmament debate, by the lack of contemporary policy demand for its services? The rise of a clearly rival powerful polity, even if only a rival in one region, must work wonderfully to concentrate the mind. Raymond Aron expressed the matter appropriately in one of the finest essays ever written on strategy. In Aron's words, "Strategic thought draws its inspiration each century, or rather at each moment of history, from the problems which events themselves pose."[54] Strategic theorists and defense planners today have no little difficulty thinking and planning in a focused way about and for either an age that lacks a central strategic focus[55]—the current one—or an age yet to emerge—a third nuclear age. The origins of this book lie in appreciation of the loss of compass among those who should, and those who might, think coherently about nuclear and other WMD issues.

Contrary to appearances, perhaps, I am not casually dismissive of futurist theory that is fundamentally skeptical about the continuing vitality of realist assumptions. One can paint a picture of

the twenty-first century wherein world politics has been so transformed by the several processes of globalization that great states
no longer behave in the opportunistic, let alone predatory, way
that frequently was true in modern history (from, say, 1648 to
1991). Admittedly, it is possible that neoclassical realist theorists
like myself may be misunderstanding the general course, character, terms, and conditions of world politics, much as we—and
everyone else—misunderstood the resilience of Soviet power in
the 1980s. It is an appealing thought. This realist, for one, would
be delighted to be convinced both that political peace truly is
breaking out all over the world and that strategic history genuinely has ended. As yet, I am not convinced.

A scholar who seeks to treat nuclear policy in the manner of
policy science, which is to say for the purpose of exploring the
structure of a problem area for policy, is assailed by the calls of
variously "endist" visions and aspirations. The distinguishing mark
of the endist claim is the assertion that times have changed radically. This form of eschatological argument, if permitted, effectively can disarm all rivals. The endist theorist does not need to
debate nuclear strategy in any detail; he or she is self-licensed to
consign rejected arguments into the bin marked "irrelevant," because a world is posited that needs no nuclear strategy.

There is no licensing authority for endist claims, so the short
list below is open-ended (no pun intended). Endist theory is more
than marginally relevant to the nuclear future (or less nuclear future) when it proclaims the following:

1. Strategic history has ended, in that force in large scale of
   application, and perhaps even of threat, no longer is a useful instrument of grand strategy; it is markets that bring
   profit and perhaps security, not the conquest of territory or
   people.[56]
2. History has ended, in that the international history of ide-
   ologically fueled rivalries has been concluded by the definitive victory of liberal democracy and the spirit of market
   economy.[57]
3. Strategic history has ended because popular democracy is
   globally in the ascendant and the record appears to show
   that democracies do not fight each other.[58]

If any of the leading *optimistic* endist theories are credited with
dominant insight, then the only policy question remaining to ask

of the nuclear arsenals is how most safely we can effect their definitive demise. One must introduce the adjective "definitive," because one cannot ignore the fact that nuclear innocence is no longer possible. Even if nuclear and other WMD were to be eschewed, what would prevent an abrupt reversal of policy on nuclear possession at some future time of acute national need?

To be fair, an endist claim is an endist claim. I have some difficulty intellectually with endism, because although I can cope with the existential fact of a unique course of history, I am deeply skeptical of claims for definitive historical endings. As a realist (but not neorealist) analyst and theorist of strategic history, I am all but culturally inbred with the expectation that history will repeat itself, by irregular cycles, in the situations that it creates and re-creates and re-creates, etc.

* * *

This book suggests that the political context for a second nuclear age is not a progressively benign condition of globalization. There is no strong reason to believe that the United States, the China, and the Russia of the early twenty-first century will behave in ways radically different from times past. The transculturally obvious fact that the political costs of major war could hugely outrun the worth of hoped-for benefits does not contribute a fatal indictment of classical realism. The most central precept of the realist perspective is prudence.[59] The fact that polities are more reluctant to fight when they anticipate assault by WMD, or even just lengthy hostilities, is not evidence of some "new way" in politics; it is simply classically realistic prudence.

Sadly for the authority of my argument, though, I recognize that each school of thought on world politics will define the contours of prudent policy in ways that fit the paradigm already preferred. There is no way in which I can demonstrate beyond a reasonable doubt the superior merit in my understanding of behavior toward WMD that is prudent for this second nuclear age. If some readers elect to believe that we are living through some great antistrategic transition that will—not just distantly might—consign the precepts and practices of classical realism to the garbage heap of history, such is their right. To close this discussion with an analogy, some people decline to wear seat belts in cars: they believe that they are immortal, accident-proof, or perhaps divinely blessed with perpetual good luck. Alternatively, there may be people around who believe that if drivers wear seat belts, they will acquire a false sense of security and drive more aggressively.[60]

NOTES

1. Familiar to English readers, at least. The original of the aphorism holds that "they cannot know cricket, who only cricket know." U.S. readers who might be intrigued, if not baffled, by this claim could do a great deal worse than consult the brilliant little book by Nandy, *Tao of Cricket.*
2. An excellent study warns its readers that "for much of the period between 600 and 1025 only one account of events has been preserved—or at least only one with minor variations. This does not mean that it can be regarded as basically correct." Whittow, *Making of Orthodox Byzantium,* p. 9.
3. For recent examples, Gaddis, *We Now Know;* and Fursenko and Naftali, *"One Hell of a Gamble."*
4. Which is not to deny that Holger Herwig succeeds in making an exceptionally strong case for Vienna's war guilt. See his masterly study, *First World War.*
5. David Dunn, *Politics of Threat.*
6. Clausewitz, *On War,* p. 131.
7. Domestic motives for nuclear acquisition figure prominently in Scott Sagan, "Why Do States Build Nuclear Weapons?"
8. Policy orientation is not synonymous with policy relevance. This book is policy oriented. In principle, an author could write a strategic historical study of, say, the Peloponnesian War that would not be policy oriented for today but that would be policy relevant. Kagan, *On the Origins of War,* is a work that is policy relevant but not (quite) policy oriented.
9. Murray and Grimsley, "Introduction: On Strategy," and Knox, "Conclusion: Continuity and Revolution in the Making of Strategy," are essential reading.
10. Speier, "Magic Geography;" Spykman, *Geography of the Peace,* ch. 2.
11. See Brodie, *Absolute Weapon;* Jervis, *Meaning of the Nuclear Revolution;* and Paul, Harknett, and Wirtz, *Absolute Weapon Revisited.*
12. Clausewitz, *On War,* p. 566.
13. Strategic effect refers to the effect upon the course of events of the threat or use of force. Gray, *Explorations in Strategy,* esp. p. 11.
14. An argument important to Keegan, *History of Warfare.*
15. See Johnston, "Thinking About Strategic Culture"; Desch, "Culture Clash"; and Gray, "Strategic Culture as Context."
16. For authoritative brief analyses of U.S. strategic nuclear forces today, see William Cohen, *Annual Report,* pp. 57–61. For Russia, see Wilkening, "Future of Russia's Strategic Nuclear Force"; and Benson, "Competing Views on Strategic Arms Reduction."
17. Beyerchen, "Clausewitz, Nonlinearity, and the Unpredictability of War"; Beaumont, *War, Chaos, and History.*
18. Evidence to back up these strong words is deployed in Gray, *NATO and the Evolving Structure of Order in Europe,* chs. 2, 3. A similar judgment pervades Wallace, "Truth and Power, Monks and Technocrats"; but see Booth, "Reply to Wallace."

19. Which happens to be principally in Chapter 4.
20. Booth, "Dare Not to Know."
21. Bull, "Strategic Studies and Its Critics"; Gray, *Strategic Studies*, ch. 4; Howard, "Forgotten Dimensions of Strategy." Betts, "Should Strategic Studies Survive?" also is relevant.
22. Gray, *American Revolution in Military Affairs* and "Fuller's Folly."
23. See Aron, "Evolution of Modern Strategic Thought," p. 7.
24. Iklé, "Second Coming of the Nuclear Age."
25. Gray, "Nuclear Weapons and the Revolution in Military Affairs."
26. Betts, "Should Strategic Studies Survive?" p. 31.
27. Payne, "Post–Cold War Requirements for U.S. Nuclear Deterrence Policy," is strongly supportive of my thesis.
28. Harkavy, "Images of the Coming International System," p. 570.
29. This idea became something of an *International Security* debate. Layne, "Unipolar Illusion"; Jervis, "International Primacy"; Huntington, "Why International Primacy Matters"; Posen and Ross, "Competing Visions for U.S. Grand Strategy"; Mastanduno, "Preserving the Unipolar Moment."
30. Kennedy, *Rise and Fall of the Great Powers.* This book was celebrated in the United States as flagging the peril of military overextension to long-term economic health—and hence security tomorrow—whereas in truth it was the USSR that fell, as it were, to Kennedy's declinist thesis.
31. It is not only U.S. academics who have become in danger of intoxication by the fumes of primacy. With reference to the RMA, for example, the defense editor of *The Economist* has written that "history suggests that no country can exploit new military technologies to maintain a position of global dominance indefinitely. Ultimately, other countries will learn to counter or copy the revolution in military affairs. But there is no prospect of Russia, China or any other country having the wealth or expertise to catch up with America for decades." Grant, "America's Ever Mightier Might," p. 78. It is words like these that mandate reading of Matthews, *Challenging the United States Symmetrically and Asymmetrically.*
32. Nye, *Bound to Lead*, remains useful.
33. There is, however, rather less to this claim than might appear. One should recall that British superpower was unsuccessful in the Americas between 1775 and 1783, while U.S. superpower succeeded only in delaying North Vietnam's conquest of the South for a decade between 1965 and 1975. Superpowers can lose small wars. See Ion and Errington, *Great Powers and Little Wars.*
34. Joffe, "'Bismarck' or 'Britain'?" and "How America Does It."
35. An argument well registered in Freedman, "Great Powers, Vital Interests and Nuclear Weapons."
36. The speculative literature was beginning to boom before the Asian economic crisis of 1998. By way of an illustrative sample: Rohwer, *Asia Rising;* Calder, *Asia's Deadly Triangle;* Bernstein and Munro, *The Coming Conflict with China;* Segal, "How Insecure Is Pacific Asia?"; Shambaugh, "Chinese Hegemony over East Asia by 2015?"; and Nye, "China's Re-emergence." If anything, the regional, possibly eventually global, economic crisis enhances rather than reduces the influence of a China that appears to be weathering the storm better than its regional neighbors.
37. This question is posed and answered in Gray, *NATO and the Evolving Structure of Order in Europe.*

38. The treaty was revised in 1996 to allow for more extensive Japanese logistic support for U.S. operations in the region—a revision that met with predictable hostility in Beijing.

39. In the early 1990s, a different view was fashionable. For an exciting example, see Friedman and Lebard, *Coming War with Japan.*

40. I am grateful to Dale Walton for his insightful exploration of these ideas.

41. For example, Owens, "The Emerging System of Systems"; Nye and Owens, "America's Information Edge"; and Arquilla and Ronfeldt, *Athena's Camp.*

42. Buzan, *People, States and Fear,* was a landmark text. Also see Weaver et al., *Identity, Migration;* and Nolan, *Global Engagement.*

43. Smith and Baylis, "Introduction," pp. 9–11.

44. Huntington, "Clash of Civilizations" and *Clash of Civilizations and the Remaking of World Order.*

45. Weaver et al., *Identity, Migration.*

46. Tucker and Hendrickson, *Imperial Temptation.*

47. Shambaugh, "Containment or Engagement of China?"

48. It is almost painfully apparent that a U.S. Quadrennial Defense Review (QDR) that purportedly was keyed to the shaping of the future strategic environment in fact has nothing of much interest to contribute to policy determination on such "shaping." William Cohen, "Report of the Quadrennial Defense Review," pp. 8–14, summarizes the QDR, including its massively unrealized ambition to provide a strategy-led guide to shaping a U.S.-friendly future strategic environment. Kane, "Sins of Omission," offers a devastating critique.

49. Waltz, *Theory of International Politics.*

50. Just such a contrast is posed in Desch, "Culture Clash." Desch's view is challenged in Gray, "Strategic Culture as Context."

51. Baldwin, "Security Studies and the End of the Cold War," and Betts, "Should Strategic Studies Survive?" are important.

52. Gray, *Geopolitics of Super Power;* Leffler, *Preponderance of Power.*

53. Ball, "Development of the SIOP"; Blair, *Logic of Accidental Nuclear War,* esp. ch. 3.

54. Aron, "Evolution of Modern Strategic Thought," p. 7.

55. Glaser, "Nuclear Policy Without an Adversary"; Goldman, "Thinking About Strategy Absent the Enemy."

56. Baldwin, "Security Studies and the End of the Cold War," tends powerfully in this direction.

57. Expressed most famously in Fukuyama, *End of History and the Last Man.*

58. Brown, Lynn-Jones, and Miller, *Debating the Democratic Peace.*

59. For which the most sacred text remains Aron, *Peace and War.*

60. For a variant on this analogy, to my mind generic rejection of the policy argument in this book would be akin to shipowners ignoring national and international law and choosing not to equip ships with lifeboats, for the logical reason that they had no intention of allowing their ships to sink.

3

Beyond the Fuel Cycle: Strategy and the Proliferation Puzzle

Chapters 3 and 4 together tackle the heartland of contemporary nuclear issues. Chapter 3 proceeds from consideration of just how important, or otherwise, nuclear proliferation may prove to be, to a critical and somewhat skeptical commentary on the proliferation study industry; after detailed consideration of the principal motives for nuclear possession, the chapter presents six "signposts" that point toward areas worthy of subsequent development.

WHO CARES? AND HOW MUCH?

This is not intended to be a book about the proliferation of nuclear weapons and other WMD. The scholarly and popular literature on nuclear WMD, though not on BCW—and not quite on delivery vehicles[1]—is overabundant in quantity and in many aspects of quality also. It follows that the last thing needed by this exploration of the nuclear condition is yet another inquiry into the wells of nuclear proliferation. This is not to say that the nuclear status of polities is unimportant; quite the contrary. But it is to say that the erstwhile cottage industry of proliferation analysis, which since 1991 has expanded to a more industrial scale of enterprise, by and large can be trusted to treat competently the significant secondary matters of how, how much, and when, though perhaps not so reliably the overriding strategic questions of why, and so what.

In the years of Cold War, *the* primary nuclear problem was the menace of a World War III that could, in some variants, have ended the human experience. It followed, sensibly, that other nuclear (and WMD) problems—in Western or Eastern perspective, at least—were apt to be addressed as subsets to the dominant peril. At some risk of giving gratuitous offense, one must add that "the best and the brightest" among U.S. strategic thinkers during the Cold War devoted only a modest fraction of their time and creative energy to what then appeared to be the objectively secondary field of nuclear proliferation. The fact that more and more of the leading lights of the extended defense community have addressed questions of proliferation in the 1990s does not necessarily stand as a rebuke for their former focus on East-West concerns.

Nuclear proliferation, like "the Balkans," is an issue area that the United States should care about. But, should it care about it very much? More to the point, should it be prepared to do much about it? And, even more to the point, is there much that the United States reliably, let alone definitively, can do about its WMD proliferation concerns? Once one descends below the level of standard pieties, the answers to questions such as these become less and less obvious. The central point of the asserted analogy between the Balkans and nuclear proliferation is that in both cases the stance of U.S. policy virtue is overshadowed by the reality of unwelcome forces that ultimately cannot be denied. The United States may hold back the evil day, as it did for ten years in Vietnam, but it cannot engineer a just and lasting solution to the unpleasantness in the former Yugoslavia, any more than it can command the tide of proliferating WMD to retreat. This is not to deny in principle the contextual value of an imposed delay—indeed one can argue that U.S. intervention in Vietnam in 1965–1975 had strongly positive consequences for the region (though admittedly not for Cambodia)[2]—but it is to suggest that some missions are impracticable and hence strategically foolish. The relevant mission for the United States may well be to cope with, and survive in, a world insecurity condition wherein WMD and their delivery vehicles will proliferate. Even if I favored a distinctly muscular, preventive coercive diplomacy and direct military action to oppose the proliferation of WMD, the target intelligence and political requirements for such a policy would be unduly heroic for U.S. (or anyone else's) statecraft.

Of course, there is a problem for the United States with the proliferation of WMD, and especially of nuclear weapons. But as we shall see, that problem is both generally manageable in and of itself and of modest significance when compared with the nuclear dimension to the defining (bipolar antagonistic) political characteristic of the first, and eventually probably third (and beyond), nuclear age. WMD in the hands of "lawbreakers" carry the threat to neutralize the power and authority of the sheriff for order—that is, the practical authority of a hegemonic United States. Lawrence Freedman is right when he notes that "rather than reinforce power politics as usual, nuclear weapons in fact confirm a tendency towards the fragmentation of the international system in which the erstwhile great powers play a reduced role."[3] By raising the risks for all concerned, or all of those contemplating concern, nuclear proliferation encourages a self-regarding autarky in security practice. This means, in principle, that notwithstanding its "unipolar moment" in this second nuclear age, the United States is going to be ever more reluctant to play regional "balancer," let alone global cop, when such roles carry the risk of exposure of forces, allies, and just possibly the U.S. homeland to counter-deterrent (or retaliatory) action by WMD.

Unfortunately, balanced political and strategic judgment is apt to be the first victim of the retreat into technicity and a world of presumptive nuclear peril that often is the dense thicket of expert scholarship on proliferation. Proliferation experts have a way of being expert on almost everything except what the subject of their expertise means politically and strategically. To be fair, the whole realm of strategic and security studies is awash with such niche cases of genuine, but bounded, expertise. Theorists of seapower, airpower, spacepower, and now cyberpower vie for our respect. But are they offering a whole theory of sufficient strategic effect for success in statecraft? Or, is the *plat du jour* but one course in what needs to be approached as a balanced meal overall?

Lest I should be misunderstood, proliferation could matter to the point where vital or even survival levels of intensity of interest are engaged because of the following considerations:

1. Nuclear proliferation renders some regional neighborhoods far more dangerous than they were previously.

2. Nuclear-armed regional polities, or other actors similarly equipped, might inflict mass destruction upon U.S. and U.S.-allied forces forward deployed, upon local friends and allies, or even upon the homeland of the United States.

3. Successful use of WMD as a diplomatic counterdeterrent would undermine fundamentally the basis of the current regional/international order, which frequently amounts in practice to a (single) superpower protection system—in other words, a hegemonic system.[4]

4. In some statistical perspective, the emergence of more (declared or undeclared) nuclear powers means a rise in the possibility of nuclear "events," purposeful or accidental. The psychological, political, and hence probably strategic consequences of a, or some, "small" nuclear event(s) are not easily analyzed by mind-sets that resist nonlinear, chaotic possibilities. Again to quote Freedman, "The concept of a small nuclear war has yet to be developed. Any nuclear use still moves us into the area of unimaginable catastrophe."[5] His hyperbole is appropriate.

Valid though these points certainly are, they are not by any means the whole story.

1. Although nuclear proliferation increases the awfulness of war, it may also greatly reduce its regional incidence. One should not derive huge satisfaction from this qualifying point, because it is a theme of this text that deterrence, even nuclear deterrence, is unreliable.

2. Attempts at nuclear (or BC) use on a relatively small scale should be defeatable by the multiple layers of physical denial that the unipolar superpower could apply. Of course, the U.S. superpower might not be engaged as an active player during the nuclear (inter alia) event(s), and "friction" happens, as Clausewitz insists.[6]

3. Awful and awesome as a "small" nuclear war could be—unless thwarted by a United States armed with dominant battlespace knowledge,[7] a political decision for timely intervention, and brute force multilayered and nicely networked to prevent nuclear action—that awfulness and awesomeness is likely to be small when compared with the damage that the superpowers might have inflicted as a finale to the great Cold War.

So proliferation matters strategically. But the study of the proliferation of WMD and their means of delivery needs to be rescued from suffocation by undue technicity on the part of those who have ploughed this section of the field of modern strategic studies.

THE PROLIFERATION STUDY INDUSTRY

Contemporary scholarship, even official policy, seemingly is better equipped with impressive-sounding answers than it is with authoritative questions. Wherever one looks for clear direction on the nature and character of what has been called "the proliferation puzzle," one tends to find inconsistent suggestions. What is the problem of nuclear security in this second nuclear age? Most likely there is no single dominant problem. Anyone who has monitored the Western scholarly, and official, literature on matters of military security in the 1990s should have been impressed by the sheer volume of work devoted to the issue area of the proliferation of WMD and their principal means of delivery.[8] The literature is large, but it has a frustrating formlessness. A small army of analysts, officials, soldiers, and popular commentators are expending great energy on the subject of "proliferation," but somehow the endeavor has the appearance of an exercise in futility.

Several fundamental problems beset the proliferation study industry. First, the United States is an engineering-minded, problem-solving culture, whose analysts are ever vulnerable to cultural seduction by the challenge of yet another problem in need of solution.[9] In other words, the idea that nuclear proliferation might be a condition rather than a problem, and a diversely manifested condition at that, is not one that sits easily in the word processors of some U.S. experts. After all, if the proliferation of WMD and of cruise and ballistic missiles is researchable as a topic, as obviously it is, then that which is researchable should lend itself to treatment with conclusions that allow confident researchers to manipulate their findings with some controlling solutions.

Second, there is a Scholar's Fallacy that beguiles many more people than scholars alone. Although there is much to be said in favor of careful study of proliferation phenomena, understanding is not by any means the golden key to wise and effective policy. Logically, understanding may have to be the preceding enabler for action, but it is neither action itself nor a functional substitute for action. Both the technical and political challenges posed by the proliferation of WMD are well understood today. Many fantasies, plausible fallacies, and other myths persist—as I explain in the next chapter—but truly there are no great mysteries about NBC proliferation or about the spread of missile technologies and missiles themselves.

The somewhat uneasy contemporary guardian of global order, the United States, does not really need to expend tens of millions of dollars and hundreds of thousands of personhours to study the problem of nuclear (and other WMD) proliferation. Of course, every actual and potential case is distinctive, but each such case fits readily enough into a fairly simple framework of theory on motivation.[10] U.S. exceptionalism has a lot to answer for in the realm of helping to misinform those whom it encultures.

For reasons that seem excellent and generally valid, the United States is apt to regard its strategic choices and subsequent behavior through the lens of understanding provided by the assumption of an exceptional, and exceptionally benign, U.S. role in world politics. Many U.S. strategic commentators would be shocked to be told that there are people abroad who genuinely believe that sometimes the United States needs to be deterred. For a related point, it is surprising just how many apparently sophisticated and well-informed people in the United States are comfortable with the deeply pejorative, and prospectively perilously misleading, concept of the "rogue state"—an issue raised briefly in Chapter 1.[11] What is a rogue state? How would a particular polity qualify to be so classified? The answer, stolen as an analogy with the misbehavior of some large mammals in the wild animal kingdom, is a state that behaves in a grossly antisocial manner—always assuming that the concept of an international society of states has some authority, of course. In practice, the problem is that the spectrum of antisocial behavior in world politics can range from regimes that set out to conquer the world—truly the neighbors from hell—through regimes whose security demands are incompatible with the reasonable needs of other regimes in the immediate region, to regimes whose principal sins fall in the category of an honest and not unreasonable definition of national interests that is at some odds with contemporary preferences in U.S. foreign policy.

A significant problem promoted by the U.S. thesis of exceptionalism is that it lacks a natural frontier. Leaving aside the large and potent ideological cultural dimension to the claim for U.S. exceptionalism, even the fairly raw and brutal realpolitical claims for exceptional global license that flow from hegemonic, or unipolar, superpower status are prone to mislead the unwary. A United States that is profoundly exceptional in U.S. self-assessment is not exactly a United States well equipped to distinguish the universal from the exceptional in its strategic reasoning. A hegemonic superpower is apt to suspect "roguery" when what it sees is not so much roguery as it is common political thought and behavior on the subject of security.

For strategic cultural reasons, the argument that follows can be difficult to explain to a U.S. audience. Some of the reasons the United States is, and in my opinion should be, the most lethally militarily equipped polity in the world pertain to the unique political condition of the United States as the global hegemon. But other important reasons the United States is an abundantly nuclear-armed polity are reasons that find resonance in many regions around the world. To Americans, and indeed to non-Americans who are sympathetic or committed to the U.S.-protected world order, it is all but self-evident why the United States should enjoy counterdeterrent effectiveness at worst and escalation dominance at best in all categories of weapons and classes of conflicts. The point is that some of the more important reasons the United States chooses to remain a nuclear weapons state (NWS) are common to a range of polities and, frighteningly, even to some would-be polities around the world.

The political and strategic logic that underpins the preceding paragraphs is probably easier to grasp if one is not American. The problem for Americans is how to grasp what is not at all exceptional in their basket of strategic cultural beliefs. The careful U.S. study of WMD proliferation thus is likely to run afoul of the problem, or condition, that beliefs and behavior that are roguish to Americans are simply prudent to the "natives."

The study of nuclear (inter alia) proliferation is unlikely to yield significant benefit to Western clients so long as the motives of "threshold" states, and other presumed would-be proliferants, are framed by a theory of roguery. For every genuine rogue state there will be a handful of candidate proliferants whose core motives for WMD acquisition are entirely congruent with some large fraction of U.S. motivation. Some of the reasons currently authoritative for the effectively indefinite maintenance of British status as an NWS look distinctly attractive to polities geostrategically far more exposed to danger than Britain is likely to be during the next half century.[12]

U.S. scholars need to be warned of two perils to the value of their scholarship. On the one hand, they are potentially vulnerable to the effects of the ubiquitous Scholar's Fallacy, which encourages the view that study of a problem is equivalent to its effective treatment. Study is not the moral or strategic equivalent of action. On the other hand, those U.S. scholars need to be alerted to the strategic cultural fact that they are U.S. scholars, and that much of what they believe to be U.S. strategic truth happens also to be geostrategic common sense, worldwide.

The third problem area worth highlighting about the study of proliferation is the challenge of local diversity. This point can be made most clearly with the aid of an analogy from international relations theory. It is obvious that the many scholarly endeavors committed to the study of the causes of wars (or war) and the conditions for peace over the past eighty or so years have produced no single dominant, let alone plausible, solution or answer.[13] The principal reason may be that the scholars involved have not been good enough scholars, but one doubts if that is the key explanation for failure in theory building. The leading reason scholars have failed to develop a compelling dominant theory of the causes of wars/war is because the subject does not lend itself to the aggregation and reduction that theory needs. Modern scholars have not really improved upon Thucydides' insistence in *The Peloponnesian War* that the will to fight for empire rests upon "three of the strongest motives, fear, honor, and interest."[14] These three universal and enduring motives explain war yet leave almost everything to be understood about any particular conflict. Theory building about the proliferation of WMD runs into a like difficulty.

"Fear, honor, and interest" explains both everything and nothing about proliferation. There are generic reasons encouraging nuclear weapons status that transcend geopolitics and strategic culture—as we shall see in the next section of this chapter—but those generic reasons (e.g., security or fear) themselves explain nothing in particular. Even the most general, adaptable, and seemingly reasonable of rationales for nuclear acquisition transpire in practice to explain nothing very much. For example, although there is a host of fairly plausible specific explanations for British retention of its strategic condition as an NWS, the core of the matter is to be found neither in any one of those explanations, nor even in a coherent assembly of them all. The true explanation for Britain's persistence as an NWS into the twenty-first century lies in minor key in domestic politics ("New Labour" is determined to look responsible on national security to its domestic constituency) but in major key (in Aron's cardinal principle of prudence) in statecraft (as that principle is defined by a classic realist).[15] Because the future is open-ended, unknown, and unknowable, and because even the recent past alerts us to the possibility of peril and tragedy on a heroic scale, it is responsible for the British government to face the uncertainties of the next century nuclear armed, particularly when currently there are no compelling arguments for unilateral national nuclear disarmament (the Strategic Arms Reduction Talks [START] process may yet produce such arguments, of course).

Local circumstances of history, geopolitics, and culture, however, have the probably net fortunate effect of denying British prudential logic any general authority. British reasoning on the permanent merit in national nuclear armament could appeal to every polity in the world; the logic is not by any means specific to Britain. Whereas politically and strategically it was entirely unremarkable that the Britain of the 1950s should become the world's third nuclear weapons state, few if any polities today or tomorrow could approach the nuclear option as if it were just another, albeit unusually expensive,[16] decision in the realm of force planning for national defense.

What we find, and this is one of the general themes of the book specified in Chapter 1, is that one size does not fit all via a general theory of nuclear (and other WMD) proliferation. Local and regional conditions differ and as a consequence have different implications for the likelihood and probable consequences of particular policy choices. Much as can be said of the scholarly literature on the causes of war, more and more study of proliferation problems is unable to yield a general wisdom beyond the injunction to be attentive to local detail. To repeat: one size of theory, or of U.S. counterproliferation policy, does not appear to fit all actual or potential examples of the phenomenon to be opposed (with variable energy).

The implications of this argument are not particularly happy, but they do help explain the deeply unsatisfactory character of the expert literature on nuclear (and other WMD, and their means of delivery) proliferation. General theory is only that and applies as general theory to no particular case in any self-evident fashion. The result is that academics, such as Scott D. Sagan and Kenneth Waltz, are at liberty to conduct an essentially meaningless expert scholarly debate about the general merits and the general perils of nuclear proliferation.[17] Proliferation is always specific to time, place, and circumstance. To debate proliferation as if it were in limbo is as foolish as to debate war per se. War is massively undesirable, unless one has no superior alternative at hand. Similarly, WMD proliferation is never an abstract topic pertaining to strategic truth but invariably a topic with a specific context.

It appears to me that the cottage industry of proliferation studies is unduly prone to march down two blind alleys. The first such blind alley is the quest for *the* theory and *the* policy, when the actuality is that real-world diversity denies governments the luxury of adopting "golden key" policy and strategy to cover all significant corners of the proliferation field. The second blind alley, which really is a consequence of the necessary frustration of the first one, is the retreat into detailed technicity. Lest one should be accused of unfair victimization of proliferation studies, one must hasten to add that the U.S., and indeed the transnational, community of arms control scholars is wont to retreat into expert detail on a whole range of topics.[18]

What we have here is operation of the Law of the Instrument. Scholars and officials do what they know how to do. These experts do not really understand whether or not a particular polity will exercise its nuclear option as a threshold state, so they do what they can do. What the experts can do, and do at great length in an ever burgeoning library of descriptive effort, is "tell the story" of the fuel and weaponization cycle(s) in question and of the pertinent political, administrative, and industrial quests after nuclear (and other WMD) prowess. Much of this study effort is well conducted, indeed truly expert. Unfortunately, it has generically the same weakness as did the hugely technical literature on strategic arms control between the superpowers in the last two decades of the Cold War. Specifically, the deeply technical analysis available in the classified and open literature was all but comprehensively irrelevant. Until the Soviet polity changed politically in a fundamental way, arms control worthy of note was impracticable. Readers may recall a classic definition of fanaticism: the redoubling of effort long after the purpose of an enterprise is forgotten, or perhaps long after the practicability of an enterprise has been assumed as an item of faith. The industry of proliferation studies, though genuinely expert, itself has become something of a barrier to clear-eyed policy and strategy on its subject. A central reason for this condition has been inferred already and warrants recognition as the fourth general point.

My fourth general problem with the industry of proliferation studies is that it has been captured by a tribe of some distinctly prosaic, if undoubtedly expert, people for whom it has become a permanent rice bowl. It may be unjust to single out proliferation studies as being particularly plagued by uninspired, and uninspiring, data collectors and technicians; nonetheless, this area of scholarly endeavor in strategic studies has become a meal ticket for thousands of people. Part of the problem lies in the character of "the American way" of government by consultancy. Officials with public money to spend will always find willing fundees. A million dollars of study effort is likely to reward the funding agency with the "insights" that a polity that has a serious national security problem may well consider pursuing a nuclear option, and that the less well heeled of would-be WMD proliferants should find that biological or toxin weapons offer the most cost-effective lethality (and terroristic-coercive return) for the buck.

The proliferation study industry is vulnerable to challenge by the same quintessentially strategic question that can embarrass a wide range of fields of enquiry: So what? The mountain of facts, quasi-facts, and possible facts about near, or undeclared but actual, "proliferants" amounts to what? Proliferation, nonproliferation, antiproliferation, and counterproliferation studies have nothing of much interest to tell us beyond what Thucydides offered: the motives of "fear, honor and interest" rule.

Finally, a fifth general difficulty with the proliferation study industry is that it tends to exhibit, and be driven by, an all but self-parody of parochial Western attitudes. I share many of those attitudes. Nonetheless, a certain strategic cultural self-awareness can be a useful check against overambitious expectations. There are reasons—pertaining to robustness of command and control arrangements,[19] the technical safety of weapons, possible proclivities to take extreme risks, and the general unreliability of deterrence—that it is sensible to affirm the principle that the best WMD proliferation is the least WMD proliferation. Nonetheless, that principle is by no means necessarily authoritative for all cases of conflict, and even when it is commanding in its apparent prudence, it rests upon shaky political, strategic, and ethical foundations.

The Western professional and popular literature on proliferation tells us almost as much about ourselves as it does about the subject. Moreover, the very concept of proliferation itself has a less-than-helpful pejorative ring to it. The point is not that the further spread of WMD and their means of delivery should be regarded generally with equanimity, let alone should be welcomed, but rather that our attitudes can blind us to the necessary strategic understanding of what is going on. It may be useful to prestigmatize nuclear acquisition by "threshold" nuclear weapons states, but not if we immunize ourselves against comprehending where this second nuclear age is tending.

Overall, there are grounds for concern lest the Western proliferation study industry is spending too much time, and too much of the taxpayers' money, massaging and trumpeting its/our values and prejudices, and too little time trying to come to grips with the phenomenon at issue. That phenomenon is best understood as an expression of the political demand for security as locally and regionally defined. It is high time for this analysis to move directly into the country of motivation, into the key area that is the demand side of the proliferation puzzle.

SECURITY DEMAND IS KING—OR IS IT? _____

In the understructured new security environment characterized by U.S. hegemony, technical hindrances to the spread of WMD and missile means for their delivery are distinctly inadequate to cope with heroic challenges. A heroic scale of challenge can be defined as a policy demand for WMD assistance in protection of core security values. If a polity is determined to acquire nuclear weapons, for example, and if that polity has access to large funds, supply-side constraints from the global nonproliferation regime in its several dimensions will not succeed;[20] at least, supply-side constraints on scarce materials, technologies, and skills ultimately will not succeed in denying nuclear acquisition. Those constraints, especially with reference to the supply of plutonium or highly enriched uranium—the most key of scarce materials[21]—can succeed, however, in raising the costs, delaying program completion, and impairing the quality of a national program to acquire WMD. Those qualifications to a failing endeavor at control may be important. To buy time is perhaps to buy time that allows for a suddenly or cumulatively dramatic change in political context. After all, South African–type political miracles do happen, albeit not often, not predictably, and not necessarily always to a definitively benign outcome.[22]

It is important to emphasize the significance of an argument I advanced in a controversial book I wrote a few years ago. In *House of Cards: Why Arms Control Must Fail,* I suggested that efforts to achieve arms control and disarmament—as contrasted with the control of arms, which fortunately is a different and more practicable matter altogether—rested upon a critically debilitating fallacy.[23] I argued that there is an "arms control paradox" that holds that the more urgently a conflict relationship is in need of the services of arms control medicine or surgery, the less likely is it to be able to enjoy those services. Why? Because the political antagonisms that fuel a war-prone condition work to preclude that meaningful measure of cooperation between adversaries that is the core activity of an arms control process.

The proliferation puzzle is at risk to the same genus of fallacy as are other regions of arms control. Nuclear and other WMD proliferation phenomena are driven by demand-side forces, not by the availability of relevant technical supply. It would be difficult to exaggerate the salience of this point. The superordinate importance of demand over supply applies not only to narrowly contemporary matters of attempts at enforcement of nuclear restraint, but also to the prospects for nuclear weapons acquisition in the most distant future. There is no great nuclear secret that can be protected against polities or other agencies who have determination and money; and no matter how successful the NPT regime may be in slowing the pace of proliferation, the nuclear era is here to stay. Nuclear denial and nuclear self-denial are both reversible in future strategic history. The belief, or hope, persists that the nuclear era can be ended by some grand global human achievement in nuclear self-denial. Such an exercise in "abolition," even if feasible, would endure only until it was contradicted by a desperate security need. Polities could agree only to forgo the benefits of WMD until they were obliged by circumstances to change their minds.[24]

The scholarly literature on the proliferation puzzle, properly sifted to sideline the tendency to undue technicity, is quite unambiguous and generally persuasive in its treatment of the motives behind nuclear acquisition. It will come as no great revelation to readers to be informed that polities want to acquire nuclear (and other) WMD because they seek security, in the hope of gain, because the institutional interests that contend in their domestic processes find WMD advantageous to their substate level of stakes, and because there can be symbolic value in nuclear weapons status. Scholars have tended to revel in their discerning of the obvious about the motives to proliferate, but nonetheless they have grasped some of the essentials of the topic. What remains to be accomplished is the highlighting of the dominant basket of motivation—which is to do with security—and definition of the challenges that that dominance implies. Specifically, how best can we cope with and in a persistently nuclear (and BC) future that likely has at least some terms and conditions notably different from those that obtained in the first nuclear age of the great Cold War (though that future will share with the Cold War years an unhappy unreliability of deterrence)?

Arms are not the problem; rather it is the political demand for arms. Salvador de Madariaga wrote in his memoirs:

> The trouble with disarmament was (it still is) that the problem of war is tackled upside down and at the wrong end. Upside down first; for nations do not arm willingly. Indeed they are sometimes

only too willing to disarm, as the British did to their sorrow in the Baldwin days. Nations don't distrust each other because they are armed; they are armed because they distrust each other. And therefore to want disarmament before a minimum of common agreement on fundamentals is as absurd as to want people to go undressed in winter. Let the weather be warm, and people will discard their clothes readily and without committees to tell them how they are to undress.[25]

The transnational arms control community has long had intellectual, emotional, and even some ethical difficulty with the following points: arms control is not identical to the control of arms; arms are tools of political purpose; and humans and their polities are remarkably flexible and adaptive in their willingness and ability to find ways to hurt other humans and polities.

It is easy to be misunderstood. I do not despise efforts at a supply-side approach to the proliferation puzzle. The argument here is not that supply-side action is without merit, but rather that the demand side of the proliferation challenge is so dominant—especially today when access to a supply of key skills, materials, and technologies is feasible, if not always easy and rarely cheap—that any approach that seeks to sideline demand-side issues is certain to fail.

For a powerfully apposite analogy to nuclear proliferation, consider the challenge posed by the "drug problem." What is the drug problem? Is it, for example, the fact that Andean peasant farmers can make far more money growing coca plants than growing coffee? Or is the problem the demand for drugs that guarantees that those Andean peasant farmers will be able to sell their coca crop to the agents of the Medellín or Cali cartels? Some defoliation action in the Andean foothills will have a temporary effect on drug prices as supply and demand readjust. But in a world where coca itself, and several coca substitutes, can be grown over a large area, a supply-side assault on the drug problem must fail. This analogy is extreme, but it does make the necessary point with uncompromising clarity. Just as we have to cope with drug addiction because we cannot solve the "problem" of the demand for drugs, so we have to cope—as an extension of the ways in which we do at present—with a more nuclear-, indeed more WMD-proliferant world, because we cannot solve the "problem" of local and regional political demand for the security that is believed to flow uniquely from possession of such weaponry.

As theorists, scholars are addicted to drawing distinctions that have the potential to mislead as well as inform. Such may be the case here. What follows is a summary, though critical, analysis of the conclusions of scholarship about the motives for nuclear proliferation. Scott Sagan's generally excellent writings necessarily figure here prominently, but this presentation is not simply a précis of his recent scholarship. He has provided three "models" that can explain nuclear proliferation.[26] These are useful, but I elect to add a fourth "model" (which codes as Security II), and I would record unease about an academic exercise that risks distinguishing matters that more truly are one, whole phenomenon.

It is instructive to march the four models in explanation of nuclear weapons status past a British policy reviewing stand. Polities endorse nuclear status for reasons of Security I (external danger); "Security II" (hope of external gain); domestic politics; and symbolism. Britain's (semi-)independent nuclear deterrent—four Vanguard-class SSBNs armed with Trident II SLBMs—certainly enjoys political cover with a dominant security (I) argument. That argument reduces to the thoroughly plausible claim that the future (a long time!) is deeply uncertain and—who knows—a British nuclear force one day might be useful for British security. But in addition to the usefully opaque Security I rationale, persistence of the British nuclear deterrent also can be explained with reference to British domestic politics. A New Labour government is committed to appearing, and being (to be fair), realistically "prudent" in policymaking for national security. Given that unilateral nuclear disarmament is a ghost that lurks in the wings only slightly off stage for Tony Blair's administration, the commitment by his Labour government to a nuclear future for British defense policy has obvious domestic, as well as international, policy resonance.

Scholars of international relations, or world politics, often seem to forget that the world is organized into polities, as security communities. The rigorous semi-nonsense of Waltz's neorealism would have us treat the actors in world security politics largely as if they were black boxes,[27] but all knowledge is local knowledge, all policy is made domestically, and every maker of policy and strategy has been encultured by a particular tradition and society. So why do polities, or other security communities, seek WMD?

Security I: To Cope with Perceptions of External Threat

The external threat that is perceived, or anticipated, is determined according to more or to less expansive definitions of the requirements of national security. For example, compare the relative strength of the security challenge to U.S., as contrasted with French, definition of needs for nuclear forces. Insofar as there is an external security rationale for French national nuclear forces, it pertains to a generalized raising of risks for any polity that might imperil core French security values. In the gloriously apposite phrase quoted by Michael Quinlan, "A nuclear state is a state that no-one can afford to make desperate."[28] The commonsense appeal of this strategic logic has not been lost on Iraqis, Libyans, and Iranians. France believes it requires nuclear forces for the mission of what Herman Kahn called "Type I deterrence": deterrence of direct attack on the homeland.[29]

The United States, by contrast, requires in addition to Type I deterrence some potency in Type II deterrence, the deterrence of attack upon distant allies and friends. This "extended" form of deterrence typically raises questions of credibility that have profound implications for nuclear doctrine and force planning.[30] A nuclear force posture judged good enough to send a putative foe's risk calculus healthily into the red zone may well be far from good enough to extend protection over a distant ally who faces the prospect of defeat in a conventional war. This analysis is edging close to the basic geostrategic problem of NATO's defense during the Cold War. For an extended nuclear deterrent to be sufficiently credible (to the deterrer, the intended deterree, and to the would-be deterrer's security clients), yet tolerably reassuring (again, to all interested parties), it has to appear to offer an all-but-seamless web of possible scales of action, useful major uncertainties, and above all the absence of any catastrophic cliff edge over which the would-be extended deterrer promises to throw all parties (including itself).[31]

Although the scale and character of the U.S. nuclear force posture can be explained in good part with reference simply to the size (and wealth) of the United States and the size (and erstwhile wealth that could be devoted to defense functions) of the USSR, somewhat redundantly perhaps one also has to point to the challenging mission of extended, Type II deterrence that the United States long has accepted. The security rationale for nuclear possession, in part at least, is deeply subjective in particular definition. If a polity's foe is a nuclear weapons state (or a nuclear threshold state), then the strategic case for a nuclear deterrent to cover core national values can be qualified only by a policy willingness to acquire some kind of effective offset to that perceived nuclear threat. Many countries discern good enough alternatives to national nuclear arsenals; some authoritative facsimile of a security guarantee is the most popular, if also the most difficult, to achieve. Nuclear weapons states, no matter how well armed, are understandably reluctant to underwrite the security of distant polities against threats from WMD.

The Security I motive for the acquisition or sustainment of a national nuclear weapons arsenal is therefore in principle as variable in its implications for force planning as it is common in its basic strategic logic. Notwithstanding the points just made, the actual contemporary practice of nuclear strategy sees only one polity more or less—and it is becoming less and less—committed to extending nuclear deterrence: the United States. None of the world's other nuclear weapons states (Russia, China, Britain, France, Israel, India, and Pakistan) or nuclear threshold states (certainly North Korea and possibly Iran) have any intention, no matter how improbably contingent, of engaging in extended nuclear deterrence. Nominal caveats to that judgment include British and French obligations under the NATO and Western European Union (WEU) treaties, and residual Russian obligations, legal and less so, to protect her "near abroad" in the ever more shadowy Commonwealth of Independent States (CIS).

Security, like deterrence and stability, is one of those essentially contestable concepts that lends itself to cynical manipulation yet points to the most basic area of a polity's responsibility to its citizens for an uncertain future. Although every polity that affords large conventional forces could find merit in the fundamental security case for national nuclear armament, in practice very few polities have elected to cross the line to become either a declared, or an undeclared, nuclear weapons state. National security may well diminish as a result of nuclear possession. The considerable force of that argument, however, with its allusion to the perils of "pariah" status and to the licensing of WMD threats against oneself, should not be taken as a blanket strategic truth. There will be occasions when polities under threat will decide that they should accept no substitutes for nuclear forces. (Chemical, and especially biological, WMD certainly are much cheaper and generally easier to acquire than are nuclear weapons, but they are less reliably predictable in their effects as weapons.) That thought is unfashionable today and heroically politically incorrect for a second nuclear age that in 1996 signed up for indefinite extension of the 1968 NPT treaty; nonetheless, that unfashionable thought has strategic merit.

Security II: To Make Gains

Geostrategic judgment is so subjective that it would be difficult to demonstrate unambiguously that Security II was the dominant, "roguish-looking" motive for nuclear acquisition. Conceptually, the distinction between Security I and Security II is plain enough. Security I motivation points to the fact, or perceived fact, that a polity is threatened from abroad. That threat may be nuclear, conventional, or of some other in kind, but this logic proposes nuclear armament as a solution.

Security II motivation envisages a polity electing to acquire nuclear weapons in order to enhance its external security space at the expense of the security of others. In practice it is frequently less than clear exactly where, or on what terms, the security spaces of geostrategically rival polities meet.[32] At the level of the tactical grammar of nuclear strategy,[33] launch after attack (LAA) can slip apparently prudently into a mode of launch under attack (LUA), which—again apparently prudently—may slip back temporally into a character of launch on warning (LOW), which for sensitive and itchy trigger fingers might translate as launch on suspicion (LOS). Conceptual clarity of distinctions becomes fuzzy in the messy and seamless world wherein those conceptual "thresholds" are hard to locate unambiguously.

Nuclear acquisition for defensive reasons of Security I may give a polity a nuclear force posture that appears to open up newly expansive options in statecraft, no matter how modest the original motivation for nuclear possession may have been. Also, the inherently subjective character of policy definition of security requirements means that even the most genuinely "roguish" of polities— by reasonable assay and with all my previous caveats noted—will have a nominally modest Security I rationale to advance. Both Iraq and Iran, examples chosen not entirely at random, have Security I stories to tell (stories some people will find reasonable) in praise of their unacknowledged bids to become nuclear threshold(-plus) states. Each of them faces genuine external security menace from the other; each has at least a case for the nuclear (and other WMD) option as a counterdeterrent to U.S. intervention and influence in the region; and each can argue that it seeks to use its wealth and skills as a protecting power on behalf of much of the Islamic world writ large in the struggles that that world cannot help but pursue against Zionism and other agencies of the devil, and so on and so forth.

Recall the words of the imperial German chancellor, Theobald von Bethmann Hollweg, to the Reichstag on 4 August 1914. The chancellor proclaimed that "we are now in a state of necessity, and necessity knows no law."[34] With appeal to the ethic of necessity, which if any actions could not be justified or at least rationalized? The same nuclear option that might protect Iraq against further U.S. intervention in the Gulf region also could serve as the strategic basis for a renewed bid for Iraq's regional hegemony. Self-serving Security I explanations for Security II ambitions are always to be found, and perennially there will be a credulous audience.

Domestic Interests and Politics

Nuclear proliferation may be more the product of contending domestic interests with domestic stakes than the policy result of a process of careful assessment of external menace. More than twenty-five years ago I suggested that arms race theory needed to take "domestic process" theses a lot more seriously than then was doctrinally fashionable.[35] At the time, in the early 1970s, it was almost mandatory for U.S. defense analysts to believe that the superpower "arms race"—if it was such[36]—worked according to a mechanistic process of action and reaction. The ghost of now long discredited action-reaction theory does, however, still linger in the shadows of scholarly proliferation country.

Scott D. Sagan has (re)discovered the obvious, but he has done so with characteristic flair, when he writes that "nuclear weapons programs are not obvious or inevitable solutions to international security problems; instead, nuclear weapons programs are solutions looking for a problem to which to attach themselves so as to justify their existence."[37] This domestic process (partial) explanation of proliferation does not deny the existence of external threats, even genuine external threats. But the model suggests that the genuine perception of external threat is a necessary convenience for domestic interests that see benefit for themselves in the national pursuit of WMD. Among the more obvious difficulties with this view of proliferation is that it tends to have a circular, self-reinforcing logic. A program for nuclear acquisition, regardless of the balance of arguments and interests prior to the decision to proceed toward threshold condition, must garner vested interests as it proceeds. The argument can become perilously existential; there is a powerful clutch of domestic interests supporting a nuclear program, but those interests have to exist because a nuclear program

requires the devotion of a large scale of resources over a long period. Every active WMD program in the world must have an extensive baggage train of vested domestic interests (that train will be
more extensive for nuclear than for BC weapon programs). But to
argue that there are domestic processes dependent upon an active
WMD program is only to state a necessary truth. This is one of those
occasional scholarly cases wherein the needs of theory building col-
lide with the inconvenience of many facts that just are as they are.

The domestic focus of some recent theoretical work on motives for proliferation has something important to say. It is all too
easy for international relations theorists to forget that all strategic
security policy is made at home somewhere, and that all politicians have first to be parochial politicians if they are ever to be unleashed as statespeople on the world scene. The domestic interests
and politics model of WMD proliferation thus not only expresses
a necessary truth but also probably usefully redirects our attention
to the policy (inter alia) processes that actually make and sustain
momentous official decisions. Few cases are likely to be as dramatic as has been that of South Africa over the course of the past
decade, but even in polities whose political and social history is
distinctly linear, the keys to nuclear weapons status may repose
more at home than in perceptions or anticipation (again at home,
admittedly) of threats from abroad.

Honor

With due acknowledgment of the continuing potency of Thucydides' analysis of motives in world politics, one must recognize the
salience of honor (status, reputation, and prestige) as a prime mo-
tivator in a bid for nuclear armament. It is true that the NPT
regime denies honor to new nuclear proliferants. In a classic example of sensible international discrimination, the NPT recognizes only five declared (as of 1967) nuclear weapons states. The
treaty has had the generally beneficial effect of helping to drive
underground at least "opaque" new national endeavors to achieve
the ability to exercise the nuclear option. From being a badge that
a state was eager to wear in the 1950s and early 1960s, nuclear-
weapons status evolved under the legal-political-ethical glare of
NPT lights into something furtive that, while not denied, was better not confirmed. Hence, one finds the phenomenon of "opaque
proliferation."[38] We sin, and we enjoy the benefits of sin, but we
do not boast about it.

It is true today that strong international suspicions that one is seeking a nuclear threshold condition would yield all the "honor" of guilt by association with Iran and North Korea. Nonetheless, modest or even negative though the honor accruing from nuclear prowess may be, a different view of honor yields a different judgment. The NPT regime effectively has closed the nuclear club as an association that confers honor with membership. But the comfortable and convenient beliefs that are promoted by that regime do not speak to the whole of future strategic history. If nuclear weapons are singularly stigmatized, then a willingness to flout the nonproliferation convention is all the more shocking and possibly strategically effective. One of the concerns that drives this analysis is the suspicion that the contemporary and massively Western-fashionable set of antinuclear attitudes is perilously vulnerable even to relatively minor perturbations from the zone inhabited by "lesser breeds without dominance in cyberspace" (translated as poorer polities unable to compete in information-led conventional capabilities for conflict).

Honor should not be despised as a leading motive for nuclear possession. A high reputation for effectiveness in statecraft, pursued by whatever mix of grand-strategic instruments, translates as a reputation that generally will not be challenged. As a rule, honor cannot be secured by "smoke and mirrors," but if a polity is credited with particular strategic prowess, challenges are apt to be rare and inadvertent. States aspiring to nuclear weapons, or at least nuclear-threshold, status can aim for honor confident that the terms of engagement in world politics will recognize the value of their achievement.

If the concept of honor is expanded, perhaps stretched, to include those "honorable in notoriety," it becomes readily apparent why the strategic value of pariah status should not be dismissed peremptorily. To be armed with WMD, even just to be suspected of being so armed, is to induce respect. Respect, as well as approval, can be an adequate basis for honor (and prestige). The honor and prestige pertaining to (newly achieved) nuclear weapons status, even though in some ways offset by the values of the NPT regime, remain consistent with the gold standard of strategic effectiveness in world politics. It is difficult to equate non-nuclear WMD status with honor and prestige, at least as those potent concepts normatively are usually understood. Nonetheless, to be known to be armed with anthrax bombs or with nerve gas weapons may well induce the respect that rests upon fear.

To risk being unduly crude, how much does it matter that the G8 world would prefer the list of nuclear weapons states to remain as it stands at present (even as recently expanded, with India and Pakistan)? A new nuclear weapons state, or a threshold nuclear weapons state, obliges established relations of nuclear-led power to adjust, much as the rise of new wealth obliges established societies to accommodate and adjust, no matter how reluctantly. Two general points about honor are widely misunderstood.

First, polities do not seek honor, prestige, or status through the acquisition of nuclear weapons as empty trappings (ceremonial nonsense) attending their search for security. Honor, prestige, and status are valued not because they induce some empty flattery but because they translate as influence when and where it counts. Second, those who stigmatize and singularize nuclear weapons risk achieving precisely the opposite of their generally worthy policy intentions. The problem is akin to that faced by a super/great power protector who seeks to discourage local allied demands for nuclear capability by providing the reliable assistance of an extended *nuclear* deterrence.

Much as Carl von Clausewitz insists that there is an ever dynamic set of complex relations among passion, chance, and reason that always makes "war a remarkable trinity,"[39] so the four classes of motives for proliferation discussed above also interpenetrate and have unstable interconnections. Motives to proliferate invariably will be mixed, and every historical case will be distinctive, albeit distinctive within the general architecture just analyzed. There is a "proliferation puzzle" in that the pieces that compose the total picture even for a single historical case usually will not all be accessible for study, let alone influence, and the exact pattern the many pieces make up will be difficult to understand.

ONWARD AND UPWARD? SIGNPOSTS AND PRINCIPLES —————————

In the practicably constrained world of statecraft, efforts to counter presumed endeavors to achieve nuclear possession among possible WMD arsenals take the form more of a series of obstacles than of the devising of an impassable barrier (biological and chemical weapon capabilities are much more difficult to deny than nuclear). The scholarly literature is awash with references to "proliferation pessimism" and "proliferation optimism."[40] I probably tend on balance to the side of pessimism, though such a description risks doing violence to a view that is far from resigned to the certainty of policy failure. However, it is less than completely clear where policy failure, or policy success for that matter, would lie. Nuclear proliferation may be generally, if not quite invariably, undesirable; but how important is it when compared with the complex policy goal of peace with security? It may be recalled that this chapter began by posing the following questions: Given that we care about nuclear (and other WMD) proliferation, just how much do we care or should we care? And can we care deeply about a problem that is really a condition with which we need to learn to cope?

With Chapters 3 and 4 together focusing upon key aspects of the broad subject of proliferation, and principally upon nuclear proliferation, it is useful at this halfway point to suggest some "signposts" to guide further discussion. By signposts this author has in mind very much what Clausewitz intended when he had this to say about "principles and rules":

> If the theorist's studies automatically result in principles and rules, and if truth spontaneously crystallizes into these forms, they will not resist this natural tendency of the mind. On the contrary, where the arch of truth culminates in such a keystone, this tendency will be underlined. But this is simply in accordance with the scientific law of reason, to indicate the point at which all lines converge, but never to construct an algebraic formula for use on the battlefield. Even these principles and rules are intended to provide a thinking man with a focus of reference for the movements he has been trained to carry out, rather than to serve as a guide which at the moment of action lays down precisely the path he must take.[41]

Six signposts serve both to summarize much of the argument of this chapter and to point the way to discussion necessary in the next one.

Signpost 1: world politics must always be conducted in the shadow of nuclear peril, actual or potential. Whether or not nuclear weapons are present in a region, indeed whether or not nuclear weapons were to be "abolished," there are no longer any true nuclear secrets the control of which could thwart bids for nuclear possession. The nuclear era has come to stay.

Signpost 2: nuclear weapons are useful. In addition to the scientific, technological, and industrial truth expressed in the first signpost, a political-military—which is to say strategic—truth was implied also.

For reasons probed in later chapters, nuclear weapons have unique strategic properties that find favor with policymakers. On the basis of the history of the nuclear era to date, one can affirm with high confidence that even if nuclear weapons do not readily lend themselves to effective use an as instrument for advantage, assuredly they provide a great measure of insurance against the probability of suffering large disadvantage. That important, though bounded, formula should not be taken as an eternal truth governing the domain of the strategic utility of nuclear weapons. Adolf Hitler did not command a nuclear arsenal, but he might have done; and who can say with assurance what a Hitler-like—if that is possible, which I believe it is—policymaker might attempt if nuclear armed? Today's nuclear weapons and nuclear weapons threshold states have not drifted into or toward nuclear possession, nor have they remained in their nuclear condition by the power of inertia alone.

Signpost 3: proliferation is more akin to a puzzle to be assembled for understanding than to a problem in need of solution. Careful political, strategic, and technical study of particular candidate cases of proliferation points to tactics that can harass, and therefore slow and render more expensive (and probably less sophisticated), the flow of military-technical achievements that cumulatively constitute a successful program leading toward the possession of nuclear weapons. In addition, empathetic consideration of the policy demand side of particular proliferation cases may, though more problematically, lead to identification of policy initiatives for security that could at least deflect, if not reduce radically, erstwhile local insistence upon national nuclear weaponry. Motives for overt or unannounced nuclear possession, or near possession, will be mixed. It follows that even superior-seeming solutions to some of the security problems, for example, which figured importantly among the motives that favored nuclear weapons, may not be answer enough to the full range of policy demands. France may well be strategically secure beneath the friendly umbrella of U.S. extended (nuclear) deterrence. But what of the security of the French people's self-respect in such a dependency condition?

Signpost 4: counterproliferation policy—one size does not fit all. Each case of possible nuclear proliferation is unique in the detail of its multicausality and distinctive in its security implications for world politics. It is probably true that every known case of achievement of nuclear threshold status is a standing challenge to the non- or even antiproliferation norms of the NPT regime. Nonetheless, beyond some generic undesirability about further proliferation, every individual instance requires understanding and, just possibly, policy treatment by a concerned international community—always excepting most of "the usual suspects," of course. Given that for obvious reasons proliferant powers tend to grow in pairs (most recently, India and Pakistan in 1998), if not quite batches, one way for the forces of international order to help cope with, say, a very near-nuclear Iraq would be to ensure that such an Iraq could be balanced by a suitably nuclear-threshold Iran. Notwithstanding some reasonable political and technical anxieties about putative Iraqi and Iranian nuclear arsenals, still one may judge that in the medium term, nuclear balance is preferable to nuclear imbalance—if, that is, nuclear possession cannot reliably be denied both parties. Reassuring thoughts about nuclear balance, even if militarily well founded, do need to be interrogated by the implications of the less reassuring thought that deterrence is not thoroughly reliable. Nuclear armament by a pair of regional rivals could mean not a near guarantee against war but rather a guarantee that their next war will be a nuclear one.

On balance, however, with the caveat noted about the reliability of deterrence, some cases of proliferation should benefit regional stability. British and French nuclear acquisition may have had positive consequences for security in Europe during the Cold War.[42] Again in the context of the Cold War, Chinese nuclear weapons status was as essential to the balancing of Soviet power in central and northeast Asia as it was strategically complementary to the U.S.-led security order in the East Asian region in the 1970s and 1980s. As for the nuclear arsenal of Israel, if the United States did not bequeath it—which was not the case—at least the United States can be grateful for it. There is a military and technological peace in the Middle East (as it focuses upon Israel), which is the most that is attainable pending eventual achievement of a political peace. Finally, it is difficult realistically to be critical of the ill-matched nuclear-armed pair in the subcontinent, India and Pakistan. What could not be prevented at a reasonable cost proportional to the stakes—in this instance, nuclear acquisition by India and Pakistan—should be publicly deplored after the fact only in muted tones. One should not make a political and strategic virtue of the necessity of unstoppable nuclear weapons programs. But scarce policy resources should not be squandered in lost causes of strategically arguable merit.

Signpost 5: accept no substitutes—only nuclear weapons will do. Notwithstanding the considerable effort devoted by the proliferation studies industry to biological and chemical weaponry, these

weapons—most of which mercifully are probably still only potential—are not well understood militarily or strategically.[43] The leading problems that have inhibited strategic comprehension include
the following: uncertainty over how each category of BC, toxin,
and radiological weapons could perform usefully as a weapon—
tactically, operationally, strategically; at least dim recognition that
each broad category of these weapons contains many distinctive
technical options with no less distinctive technical-tactical features; a happily severe shortage of historical experience with BC
weapons to use as a basis for theory and doctrine building (indeed, the confirmed category of biological warfare in modern
times is restricted to Japanese misbehavior in China); and profound uncertainty over how BC weapons relate strategically to nuclear weapons. Contemporary strategy recognizes, albeit barely,
that grouping NBC weapons as WMD and conveniently treating
BC weapons simply as lesser but included cases of whatever one
thinks one knows about nuclear weapons is wrong, or at least un-
wise. Strategically, what does one need to understand about BC
weapons issues, especially in their relation to nuclear arms?

Arms control is especially unhelpful with respect to BC
weapons. The widespread manufacture of industrial "precursor"
or starter chemicals for innocent functions renders many CW-
capable production facilities beyond reliable inspection and control. Difficult though it has to be to identify illegal chemical
weapons production facilities, that difficulty is all but trivial when
compared with the problems of monitoring for illegal BW research. Medical research, the proper activities of a pharmaceutical
industry, and largely approved research on BW for defensive purposes yield a condition that is beyond useful control by multinational agreement. Signature to the Biological and Toxin and
the Chemical Weapons Conventions (1972, 1995, respectively)
may help make one feel more comfortable, but really it should
not. BC, especially biological, weapons programs are relatively
easy to hide, or at least explain away. The net effect of arms control conventions concerning this strategic area is to discourage vig-
ilance and active responsive preparation on the part of potential
victims. It is unlikely that any polity could be denied BC weapons
because of the additional barriers that the legal conventions sup-
posedly erect. (The Biological and Toxin Weapons Convention of
1972 does not even pretend to a verification and enforcement
regime—which is at least honest, if not reassuring). As usual, the
overwhelming problem with arms control is simply that it does not

work when and where the international community needs it badly. The BC conventions will be obeyed more or less faithfully by all the countries not strongly motivated to behave otherwise.

BC weapons continue to be insufficiently controllable in their tactical domain of action to be very useful *military* weapons. There are actual, and certainly potential, exceptions to this point, but nonetheless the rule holds well enough. Both chemical and biological weapons lack the reliability of predictable military effect that is characteristic of nuclear weapons. Chemical weapons, as with many biological weapons, can be defeated by an enemy's protective measures. Although biological, unlike chemical, agents do not need to be produced and delivered in huge quantities, and notwithstanding their potential to outperform even nuclear arms as killing mechanisms, "friction" produced in storage, in mechanical delivery, from the weather, or from uneven terrain could result in catastrophic strategic failure. Moreover, contrary to some popular fears, BW contamination of public water and food supplies is extraordinarily difficult to achieve to the necessary level of strategic effect. Whereas chemical and toxin weapons incapacitate or kill promptly, biological agents can work only at the speed of incubation and reproduction in the victim-host. Conservative war planners will know that a great deal they do not favor can occur between the initiation of aerosolized, explosive, or other release of BW agents and the maturity of the strategic mission of those agents. Nuclear-armed missiles are swifter, more reliable, and more predictable in their military consequences. But as weapons to terrorize and to punish—increase casualties and thereby raise the political stakes precipitously—BC armament represents strategically unknown territory that ought to worry governments.

There are some excellent reasons that the most appropriate responses to prepare against BC threats should be asymmetric to those threats. In other words, unconventional special warfare, conventional action, or nuclear action should be the first lines of defense for deterrence and denial. But deterrence may fail, or fail to apply, and military action of whatever character could be attempted too late, after the fact of BC assault. It is politically convenient to adopt a policy that specifies arms control and passive defensive measures as the twin thrusts of a counter-BC strategy. The problem is that arms control must prove extremely unrewarding for the diminution of BC menaces, while passive measures—immunization, protective clothing, air-filtered vehicles and facilities, evacuation—will be notably attriting of military effectiveness, most likely will not be practicable for all of the "targets" potentially at risk, and may not meet the political mail. There is no simple strategic solution to BC threats. But some combination of deliberately rather heavy-handed nuclear counterthreat, active defenses at least against air-breathing and ballistic means of BC delivery, and very prompt military preemptive—in principle even preventive—measures against the enemy's known BC armament should serve usefully to reduce the scale of the menace.[44] For technical reasons of survivability, stability, and potency of the necessary BW aerosol, reliable ballistic delivery of live and lethal BW agents in sufficient concentration is difficult to achieve. The principal threat of BW delivery is posed by aerosol spray devices on aircraft, cruise missiles, and just possibly ships (with a following wind and a dedicated crew).

For reliable terrorization and an optimal prospect of achieving counterdeterrence, there is no adequate substitute for "old-fashioned" nuclear weaponry.[45] The manifold major uncertainties pertaining to BC weapons—for example, will they survive storage and delivery, what might they deter, what damage might they do?—are considerably smaller for nuclear armament. This is not to deny the possibility that BC weapons might constitute a halfway house, or perhaps a set of eccentric options, between or aside from conventional and nuclear zones of combat. Polities could persuade themselves that BC weapons would generate exceptional international respect yet should function below the threshold for a nuclear response. So much is only speculation, though we do suspect that in 1991 Iraq may have been dissuaded by Israeli, and possibly by U.S., nuclear growls from delivering chemical warheads with its Scud missiles.[46] The United States was bluffing, though no such confidence can attach to a judgment that Israel would not have responded with nuclear weapons to another chemical assault on the Jewish people.

Overall, a great deal more analytical and defense planning effort needs to be devoted to the still somewhat opaque strategic challenges that BC weaponry predictably will pose. Until very recently, it was easy to note the obvious signs of strategic delegation of BC weapons problems to the less-than-fully serious realms of arms control and passive defensive measures. Strategic historical experience with novel challenges suggests that governments will take the BC weapons problem/condition as seriously as they ought only when dire events in the real world allow no further evasion.

Signpost 6: uncertainty rules. None of the strategic theorists and other commentators active today have known any security condition

other than one with a nuclear dimension. Familiarity can breed, if
not contempt, at least an overconfident assurance of knowledge
that flows inappropriately from long familiarity. Peter R. Lavoy is
correct when he claims that "little is known about nuclear-
weapons."[47] Nothing much has been settled about nuclear questions by the passage of time thus far. A great deal can be inferred
about the strategic utility of nuclear weapons for deterrence, and
many nostrums are believed—indeed have been all but canon-
ized—about "the requirements of deterrence."[48] But the fortunate
absence of nuclear combat presents severe difficulties of evidence
for theory, doctrine, and policy. If Lavoy, among others, is plausible in pointing to a lack of historical knowledge about nuclear
weapons in strategic action, how much more correct is he with reference to this new and second nuclear age? It is possible, and in
some respects probable, that much of what we have accumulated
as "nuclear lore" is actually little more than a bundle of hopes and
agreeable platitudes that strategic history has yet to refute definitively. It is to this dire prospect that the discussion now must turn.

NOTES

1. The scholarly literature on the delivery of WMD is less voluminous
than is the literature on proliferant WMD programs and arms control over
the same. The reason for this disparity lies, I suspect, at least partially with
the fact that the technically preferable means for delivery of at least nuclear WMD (ballistic missiles) imply for their negation a serious interest in
missile defense. The community of Western arms controllers, which is willing to beat the drum of alarm about proliferant NBC perils, is not at all enthusiastic about Western ballistic missile defense (BMD). The monograph
series from Lancaster University's Centre for Defence and International Security Studies (CDISS) is particularly informative on the subject of delivery
vehicles for WMD. For example, see Ewing, Ranger, and Bosdet, *Ballistic
Missiles;* Ewing et al., *Cruise Missiles;* and Ranger, *Devil's Brews I.* Also useful
are Nolan, *Trappings of Power,* and Aaron Karp, *Ballistic Missile Proliferation.*
2. The ten-year delay that U.S. intervention imposed on Hanoi's
schedule in Vietnam was vital for the development and modernization of
Southeast Asia. Much of the eventual economic achievement by East
Asia's "tiger" economies in the 1980s is plausibly attributable to the security cover that they gained because of the U.S. venture in Vietnam. The
Asia of 1975, when Hanoi finally acquired Saigon, was not the Asia of
1965; those ten years really mattered. It is strangely ironic to suggest that
the United States may have lost the war, but—for once in the twentieth
century—it probably won the peace.
3. Freedman, "Great Powers," p. 37.
4. See the discussion in Posen, "U.S. Security Policy in a Nuclear-
Armed World."

5. Freedman, "Great Powers," p. 39.

6. Clausewitz, *On War,* pp. 119–121.

7. Johnson and Libicki, *Dominant Battlespace Knowledge.*

8. The literature is huge and hugely repetitive. The following is merely the shortest of short lists I personally favor. First, I recommend two quasi-official "primers" from the U.S. Congress, Office of Technology Assessment (OTA): *Proliferation of Weapons of Mass Destruction* and *Technologies Underlying Weapons of Mass Destruction.* Second are two explicit "primers": Gardner, *Nuclear Nonproliferation,* and Forsberg et al., *Nonproliferation Primer.* Third, there is an excellent trilogy from the fecund pen of Kathleen Bailey: *Doomsday Weapons in the Hands of Many; Strengthening Nuclear Nonproliferation;* and *Weapons of Mass Destruction.* Fourth is a handful of especially thoughtful studies: Dunn, *Containing Nuclear Proliferation;* Davis and Frankel, "The Proliferation Puzzle"; Sagan and Waltz, *The Spread of Nuclear Weapons;* and Scott Sagan, "Why Do States Build Nuclear Weapons?" These items are but the small tip of a mighty iceberg. I am grateful to Davis and Frankel for the inspiration for the title to this chapter.

9. Hoffmann, *Gulliver's Troubles,* Part II; Gray, "Strategy in the Nuclear Age," esp. pp. 592–593.

10. Scott Sagan, "Why Do States Build Nuclear Weapons?" is sound and basic and can be supplemented usefully by two particularly innovative ventures: Lavoy, "Nuclear Myths and the Causes of Nuclear Proliferation"; and Flank, "Exploding the Black Box."

11. See the discussion of potential "rogues" in Klare, *Rogue States and Nuclear Outlaws,* ch. 5. It is encouraging to note that by 1998 the U.S. government by and large no longer was referring to "rogue states." Unfortunately, "rogue state" appears to have been replaced by another highly charged formula—"aggressors." See William Cohen, *Annual Report,* esp. pp. 2–8.

12. As a university professor who teaches strategic studies, and especially as one who contributed to the British government's Strategic Defence Review in 1998, from time to time I am asked by foreign students why it is that Britain, a country almost entirely unmenaced at present by other than domestic Irish "rogues," is determined to remain nuclear armed. I have been surprised, and even on occasion alarmed, by the approving comments I have received in response to my standard explanation. Some of those students come from countries with far stronger security motivation for nuclear armament than has Britain.

13. This point is all but admitted in the conclusions to the most recent rigorous study of the subject. Suganami, *On the Causes of War.*

14. Strassler, *Landmark Thucydides,* p. 43.

15. As explained magisterially in Aron, *Peace and War,* esp. pp. 580–585.

16. Solingen, "Political Economy of Nuclear Restraint."

17. Sagan and Waltz, *Spread of Nuclear Weapons.* See "The Kenneth Waltz–Scott Sagan Debate" and "The Kenneth Waltz–Scott Sagan Debate II."

18. Every scholarly discipline has its *déformation professionelle.* Historians, for example, when troubled by big concepts, have been known to retreat into the narrative mode.

19. Seng, "Less Is More"; Feaver, "Neo-optimists and the Enduring Problem of Nuclear Proliferation"; Seng, "Optimism in the Balance."

20. For reasons superbly, and admirably tersely, laid out in Bailey, *Strengthening Nuclear Nonproliferation.* In Bailey's trenchant words, "The key conclusion drawn from the Iraqi case is that the nuclear nonproliferation regime cannot prevent a determined proliferant, even when that nation is a participant in the regime. Iraq was a party to the NPT and placed its declared facilities under safeguards" (p. 34). A classic treatment of this case is Kay, "Denial and Deception Practices of WMD Proliferators." Trevan, *Saddam's Secrets,* is also useful.

21. U.S. Congress, *Technologies Underlying Weapons of Mass Destruction.* Also good on nuclear weapons "basics" is Grace, *Nuclear Weapons.*

22. Stumpf, "South Africa's Nuclear Weapons Programme."

23. Gray, *House of Cards.*

24. For views more friendly to the prospects for some variant of nuclear abolition, see Rotblat, Steinberger, and Udgaonkar, *Nuclear-Weapon-Free World.*

25. Madariaga, quoted in Quinlan, *Thinking About Nuclear Weapons,* p. 67.

26. In Scott Sagan, "Why Do States Build Nuclear Weapons?"

27. Waltz, *Theory of International Politics,* is *the* sacred text of *neo*realism. My strong preference is for the more sophisticated, if frequently less theoretically rigorous, classical realist wisdom to be found in Aron, *Peace and War,* and Morgenthau, *Politics Among Nations.*

28. Quinlan, *Thinking About Nuclear Weapons,* p. 19.

29. Kahn, *On Thermonuclear War,* ch. 4.

30. Huth, *Extended Deterrence and the Prevention of War.*

31. Howard, "Reassurance and Deterrence."

32. The concept of security space is one that I find useful. The Caribbean, for example, is within the U.S. security space, psychologically speaking at least. It was Nikita Khrushchev's misunderstanding of the force of this point that made the Cuban missile crisis of October 1962 so dangerous. At the present time, it is less than clear just what is, and what is no longer, within Russia's security space from among the lost lands of the old USSR.

33. With gratitude to Clausewitz, *On War,* p. 605, with his powerful distinction between the grammar of war and the logic of policy for war.

34. Bethmann Hollweg, quoted in Walzer, *Just and Unjust Wars,* p. 240.

35. In Gray, "Arms Race Phenomenon" and *Soviet-American Arms Race.* Also see the discussion in Buzan and Herring, *Arms Dynamic in World Politics,* ch. 7.

36. Gray, "Arms Races and Other Pathetic Fallacies."

37. Scott Sagan, "Why Do States Build Nuclear Weapons?" p. 65.

38. Frankel, *Opaque Nuclear Proliferation.* Reiss, *Bridled Ambition,* also is pertinent.

39. Clausewitz, *On War,* p. 89.

40. For example, Karl, "Proliferation Pessimism and Emerging Nuclear Powers."

41. Clausewitz, *On War,* p. 141.

42. No country cares as much about another as it does about itself. For stable deterrence it was useful for Soviet leaders to have to take

account of the political fact that there were three independent nuclear decisionmaking processes within NATO, two of which were in Europe.

43. U.S. Congress, *Proliferation of Weapons of Mass Destruction*, ch. 2, is outstanding. Other useful studies include Spiers, *Chemical Warfare;* Wright, *Preventing a Biological Arms Race;* Grove, *Banning Chemical Weapons;* Spiers, *Chemical and Biological Weapons;* Dando, *Biological Warfare in the 21st Century;* Shubik, "Terrorism, Technology, and the Socioeconomics of Death" (though path-breaking and suitably deeply troubling, this article needs to be taken with a dose of strategic salt with respect to the practical operational dimension of its subject); Cole, *The Eleventh Plague;* Betts, "New Threat of Mass Destruction"; and Falkenrath, "Confronting Nuclear, Biological and Chemical Terrorism."

44. Cohen, *Annual Report,* p. 21, is quite encouraging: "The Joint Staff and CINCs are developing a Joint counter-NBC weapons operational concept that integrates both offensive and defensive measures." Concepts and doctrines are important; they are not, however, synonymous with capabilities or actions.

45. Gray, "Nuclear Weapons and the Revolution in Military Affairs."

46. See Payne, *Deterrence in the Second Nuclear Age,* p. 85.

47. Lavoy, "Nuclear Myths," p. 200.

48. Kaufmann, "Requirements of Deterrence," remains classic.

4

To Confuse Ourselves: Nuclear Fallacies

This chapter, which focuses primarily on proliferation-oriented topics, is designed to serve as a master filter for judgments on nuclear ideas and policy. So much of the professional literature today barely lifts its level of concern from the weeds of the erstwhile marshes of southern Iraq, or ventures beyond the containing walls of nuclear reactors, that major effort is required to escape capture by technical and diplomatic detail and local context. I am concerned lest these early years of the second nuclear age should be squandered by a transnational, extended Western defense community that is not equipped theoretically to understand the strategic history that is at hand, let alone the strategic history that may be.

The main body of the discussion in this chapter explores what is labeled, undeniably with deliberate malice, as "eight nuclear fallacies." The choice of eight is not significant. What is significant, however, is the spirit of the analysis and discussion. This spirit is skeptical, irreverent, unapologetic, and yet deeply serious about the emerging perils to national and international security posed by WMD. Some readers will know that I have a "past," as the ominous phrase will have it. It is precisely because I have a "past" that this chapter is especially important. Some of the strategic controversies with which my name is closely linked—nuclear strategy and strategic arms control, in particular[1]—may appear to pertain only to the now closed context of the Cold War. In this chapter, the nuclear fallacies discussed are fallacies about today and tomorrow. These fallacies have some minor resonance for all nuclear history, but they have major resonance for this second nuclear age.

The fallacies identified and discussed below comprise a mix of beliefs and arguments, some of which are advanced explicitly in the literature (e.g., on nuclear abolition, on virtual arsenals, and on a nuclear taboo); others either are implicit in much public debate (e.g., the reliability of deterrence, the infeasibility of defense, and the ability of the current international security system to cope well enough with a small nuclear war) or at least—in my opinion—loom as important topics likely to attract attention before very long. Whether the extant literature on a "fallacy" is large or small, the belief in question inherently is important, either because it addresses a matter structural to this second nuclear age or because it attracts adherents who might succeed in influencing nuclear policy in significant ways.

FALLACY 1: A POST-NUCLEAR ERA HAS DAWNED _____

Neither the nonproliferation regime that has the NPT as the jewel in its crown nor strategic trends of other kinds (e.g., keyed to the political, ethical, or technological dimensions of strategy) are in the process of aborting the nuclear character of this second nuclear age. Nuclear deterrence is not at present actively intended in great power relations, but it remains a background element. It is useful for Michael Quinlan to distinguish between a policy toward nuclear deterrence that has shifted comprehensively into generality—"to whom it may concern" as the unnamed addressee[2]—and one that absolutely renounces nuclear war. As Quinlan notes, most countries' armed forces, most of the time, are not specifically "addressed" as threats to particular putative foes. However, the popular notion of general deterrence, and especially general nuclear deterrence, can be overappreciated.[3] Nonetheless, U.S. nuclear weapons do help frame, or backstop, U.S. diplomacy for the (pre)containment of China, they are obviously a factor in any Russian speculation about the staging of some return of imperium, and they would be inalienably on the board of statecraft in roles supporting any U.S. military intervention against regional foes. The U.S. policy stance today is decidedly unenthusiastic about nuclear weapons,[4] probably unduly so, but no matter how bland and general that policy is, actual or potential enemies of the United States have to ask the question, What do U.S. nuclear weapons mean for us?

Identification of this first fallacy is not intended to invite an argument about current trends. Most trends are reversible. The political and military-technical tide certainly would seem to be leaving nuclear options "on the beach"—with apologies to the late

Nevil Shute for the reference to his apocalyptic novel.[5] The indefinite extension of the NPT at the latest review conference (1995) assuredly was a great success for the nonproliferation regime and was, at least apparently, a boost to the norms promoted by that regime. Moreover, the surge in precise military lethality that is allowed by the clutch of capabilities developed for information-led warfare would seem to place nuclear weapons at a discount. One can argue that the quest for precision in bombardment has been motivated in part by the strong desire to escape from the grip of military rationales for nuclear weapons.[6] All that appears to beckon, however, may not really be on offer.

The numbers of nuclear weapons and nuclear threshold states remain much lower than proliferation pessimists were predicting in the 1950s and 1960s.[7] There is no question that the pace of proliferation has been slow and at present shows no thoroughly convincing signs of a prospect for other than a distinctly steady acceleration. But this trend, if that is what it is, of a deliberate pace in proliferation is vulnerable to nuclear learning from any crisis, anywhere, that seems to demonstrate a strategic necessity for nuclear arms. The trend that has produced only five NPT-"licensed" nuclear weapons states (which happen to be the five permanent members of the UN Security Council), three "unlicensed" nuclear-weapons states (Israel, India, Pakistan), (at least) one near—nuclear weapons threshold state (North Korea), and three would-be nuclear weapons states (Iraq, Iran, Libya) is indeed impressive. Also, it is impressive that, inter alia, Sweden, Switzerland, Japan, Argentina, Brazil, Egypt, and Taiwan have stepped back from active pursuit of the military nuclear option.[8] More noteworthy still was the renunciation in 1990 of actual, as opposed to virtual, nuclear weapons by South Africa, whose internal and external security condition has been transformed by and large for the better,[9] and by the distinctly insecure extra-Russian legatees of part of the erstwhile Soviet nuclear arsenal.

Unfortunately, the problem is not with the fact of a slow pace of nuclear proliferation. The problem lies rather in knowing what that fact means. Are we witnessing a trend in nuclear reduction toward zero—a high policy goal embraced formally, if insincerely, by the extant nuclear weapons states—toward an existentially postnuclear era? Or does what we see signify nothing in particular about the strategic salience of nuclear weapons? Just one undeterrable, or deterrable but not deterred, nuclear act could revolutionize the terms of debate over nuclear policy in several countries.

Quantity and quality should not be confused. The small number of nuclear weapons, and near nuclear weapons, states is less important than is their identity, the potential for infectious further proliferation that they bear, and the implications for character of conflict that they carry. The principal reason that nuclear proliferation is dangerous, even if occasionally it can make a net positive contribution to regional peace with security, is exactly the reason that arms control usually disappoints. The global nonproliferation regime cannot handle the hardest of hard cases. Even if there are only a handful of predictably near-threshold states, that short shortlist happens to include polities with exceedingly serious security problems—which is, of course, a leading reason they resist the force of the control regime. The polities in question are at present only North Korea, Iraq, Iran, and perhaps Libya. In 1998, India and Pakistan left the realm of "threshold" states to enjoy the uncertain mixed blessings of full-blown nuclear weapons standing.

A significant reason this second nuclear age is not in the process of radical transformation into a postnuclear era has been identified with some hyperbole by Martin van Creveld. "By the time the cold war ended, any state in possession of even a halfway modern conventionally armed force was also capable of manufacturing, begging or stealing nuclear weapons."[10] Van Creveld exaggerates, but not by much, and the exaggeration is merited because it highlights a point of the utmost importance. The newfound effectiveness of regular Western conventional arms is the very reason those who are conventionally challenged find NBC arms of great interest.

FALLACY 2:
NUCLEAR ABOLITION IS FEASIBLE AND DESIRABLE _____

Two problems with nuclear weapons have the effect of acting like forces of nature. The first problem is the persistence of the strategic (i.e., force-related) element in human history; the second is the elemental fact of "the nuclear discovery."[11] The synergy between these two "problems" creates the condition this book analyzes. One can imagine a world wherein the undesirable and admittedly irreversible fact of the nuclear discovery would be entirely unimportant; but if readers recall the discussion of political context in Chapter 2, they will appreciate that the kind of world that generates no policy demands for nuclear arms is not a world likely to be on offer anytime soon. For reasons of both general humanity and particular Western interest, the desirability of attempting to "marginalize" nuclear weapons as a central thrust to our security policy is fairly obvious.[12] But the difficulty with "marginalization" is that it cannot succeed if those security communities that are conventionally challenged logically see in NBC arms the prospect of a great equalizer. One need not master the finer points of Sun Tzu's *Art of War*,[13] or even invest much time in the design of cunning plans, to appreciate that the highest of high roads to success lies in attacking the enemy's strategy. In 1991, the United States taught would-be regional hegemons a master class in why nuclear armament is not a dispensable luxury if one chooses to act in ways the United States strongly deplores.

Marginalization may warrant classification as a fallacy—certainly it is a candidate fallacy—but at least it has the merit of being desirable for the United States, and it may even be feasible in a few cases that matter to the United States. That judgment is not intended as a ringing endorsement of the thesis that nuclear weapons can and should be marginalized in local, regional, and world politics, but it notes that this modest notion has some modest strategic utility. The contrast with the abolitionist position could hardly be more stark.

Two linked arguments on the feasibility of nuclear abolition should render moot any subsequent discussion about desirability. First, the nuclear discovery of 1945 means that nuclear weapons cannot really be abolished forever. One could speculate about abolition only if one toys with the notion that somehow, as with the formula for the Byzantines' wonder weapon "Greek fire,"[14] human beings will lose the nuclear knowledge. But unless knowledge even of the fact of the erstwhile nuclear discovery also was mislaid, why would nuclear rediscovery not occur? "Virtual nuclear arsenals" by definition would lack physical presence, but they would constitute nuclear arsenals possible in the future.[15] (The distinctive fallacy of purposefully virtual arsenals is discussed below.)

The second argument against the empirical and logical integrity of the abolitionist thesis is the persisting and reliably predictable fact of policy and strategy demands for the services of nuclear arsenals. Notwithstanding Lavoy's interesting emphasis on the manufacture of "nuclear myths"[16] (which he defines as unverifiable rather than false beliefs) by key individuals, strategic history shows that proliferant polities "go, or approach, nuclear" for a mix of deeply serious reasons. Whether or not Western would-be nuclear abolitionists find these mixes of reasons deplorable, or on balance imprudent, is beside the point.

If nuclear abolition were politically feasible, it would not really be necessary. For a global security regime, perhaps an antisecurity-regime regime in which there was robust (lasting? everyone who mattered?) consensus on the irrelevance of nuclear weapons (and BC weapons, of course), there should also be a no-less-robust consensus on the irrelevance of weapons of any kind, save those necessary for local security. With respect to nuclear weapons, in principle one can conceive of a world wherein the nuclear revolution is rendered obsolete, not merely obsolescent, by transformational changes in technology. That is a less-than-compellingly persuasive thought, one must hasten to add. There are strategic historical precedents for whole classes of weapons being abandoned—at least by the practitioners of "civilized" and regular warfare—because they have ceased to be effective. It is difficult to imagine how nuclear weapons writ large and various, which is to say not only as deliverable by ballistic or air-breathing vehicles, might be rendered globally obsolete; but one should have sufficient respect for the power of history to offer surprises as to recognize the distant possibility. However, I do not recognize even the distant possibility of a global community that does not need to be a strategic security community because it has come to embrace all possible earthly security communities. Such a global community is more likely to be achieved in the form of a dictatorial world empire than by the effect of some stain-like spread of a zone of political peace.

Nuclear abolition is impractical because, unless time travel becomes feasible, "the nuclear discovery" by the Manhattan Project in World War II cannot be undone. To argue for a policy that is inherently and permanently impractical has to be foolish, given that it can raise public expectations that cannot be fulfilled, it wastes scarce intellectual effort, and it can serve as a counsel of perfection that destabilizes more sensible nuclear policy.[17] The idea, or standard, of abolition is not merely irrelevant to the security challenges that attend nuclear armament, however; it is irrelevant in ways that could damage security. Readers may recall that although the Intermediate-Range Nuclear Forces (INF) treaty of 1987 was overtaken rapidly by the political events of the meltdown of the Soviet empire, during the years of its negotiation it was a menace to the political legitimacy of NATO's nuclear-dependent defense doctrine.[18] Given that arguments for nuclear abolition plainly are impractical and that many of those who have associated themselves with abolitionist sentiments are genuinely nuclear experts, one is at a loss to know how to characterize those people's views other than uncharitably.[19] Experts, those whose reputations for expert knowledge lend credibility to a debatable cause, should not advocate a process that looks to accomplish complete nuclear disarmament when they know that that process must fail.

FALLACY 3: VIRTUAL ARSENALS

"The thinking person's" variant of nuclear abolition is the proposal for a transition to virtual nuclear arsenals.[20] Recognizing the permanent force of the nuclear discovery, and indeed leaning upon its dissuasive power, at least the virtual nuclear warriors would not be seeking impracticably to reverse strategic history by declaring nuclear facts to be nonfacts. As with many of the fallacies treated in these pages, this idea of movement toward virtual nuclear arsenals is not bereft of all merit.

Lest there be any misunderstanding, "virtual arsenals would identify as a goal a situation in which no nuclear weapon is assembled and ready for use."[21] Rephrased, "for nuclear-weapon states, creating such a cushion [of time between a given stage of nuclear technology and a deployed nuclear force] means banning the existence of assembled, ready-to-use nuclear weapons."[22] Virtual and opaque nuclear weapons status should not be confused. If India and Pakistan prior to spring 1998 were adherents to the former, then Israel plainly enjoys the latter. A virtual nuclear arsenal is an arsenal that could be used in action quite soon. An opaque nuclear arsenal is a nuclear arsenal that is probably entirely real but whose owners choose to leave it formally unannounced or unarguably authoritatively verified.

The proposal for virtual nuclear arsenals does have its attractive features. For example:

1. Disassembled nuclear weapons cannot detonate.
2. A move toward virtuality in nuclear arsenals should help marginalize nuclear weapons as a consequence of removing them from active military inventories. Any measure of nuclear marginalization must enhance the prospective potency of the conventional weaponry in which the West currently

enjoys a long lead. Military planners must discount the political availability of weapons that policy has insisted must
be only virtual.

3. Nuclear virtuality should reinforce the NPT regime by dis-
arming the world's active military inventories of nuclear
weapons.

4. Virtual nuclear weapons would be "weapons" unready for
prime time in the hands of terrorists, criminals, or dissident
generals.

5. An only virtual nuclear arsenal would be an arsenal whose
"mobilization" lead time (i.e., assembly and perhaps trans-
port) might serve usefully to slow down the pace of a crisis
slide toward catastrophe.

Nonetheless, granted its apparent attractions, there is much that is
unattractive about this proposal. A first-order problem with virtual
nuclear deterrents is that their post- (perhaps pre)existentiality is
most vitally dependent upon the ability and willingness of policymakers in popular democracies to spot evil intention and armament in time to prepare to thwart it. A virtual nuclear arsenal has
the attractive quality that it will not explode by accident or be
stolen in a condition ready to use (*prêt-à-porter*). But if the problem
of nuclear accident leading to holocaust is slight and the risk of
theft is minimal, why chance paying a significant price in deterrence forsworn when the benefit to security from virtuality is arguable at best?

The case against virtual nuclear arsenals is not impregnable,
but it is strong:

1. Existing nuclear weapons states—the P5 members of the
UN Security Council, plus India, Pakistan, and Israel—have
judged the risks to be disproportionate to the highly theoretical benefits. That list comprises an impressive assembly
of opinions on nuclear policy.

2. The vital temporal quality and quantity of delay that makes
for virtuality represents political and military opportunity
for the foe. A near-nuclear-armed state is not quite a nuclear-
armed state.

3. When pressed beyond the level of concept, the practical
problems with a policy of nuclear virtuality assume huge
proportions. For example, strategic history shows that democracies have severe political difficulties coping with even

unmistakable evidence of malfeasance on the part of authoritarian polities.[23] There are problems at every relevant level of assay. Specifically, what is going on? What should we do about it?

The argument for negotiation of virtual nuclear arsenals is quite clever and not without some appeal, but it fails the tougher tests that strategic history requires one to apply for policy adoption. Virtual nuclear arsenals must be unattractive to policymakers habituated to real nuclear arsenals, and virtuality implies a range of gratuitous vulnerabilities.

The reasons that the proposal for virtual nuclear arsenals amounts to a fallacy are intensely practical. Above all else, perhaps, the proposal is likely to appear inherently foolish to established nuclear weapons states. There are several strands to this argument. With respect to politics, none of the existing NPT-licensed, nuclear weapons states would be strategically comfortable moving from the now familiar condition of being more or less ready for nuclear action, into some zone of only near-nuclear armament. With reference to military strategy, the virtual nuclear weapons states would worry about the prospective military effectiveness of nuclear forces that had been critically disaggregated until a time of acute crisis triggered the process of operational nuclear constitution or reconstitution. The case for a virtual nuclear arsenal would be an extremely difficult briefing to give in Washington, Moscow, Beijing, London, Paris, Islamabad, or New Delhi. I would not even attempt to deliver the briefing in Jerusalem.

This may sound a little strange, coming as it does from the pen of a fully licensed professional academic, but there are some ideas in strategic studies that are too clever, too eccentrically brilliant, or just too eccentric to be real contenders for policy or strategic adoption. Whereas a skillful strategic theorist will always find something to say in praise of any idea, especially in the nuclear field concerning which so little truly is known, strategy is a quintessentially practical realm. The proposal to move toward virtual nuclear arsenals, whatever the intellectual merit in the idea, suffers from the same malady as did Thomas C. Schelling's appallingly insightful notion of a "threat that leaves something to chance,"[24] and as also did the official U.S. plan announced in 1982 to deploy MX ICBMs in a "dense pack" basing mode.[25] Virtual nuclear arms sound silly, or at least gratuitously perilous; the taking of risks that purposefully leave something to chance sounds dangerously irresponsible, not to mention culturally opposed to policymakers' desire for control; and "dense pack" basing affronted the widespread view that one should disperse forces for survivability, not concentrate them as a clustered target.

Clausewitz wrote that "everything in strategy is very simple, but that does not mean that everything is very easy."[26] Anything in strategy, and especially anything bearing upon nuclear strategy, that appears to be distinctly odd or extremely subtle stands little chance of policy adoption. Most politicians, senior civil servants, and senior military officers are not practicing defense intellectuals. Ideas for nuclear policy that need to drive minds in the official audience far down unfamiliar paths are all but doomed to failure. The core reason is hard neither to locate nor to explain. If contingent nuclear use is the ultima ratio regis (as well as possibly the reductio ad absurdum of strategy) in the defense of basic national security values, it follows that the nuclear force posture and strategy should be guarded in a most conservative—or dare one say prudent—spirit.

FALLACY 4: DETERRENCE IS RELIABLE

Deterrence is never reliable, and this general truth applies with particular force today in the second nuclear age. In the most vigorous and rigorous assault to date on the smellier orthodoxies of both expert and popular beliefs about deterrence, Keith B. Payne offers an uncompromising view of the pertinent realities:

> In the second nuclear age, several factors are combining to change the strategic environment of effective deterrence policies: the apparent increase in threats posed by rogue states such as Iraq, Iran, Libya, Syria, China, and North Korea; the retraction of U.S. forward-based armed forces; and the proliferation of WMD. Given these features of the second nuclear age, in comparison with the Cold War, U.S. deterrence goals will have to be expanded: the list of players to be deterred has to be expanded, as do the types of behavior to be prevented.[27]

Different aspects of Payne's comprehensive proposition, as just quoted, are treated in detail at suitable junctures throughout this book. What matters most at this point, however, is to explain why it is that deterrence, even nuclear deterrence, is unreliable. Quinlan penetrates to the heart of the matter when he writes: "Deterrence is a concept for operating upon the thinking of others. It therefore entails some basic presuppositions about that thinking."[28] Deterrence, therefore, is a relational variable; it is an effect upon, or influence over, behavior—achieved and achievable only with the cooperation of the intended deterree. Deterrence is structurally unreliable for precisely the same leading reason that friction in war cannot be eliminated by wonderful new technologies:[29] specifically, there are human beings in the loop for deterrence and for the conduct of strategy in war. An individual policymaker, or a group of policymakers, may decide not to be deterred. Literally, there can be no such thing as "*the* deterrent," nuclear or otherwise. Whether or not a nuclear arsenal deters is a matter for decision by the recipients of would-be deterrent menaces, not by the owners of the putative deterrent.

At issue here is not so much the core logic of some long-appreciated deterrence theory, but rather the application of that theory to strategic historical practice and the judgments offered in explanation of strategic history. What we know, as contrasted with what we believe, about the record of deterrence in the first nuclear age of the Cold War appears less and less impressive as the archives open, as oral histories burgeon, and as scholars entertain seriously second thoughts about "nuclear history."[30]

The logic of deterrence, as propounded quite formally in a small library of books, articles, and studies since the mid-1950s, most probably is eternal and universal. But the application of that logic, indeed even knowledge of when to apply that logic, always has the potential to be catastrophically variable. To understand a problem in general terms is not necessarily the same as to understand how to solve or alleviate it. The United States in 1990 was led by a generation of Cold War–trained would-be practitioners of deterrence, could draw upon a historically unparalleled measure of scholarly expertise in deterrence theory, and happened to be at the peak of its military prowess. And yet, Saddam Hussein was not deterred from seizing Kuwait.[31] If the U.S., indeed Western, defense community of 1990 was proud of anything, it was proud of its presumed achievement in deterrence over four decades of Cold War.[32]

Deterrence per se is not the source of difficulty. The last thing the world needs is another great tome on deterrence *theory*. The problem is that deterrence is inherently unreliable because actual locally encultured human beings, deciding for any of the reasons that may move us humans, can decide that they will not be deterred. It is probably true—indeed it is very probably true—that nuclear deterrence is much more reliable than is non-nuclear, at least (extra-NBC) conventional, deterrence; but even the tilting of the playing field in favor of deterrence with the WMD qualification cannot guarantee success. For once, Quinlan is not entirely to be trusted when he judges that "only a state ruler possessed by a reckless lunacy scarcely paralleled even in prenuclear history would contemplate *with equanimity* initiating a conflict that seemed likely to bring nuclear weapons down upon his country."[33] Quinlan's intended reassurance has the reverse effect of that intended. If the rhetorical qualification "with equanimity" is deleted, the fragility of Quinlan's claim is exposed.

Forty-plus years of superpower-led Cold War may tell us little about the working of deterrence, and especially about the requirements for its successful functioning. If deterrence works at both a general and an immediate level, with the former helping to shape the course of events that might plausibly bring the latter into play, was either side specifically—which is to say "immediately"—deterred (from doing what over which issues) in the Cold War? And if deterrence is believed to have worked "immediately," just why did it work? These are questions so hard to answer with high confidence of historical accuracy that scholars must qualify their responses. The necessity for such qualification makes the point that drives this fourth fallacy. If one is irreducibly unsure as to why certain deeply undesired events did not occur during the Cold War, even though one knows the course of relevant strategic history, how much more uncertainty pertains to putative deterrent relations in the future?

Nothing, repeat nothing, can render intended deterrent effect entirely reliable. Prudent and sensibly fearful policymakers certainly should be appalled to the point of cooperation by some not totally incredible prospect of suffering damage utterly disproportionate to the prospective gains from an adventurous policy. But "should" is not "will," and even if policymakers genuinely are appalled by the risks that they believe they are running, they might decide to run those risks anyway. Western scholars who place confidence in the practice of the theory of stable deterrence are wont to neglect to factor in the political dimension of strength of motivation for inimical behavior.[34] The key problem is that even if every roguish regime in the world is deterrable over every issue on which it is contemplating bold moves, there is no way that a U.S. would-be deterrer can be certain that it would know the specific requirements of deterrence for all those cases.

A United States that, for example, wishes to achieve such deterrent effect in Beijing as may be necessary is entirely uncertain over how much, and over some questions even whether, deterrence is needed. To a significant degree the deterrence needs of the United States vis-à-vis China currently are unknowable. Some readers may be discomforted by such an open-ended argument regarding China, but that open-endedness is the very core of the difficulty that one must recognize. A China hugely in a condition of domestic turmoil is distinctly possible for the next several decades. How the desperately insecure leaders of such a China could be deterred from taking action—in a bid for national unity—over Taiwan, we cannot know reliably; and even those insecure Chinese leaders themselves cannot know reliably. Ultimately, deterrence is like that.

FALLACY 5: STABLE DETERRENCE WORKS TODAY

This fallacy has two important aspects. First, it misunderstands current conditions, and, second, it all but invites misunderstanding of some chaotically nonlinear futures.[35] At the level of general deterrence, U.S. military power casts a shadow of global domain over the cunning plans of any and every would-be "rogue," or regional "aggressor," in the world. But each would-be regional revisionist polity has to interrogate its specific circumstances, and its understanding of U.S. affairs, to inquire whether that general deterrence has any plausible, let alone probable, relevance to the adventure that it contemplates. Unfortunately for reliability of scholarship, if the general deterrence delivered by the U.S. armed forces has practical effect in immediate deterrence, we are unlikely to know about it. When lines are not drawn in the sand, there are unlikely to be footprints for scholars to photograph.

The first aspect of this fifth fallacy is the presumption that the absence of U.S. belligerency today demonstrates the successful working of a stable deterrence. On the contrary, the absence of U.S. belligerency today most probably means nothing more significant than that no polity is sufficiently motivated to challenge the U.S.-shaped world order. Perception of this probable condition is inherently inadequate as stated, because that low motivation may well simply recognize the improbability of success in the face of active U.S. military opposition.

The second, and more troubling, aspect of this particular fallacy is one that appears and reappears throughout strategic history.

Specifically, it is a common failure of the strategic imagination to
recognize how difficult it can be to deter those who are truly desperate, those who are overconfident, and those who are fatalisti-
cally resigned to submit to "History's command" or the "will of
Allah," and so forth, according to cultural predilection.[36] Usually,
the absence of conditions of acute crisis and war will not be (negative) evidence of the successful functioning of some mechanism
for stable deterrence. The leading problems of evidence for scholars are that they cannot know how much dissuasive influence U.S.
military power produces for a general deterrence that discourages
those would-be aggressors who rule out certain forms of challenge
to a U.S.-backed regional order; and that they cannot know or discover whether or not a regional power declines to be heroic in the
face of immediate U.S. deterrence, having first decided to be
brave in the face of general U.S. deterrence.

Argument by illustrative analogy is not widely favored by U.S.
scholars, but I will defy that fact. Because the Soviet leadership in
1989–1991 decided not to fight for the Soviet imperium, the Soviet empire, or even (utterly unpredictably) for the USSR itself—
even the Turkish Empire, "the sick man of Europe" for the better
part of a century prior to 1914, resisted its demise more vigor-
ously—it is widely believed that stable deterrence throughout the
Cold War must have been easily achievable. After all, if Soviet
leaders would not even contest, *à outrance,* their political patri-
mony at home, how formidable really were they over matters of
relative influence much further afield? This is not the place to debate the decline and fall of the Soviet empire; indeed, such a mission would exceed the domain of the inquiry.[37] But I am concerned lest false conclusions be drawn from the relatively painless
demise of Soviet authority. A group of Soviet leaders different
from that led by the unfortunate and incompetent Mikhail Gorbachev could well have decided that their sacred ideological duty
mandated a brutal response to the thoroughgoing challenge
posed by local opposition to Soviet imperium in East-Central Europe in 1989. Admittedly, this is counterfactual argument, but it
would not have been excessively difficult for different Soviet leaders to have licensed, one need hardly add motivate, East-Central
European satraps to suppress popular dissent. Tiananmen Square
easily could have happened in Berlin in 1989 (e.g., Alexander-
platz). If it had happened, the Soviet imperium of the great so-
cialist empire might well have been preserved, albeit in severely
damaged condition both politically and morally.

The point of the above pseudoanalogy is to emphasize that the fall of the Soviet empire probably tells us nothing of great importance about deterrence, stable or otherwise. On the basis of the perilously limited evidence available to date, one has to conclude that the East-West deterrence relationship played scarcely, if at all, in the demise of the Soviet empire. To make the point unmistakably, one needs to specify the contrary hypothesis. Specifically, Gorbachev could have asked, "can we suppress (shoot down, and so forth) the dissenters" wherever and whenever they needed suppressing? Had Gorbachev decided to roll tanks over anti-Soviet protesters throughout East-Central Europe, and had the United States and NATO decided to try to discourage such action, then we would know more about the relative ease with which the USSR could have been deterred. The problem for strategic theorists is that they do not know whether the manner of, and conclusion to, the demise of the USSR is or is not attributable to the suasive effort of nuclear-led deterrence.

FALLACY 6: CARRY ON . . . SMALL NUCLEAR WARS?

Modern chaos theory alerts us to the possibility, even probability, of discontinuities in strategic history.[38] Whereas the gunpowder revolution took more than a century, from the 1320s to the 1410s,[39] to take substantial effect, the atomic age occurred apparently after the fashion of a light being switched on. That is in some sense an exaggeration, but still it is true to claim that the atomic age exploded into political and strategic reality between the surrender of Germany and the surrender of Japan in 1945, only a three-month period. A similar shock to popular and official consciousness undoubtedly will be administered by the next episode of nuclear use in war.[40] I suggest, in the guise of yet more fallacies discussed below, that antinuclear taboos and assumptions about a persisting nonuse of nuclear weapons are apt to disappoint and mislead. The principal problem with beliefs about such antinuclear taboos and assumptions—apart from the plausible fact that they may be perilously fictitious—is that they encourage Westerners to disarm themselves against significant potential dangers. If one believes, and wants to believe, that there is a tolerably authoritative universal taboo against nuclear threats, and especially against nuclear use, one is unlikely to expend many scarce resources worrying about, let alone preparing against, actual nuclear use. This is not to claim that scholars who write about a nuclear taboo are dismissive of the possibility of its being defied. On the contrary, they emphasize the importance of the normative proscription of the taboo precisely because of the danger of nuclear war. Such scholarship, though no doubt well intended, confuses a limited truth—that nuclear weapons carry some normative stigma—with a social proscription of great significance. As we shall see, the idea of a nuclear taboo is both empirically somewhat valid yet all but irrelevant to international security.

This sixth nuclear fallacy is especially poignant because it illustrates with exemplary clarity how the path to hell can be paved with good intentions. Paradox is the problem here. The more settled the expectations of a future that excludes nuclear (or other WMD) use, the more shocking must be the events of blunt nuclear threat or of actual nuclear use. In principle this need not be the case, but in practice when antinuclear preferences influence strategic culture, as has happened in the West, readiness to cope with the stigmatized nuclear events is likely to have fallen early victim to the virus of hope. No one knows the probability of occurrence of nuclear war, but we all should know that

> whenever there is a possibility of a nuclear detonation, a vital interest is created. Whatever the prior security commitments or stakes in a particular conflict, few events would rock national, regional or global security more than even one nuclear detonation. While a war involving small nuclear powers need not necessarily raise such apocalyptical scenarios as those developed for a superpower war, with the spectre of a true end to history, *the concept of a "small" nuclear war has yet to be developed.* Any nuclear use still moves us into the area of unimaginable catastrophe.[41]

A small nuclear war is an oxymoron. While most probably it is true that a nuclear war between regional powers would have the effect of encouraging extraregional actors to keep their heads down, it is not likely that a "small" nuclear war between regional rivals would have negligible, or world system–supporting, consequences. Scholar-theorists like Kenneth N. Waltz probably are correct when they point to the readily confinable domain of a regional nuclear conflict. In Waltz's brutally realistic words: "If such [relatively weak] states use nuclear weapons, the world will not end. The use of nuclear weapons by lesser powers would hardly trigger them elsewhere."[42] No one wants to be a player (target) in other people's nuclear wars. But to argue that a small regional nuclear war is going to remain small and regional is to risk missing the point. The historical event of a nuclear war, no matter how small and tactically contained, *must* demonstrate the nonsense in the assumption that nuclear nonuse is the "rule of the road" in world politics.

The principal concern behind this sixth nuclear fallacy is that theoreticians and policymakers should not discount the strategic effect of small nuclear wars, either because such wars are geostrategically distant or because they are small relative to large. The sounder proposition is the claim that nuclear war is nuclear war. Unfortunately, it is improbable that a benign resolution to many human security dilemmas would follow from the experience of a small nuclear war. All things are possible, but they are not all equally probable. Human beings' strategic condition and proclivities, in short their humanity, have remained constant throughout history; it is therefore unlikely that a small nuclear war in South Asia, or indeed anywhere, would prompt an end to strategic history per se.

Although a small nuclear war is entirely possible, it is not, of course, certain. Moreover, such an event would be eminently survivable for most of the planet: it would be "Apocalypse now" in one or two neighborhoods, albeit leading to much peril downwind (à la Chernobyl, only probably much worse). The nuclear event, far from proving the exception to a taboo on nuclear use, would likely consign the taboo to humankind's well-stocked museum of impracticable beliefs.[43] One can argue that a small nuclear war, for all its horror—actually because of its horror—would serve usefully to underline all of the long-known, but perhaps now blandly overfamiliar, reasons why the nonproliferation regime is of extraordinary importance. In other words, a small nuclear war would be overall a readily survivable and isolatable event that, on balance, probably should reinforce the NPT regime and its associated norms. That is possible, but one argument may not suit all cases. By way of contrast to the relatively optimistic view just cited, a small nuclear war might

- demonstrate the political and military value of nuclear arms, both against a regional foe and as a means strategically to cancel out extended deterrent menaces by a superstate would-be protector;[44]
- remind all interested polities that efforts to marginalize nuclear weapons are a forlorn hope; and
- suggest plausibly, if not quite conclusively, that the nonproliferation regime largely has been an exercise in self-deception

by parties so self-interested in restricting proliferation that they have deceived themselves over the attractiveness of NBC weapons to others.

For all the speculation that the subject of this sixth nuclear fallacy could attract, at least three interdependent claims merit close attention. First, too little thought is being given to the consequences of a nuclear war, small or otherwise. Much of the world, certainly much of the Western community of defense experts, appears unwilling to face the persisting problems of a permanent nuclear era. A sense of nuclear incredulity renders many people, experts not excluded, disinclined to think prudently about nuclear (biological and chemical) *war*. Much as most civilian strategic theorists will wallow happily in ideas about security, strategy, and war in the abstract but shy away from the decidedly ugly "face of battle,"[45] so they are profoundly uncomfortable with discussion of events beyond, or through, the veil of deterrence and crisis as they relate to nuclear (and BC) war. If one's energies are focused upon the restricting or reversing of NBC proliferation and, if need be, upon (extended) deterrence of NBC-led menace in regional conflicts, it is humanly understandable, though not professionally praiseworthy, for one to be reluctant to venture into a future zone of policy failure.

The second claim about this fallacy is that, in Freedman's words, "few events would rock national, regional or global security more than even one nuclear detonation." If a major airplane accident, a large earthquake, or even just a handful of Tomahawk cruise missiles on Iraqi targets can command global attention as shaped by media coverage, what kind of notice would a "small" nuclear war attract? The question all but answers itself. One cannot predict in detail what the many consequences of a small nuclear war would be for the course of, and eventual conclusion to, this second nuclear age; but one can be certain that the shock of the nuclear event would score extremely high on the strategic Richter scale. Even if much more forethought had been devoted to anticipation of such a nuclear event than is the case to date, still the shock would be profound. Some experts may expect a small nuclear war or two over the course of the next several decades, but it is unlikely that a large fraction of the general public, their opinion shapers in the mass media, or their political leaders would share that "expert" expectation.

Third, tragedy in one arena can, though need not, sound an alarm that is heeded elsewhere. The successive tragedies that overwhelmed Czechoslovakia in 1938, Poland in 1939, and much of

Scandinavia, the Low Countries, and France in 1940 delivered a cumulative and salutary wake-up call that Britain eventually heeded. It seems most probable that a small nuclear war would not change much of the structure of the political context probed in Chapter 2, but it would change radically the terms of debate over strategy around the world, including the United States. Following some no doubt hysterically "abolitionist" immediate reaction to the fact of nuclear use in war again, the United States and many others would realize that what they would have just witnessed by way of nuclear tragedy actually could have been precluded, at least rendered far more difficult to effect, by military counterforce—offensive and (especially) defensive.[46]

One can predict that the wake-up call to deploy active antimissile defenses most probably, and sadly, will have to take the form of real historical demonstration that nuclear weapons are weapons that can be used. This second nuclear age will wake up to the necessity for treating nuclear weapons as weapons only after the nuclear-armed belligerents in some regional conflict have sounded the bell of danger as clearly as did Germany's actions from 1938 to the spring of 1940.

FALLACY 7:
DEFENSE DOES NOT WORK IN A NUCLEAR AGE _____

Of all the highways and byways of nuclear-related policy and strategy, none is so harassed by mythical perils—yesterday's anxieties promoted long past their sell-by date—and general ideological baggage as is the subject of ballistic missile defense (BMD). One of the less appreciated reasons that BMD options failed to crack the consensus barrier in the United States during the Cold War was that the prospect of actual nuclear war was denied psychologically. When the massively undesired is denied as a plausible future—it is too awful to think about—it is hugely unlikely that scarce assets will be allocated to prepare to alleviate the consequences of catastrophe. There were always some grounds for technical argument over the probable effectiveness of the BMD technologies then in contention for adoption, but the military-technical debate over BMD in the 1960s, 1970s, and especially the early to mid-1980s offers rich pickings to those in quest of barely concealed subtexts.[47] Many arguments were not quite what they seemed to be. There was no BMD deployment, no matter how sophisticated or ample in relevant redundancy and mass, that cunning offensive-force planners could not defeat, at least in theory, with their deadly vu-graphs.

This text has no interest in reopening old debates over BMD. Suffice it to say, as this seventh fallacy claims, that it is an error simply to argue that "defense does not work in the nuclear era." In this second nuclear age, the challenge is to be able to defeat missile threats far more modest in scale and sophistication than was the case in the 1970s and 1980s in the great Cold War. Both the strategic-theoretical and the military-technical-tactical referents for this subject have been transformed since 1989. Some of our arms control experts appear still to be trapped in a Cold War time warp that prevents them from thinking about BMD in a rational manner. If U.S. arms control experts would elevate their eyes to scan the political context that provides the meaning for their professional endeavors, they would notice that, notwithstanding the START process, there is no political context of real antagonism in Russian-U.S. security relations. Much of the contemporary cottage industry of U.S. arms control activity proceeds with a blithe indifference to the overwhelming political fact that—let us emphasize this—*there is no Russian-U.S. "strategic balance" today.* To risk overstatement of what should be obvious, no one cares or should care how U.S. strategic nuclear forces stack up against Russian strategic nuclear forces, because such military comparison lacks political referents of antagonism. When there is no political content worthy of the label in dispute between two great powers, their military relationship is apt to be a topic only for relaxed contemplation.

Of course, Russia today resents the U.S.-led Western victory in the Cold War; that is not at issue. It follows that today's Russia is easily seduced into a political flirtation with China, another power resentful of the contemporary U.S. hegemonic condition. None of this means, however, that there is, or is likely to be again a Russian-U.S. strategic balance of much significance. Strategic history is governed by political history. It is not impossible that the new Russian Federation should reprise the role of Soviet Problem for Eurasian and U.S. security, but it is distinctly improbable. At this writing, at least, Russia appears as a still noteworthy and still unusually nuclear-well-armed power, but one that is set solidly on the path of an enduring decline. Moreover, there are persuasive reasons of broad political context why Russian nuclear-armed forces should not be the proximate U.S. problem either in the remainder of this second nuclear age or in a third such age. Of course, one cannot be sure, but when contrasted politically and geostrategically with the China of the twenty-first century, the Russian Federation looks like yesterday's menace. This is not to deny that the brief, troubled era of Russian-U.S. cooperation now has passed. More to the point, however, is the fact that early-twenty-first-century Russia will have security problems far more serious than those stemming from resentment of a United States that is hegemonic after the Cold War.

Active defense in the nuclear era would have had great difficulty working against, say, "the Soviet threat" of 1980–1985 vintage, but that tactical judgment cannot hold vis-à-vis regional missile threats today and tomorrow. Because the United States could not have limited damage usefully in the context of a Soviet missile attack in 1970 or 1980 (if that is true), it does not follow that the (ballistic and cruise) missile threats posed by regional powers, not excluding China, could not be defeated early in the twenty-first century. There is no technically compelling connection between claims from the early 1980s that the (Soviet) missile assault will always get through[48] and parallel claims today that BMD will not work in the future.

Although there can never be any absolute guarantees, it is as certain as anything can be in this friction-fraught realm that a multitiered U.S. BMD architecture would defeat militarily any missile menace from regional powers. Nonetheless, there are particular tactical problems posed by regional foes that would stress BMD competencies. Regional nuclear wars will register short times of flight for missiles dispatched to strike targets in-theater. Short ranges translate as minimal, potentially even subliminal, reaction times even for optimally alert and well-positioned active defenses. Almost regardless of the degree of technical sophistication of the defense, short-range ballistic missiles and some medium-range ballistic missiles could pose a genuinely intractable challenge to the defense. That limiting thought aside, BMD today and tomorrow can pose a politically and militarily lethal menace to the suasive power of missile threats.

The Russian-U.S. agreement at the Helsinki Summit meeting on 21 March 1997 to prohibit the development, testing, and deployment of space basing for interceptors for theater missile defense (TMD) is profoundly atavistic.[49] In order both to help sustain the ABM Treaty regime and to hinder the pace of TMD programs, for the first time TMD is subject to explicit international control. The rationale for this backward-looking policy démarche is that allegedly there is urgent need to demarcate TMD from the so-called strategic missile defenses that are constrained by the terms of the ABM Treaty. It is difficult to appreciate the strategic wisdom in placing entirely new constraints upon BMD developed to defeat the WMD that regional powers might deliver by missile when that mission is urgent, technically feasible, and fraught with awful consequences should it fail. The difficulty increases when one finds that a leading reason for the agreement is to spare possible Russian anxieties over the survivability in flight of their long-range ballistic missiles when, to repeat, the United States is not, and is unlikely to be, in a condition of strategic balance or imbalance with the new Russia. One might observe of a United States that remains officially still committed to expansion of constraints upon BMD in a world of growing WMD menace— on official U.S. assay, please note—that those whom the Gods would destroy, they first make mad (or is it MAD?).[50]

Although I am strongly persuaded of the case for BMD, and have debated the subject for nearly thirty years, I am not contemptuous of views different from my own (appearances to the contrary notwithstanding, perhaps). Of course, there is a case against BMD; there always was. The point is that that case is not sound. Critics can argue, correctly, that today's BMD options are not militarily very impressive. That is true but beside the point; it argues for more effort and better programs. Also, one can argue, again correctly, that intelligent adversaries will attempt to swamp or evade U.S. BMD prowess. Again that is true, but irrelevant because obvious and expected. If the United States declined to build any force that foes would try to thwart, it would not build anything. The issue is not will they try but rather are they likely to succeed? Also, one could seek to oppose BMD with the distinctly sensible argument that foes thwarted with respect to missile delivery will seek to evade such active defenses by means of "irregular" insertion of WMD into the United States. As a matter of strategic logic, that argument is sound.[51] It is not sound, however, to argue that because there are several ways to deliver WMD (e.g., by ballistic and air-breathing vehicles, and by sea and across land frontiers), we should grant ballistic missiles a free ride.

Missile defense should not be analyzed in isolation. This text treats BMD in the context broadly of counterforce, in company with offensive military action against missile forces. Even when BMD is treated properly within a mix of active offensive and defensive options, still it remains a subject curiously stapled to counsels of military perfection. The strategic truth of the matter is that

BMD may well prove useful for deterrence and defense, but no defensive measures literally can guarantee the tactical negation of the offense. If deterrence is unreliable, as strategic history in general—but not Cold War strategic history—shows, then the case for active defense against proliferant powers' most probable weapon of choice, the ballistic missile, is strong indeed.[52] Reflection on the decades of Cold War yields a less-than-ringing endorsement for the thesis that nuclear-era deterrence is robustly reliable. Both sides of the argument over the military-technical perils of the East-West nuclear standoff can register telling blows in debate. Does the record of a nonwar outcome to the Cold War, notwithstanding the facts of many accidents and much mutual miscalculation,[53] reveal the reliability of nuclear deterrence, simply the authority of luck, or some indeterminate mix of the two? Because there was no Soviet-U.S. nuclear war, it does not follow that the case against BMD stands proven. Alas for scholarly rigor, the absence of nuclear war proves nothing in particular about the merit in opposing views during the recurrent debates over BMD. U.S. BMD deployment might have added complications for a rational would-be Soviet attacker that could prove definitively dissuasive; or (improbably, but who really knows?) Soviet strategic anxiety at the prospect of impending U.S. deployment of multilayered missile defenses might have triggered desperate action on the Soviet part. We are in the realm of strategic fiction, or perhaps prudent forecasting.

Much less fanciful than the above small venture into counterfactual history, however, is consideration of the merits in BMD today.

First, the unreliability of deterrence that must attend strategic relations between a U.S. superpower and some regional polity strongly motivated to assert itself in its immediate neighborhood renders actual defense much more important than it was for East-West strategic nexuses during the Cold War. Readers may recall that a significant asymmetry that helped structure the U.S. phase of the Vietnam War was the contrast in intensity of commitment between Washington and Hanoi. Basic punitive deterrence on the grand scale, though perilous in the extreme if challenged, let alone tripped into consequential military action, probably is robust in the face of broad threats to national values. But if the political will of the U.S. superpower is challenged over some matter of only arguably vital national interest—the continued independence of the Republic of China on Taiwan, for instance—vast threats of nuclear punishment are less than self-evidently deterring.[54] In confrontation with regional powers, the United States, acting as protector of a regional order, has a need to be able to deny tactical, and hence strategic, success to the aircraft and missile-deliverable NBC weapons of those regional powers. Multitiered and mobile forward-deployable theater missile defense (TMD), backstopped critically by a national missile defense (NMD) capability—to minimize the option for terroristic efforts at blackmail—should help enable the superpower to extend protection, even by extended deterrence.

Second, U.S. deployment of complementary tiers of BMD—and extended air defenses—devalues the currency of missile threats. Given that missiles have no close substitutes as terrifying, tactically reliable, and swift-delivery vehicles for WMD (even though, as noted, they are less than ideal for delivery of BC agents that must work in aerosol form), the strategic benefit to regional order from U.S. BMD is considerable. One should not advance this argument too far. There is no question but that U.S. BMD should be able to defeat the offensive missile force of any regional polity; but the workings and anticipation of friction, the enemy's cunning plans, bad luck, and strategic prudence all would function in practice to diminish the leverage that BMD and air defense deployments should yield.

Third, the ability of the world's "ordering" powers, the G8 club, to function responsibly in extended deterrence and defense roles requires that they should not be hostage to any polity, faction from a polity, eccentrically motivated military unit, accident-prone military unit, or roguishly criminal body that can brandish a tactically credible threat to deliver a few NBC weapons by plane or missile. Active missile defenses cannot banish all menace of NBC weapons. But such defenses can carry a plausible promise to defeat a threat that typically would number only in the tens of vehicles, at most. There are some NBC delivery threats that BMD cannot answer: weapons of very short range, for example, or weapons that arrive in backpacks, by car, or by boat. Nonetheless, what BMD and air defenses certainly can do with high assurance is strategically—not to say morally—well worth doing.

Fourth, and finally, with the arguable possible exception of the residual though still modernizing Russian strategic nuclear arsenal, there are no missile-armed groups in the world today, or prospectively tomorrow, whose WMD capabilities should prove beyond defeat by U.S. offensive and (especially) *defensive* counterforce means. It is not obvious on military-technical or economic grounds why the United States should be obliged to settle again for the potentially strategically paralyzing reality of *mutual* assured destruction nexuses with regional polities.[55] Acting strategically as a distant protecting power for regional security, the United States needs to deny leverage to regional owners of WMD. If both the United States and a regional foe rely heavily on a punitive deterrence, the probable asymmetry in vitality of rival interests at stake will leave the United States with a politically lethal deterrence deficit. U.S. BMD and extended air defenses can help deny hostages to U.S. behavior compliant with the wishes of regional foes. Moreover, the United States and its principal allies could commit to deploy active defenses that would stay either ahead of or at least tactically competitive with regional missile-borne threats of action by WMD. But so long as the ABM Treaty regime is permitted to prevent orbital deployments of BMD-dedicated interceptor missiles or of BMD weapons based on "other physical principles," the prospects for really effective missile defenses are short of glittering.

FALLACY 8: NUCLEAR WEAPONS HAVE COME TO BE STIGMATIZED BY A TABOO AGAINST THEIR "USE"

Reference has been made already to a nuclear taboo. Although the proposition of a nuclear taboo is both plausible and attractive, it is perilously flawed in a way that is likely to set damaging ambushes for those who have been imprudently optimistic. The idea of a nuclear taboo hovers somewhat uneasily between fact and value. Widespread endorsement of the desirability of social demotion and general denigration of all things nuclear works to hinder prudent thoughts and action on the subject of how best to cope with the permanence of nuclear facts. Commitment to the worthy idea of a nuclear taboo is wont to encourage effort devoted to strengthening the nonproliferation regime—activity that generally is sensible, praiseworthy, and often worthy of the energy expended—rather than to deal effectively with the enduring nuclear dimension to security.

The case of a nuclear taboo is one of those instances where a sound idea, as well as a culturally inescapable but not thoroughly effective proscriptive norm, has the potential to function to unanticipated dangerous consequences (the law of unintended consequences). The proposition that the global nonproliferation regime has come to be supported and is to a degree propelled forward by a nuclear taboo is an astrategic rationalization by generally unintentionally hypocritical Westerners. The fragility of Western theory about a nuclear taboo is easily demonstrated. Supported by the structurally discriminatory NPT regime, the majority of declared nuclear weapons states simultaneously reaffirm the nationally vital security functions of their WMD and condemn WMD in the hands of others—but not all others, one must hasten to add. Israel's nuclear arsenal attracts little negative comment from the West, and the newly demonstrated and declared nuclear weapons states of India and Pakistan have attracted more expressions of understanding than condemnation from other polities outside the West. It is only the third tier of would-be nuclear weapons states, deemed irresponsible if not roguish for their rejection of Western norms of civilized international (and domestic) behavior, that falls under the heavy censure of spokespersons for a nuclear taboo.

The policy inclinations fairly attributable to Iraq, Iran, North Korea, and Libya hold no appeal for me. However, that said, one should not risk gratuitous damage to international security by fooling oneself with parochial nostrums. While arguably it is true to claim that a nuclear taboo has grown that deglamorizes and delegitimizes nuclear arms, such a taboo has proved itself no reliable barrier to further nuclear proliferation. If there had ever been some danger that states capable of acquiring nuclear arms somehow would slip naturally into actual nuclear capability, then the taboo argument would have much more force. But for all its popularity, inherent attractiveness (to us, at least), and apparent political sophistication, the operation and significance of a nuclear taboo is not all that it may seem to be. One should not presume causal connection between the phenomenon of a very slow pace of nuclear proliferation and the international popularity of a nuclear taboo. The latter probably has some relevance to the former but nowhere near as much as often is implied or claimed.

Similarly, one should not presume a causal connection between nuclear nonuse and a nuclear taboo. One of the major studies of weapon taboos, for example, inadvertently illustrates the weakness of the evidential base for taboo claims. Null hypotheses are notoriously difficult to prove. For example, Richard Price and Nina Tannenwald overreach severely when they claim that "the strengths of the nuclear taboo and the odium attached to nuclear weapons as weapons of mass destruction render unusable all nuclear weapons, even though certain kinds of nuclear weapons could, from the perspective of Just War theory, conceivably be justified."[56] This is just not so. The arguments for the historical functioning of a nuclear taboo advanced by Price and Tannenwald cannot bear the strategic traffic that is run over them. In their analysis, normative proscription—taboo-related injunctions—assumes a residual value that is methodologically infeasible. "Taboo" argument tends to degrade under pressure into a residual culturalist explanation that is advanced as an unduly pervasive explanation. The problem is that a taboo does exist, but its worth as an explanation for the nonoccurrence of some undesired events is not at all powerful.

Before proceeding further into a critique of the hypothesis of a nuclear taboo, it is important to outline the apparent context of that hypothesis.

A taboo is a socially sanctioned prohibition that may, or may not, carry the force of law.[57] Contemporary discussion of nuclear weapons issues is ambivalent on the question of whether or not a nuclear taboo exists. It is significant, for example, that in a well-regarded 1991 study, Lewis A. Dunn wrote aspirationally that "the goal here should be to reduce to an absolute minimum the role of nuclear weapons *and to bring about a global nuclear taboo.*" He proceeded to refer favorably to the prospect that "[a] commitment to reducing the role of nuclear weapons *and fostering a global nuclear taboo against their use* would also contribute across the board to containing the scope of nuclear proliferation and its consequences."[58] To quote Dunn again, a global taboo against nuclear use would (1) "reduce the prestige of going nuclear"; (2) "greatly help to ensure the long-term extension of the NPT"; (3) "influence thinking among new nuclear powers"; and (4) "provide legitimacy for great power or UN Security Council actions to defuse or contain the threat of regional nuclear wars."[59] There is much to be said in praise of the taboo hypothesis. Unfortunately, the proposition that an international political taboo against the "use" (i.e., the threat or the employment) of nuclear weapons has coalesced, is coalescing, or might coalesce has about as much validity as the proposition that major war is, is becoming, or soon will be obsolete.[60] In the decent opinion of truly civilized folk the use of nuclear weapons (let alone chemical or, heaven forfend, biological weapons) may well be far beyond the pale of acceptable options for statecraft; that, however, can never be the relevant issue. Most probably there exists today a political taboo against nuclear weapons per se, and certainly against the use of nuclear weapons, that is authoritative for most people and most polities. If ruling notions for all of world politics were determined by a crude head or political unit count, then indeed it would be true to point to the power and influence of *a* or *the* nuclear taboo.

The reality of world politics in this second nuclear age is, alas, far removed from that just fantasized. Self-helping security communities cannot be influenced very usefully by a nuclear taboo, especially when the principal articulators of this taboo are citizens of contentedly and prospectively permanently nuclear-armed states. To put this concept in some context, there are social (and legal) taboos against incest (everywhere) and spitting in public (in some societies), but in neither of these cases are taboos able to cope with the truly hard cases ("necessity knows no proscriptive norms," to misquote Theobald von Bethman Hollweg).[61] The idea that embattled polities with the most serious of security problems could be influenced conclusively by a Western-led nuclear taboo is close to absurd. Less absurd is the proposition that the stigmatization of nuclear arms that is largely implicit in the global nonproliferation regime, which is capped by the NPT, might help inhibit the pace of further nuclear proliferation. A general delegitimization and "deglorification" of nuclear arms should facilitate the efforts of those who seek to impede the path of would-be nuclear proliferants. That granted, the superordinate difficulty remains that supply-side antiproliferation measures cannot succeed unless success is claimed merely for delay.

The central problem with the hypothesis of a nuclear taboo is that it endeavors to deny needs both of the logic of policy and the grammar of strategy, to resort to Clausewitzian phrasing.[62] U.S. adherents to the hypothesis of the importance of a nuclear taboo should explain why this taboo can carry authority, given that it is flatly and robustly contradicted in key senses by the strategic beliefs and policies of eight nuclear weapons states. There is a nuclear taboo that stigmatizes nuclear threat or employment. But policymakers in the eight nuclear weapons states do not equate such stigmatization—or singularization, for a less pejorative rendering—with unusability. Nuclear weapons may be weapons of last resort (for us, at least), but last resort should not be confused with no resort. More to the point, perhaps, is the question of how a nuclear taboo possibly can contribute usefully to world peace with security when this second nuclear age provides a buyer's market for fissile material, for skills in nuclear weapons design and industrial fabrication, and for ballistic and air-breathing means of nuclear weapons delivery.

To show the absurdity of the hypothesis of a nuclear taboo is akin to demonstrating the folly in the United Nations. Neither critique really is fair, because neither subject can command the merit in its destiny. Practical demolition of the value in the hypothesis of a nuclear taboo, and thoroughgoing criticism of the United Nations, ultimately are futile exercises, because both are shooting at straw targets. The United Nations cannot reform until its members reform their approaches to world politics. Similarly, a nuclear taboo cannot assume solidly reliable significance until political-military conditions are permissive, in which case it will not be needed. It is just naive to believe that nuclear arms, or other WMD, can be rendered morally unfashionable to a point of policy insignificance.

Occasionally a strategic topic arises that is so basic that it is unusually challenging of the ability to communicate pertinent considerations. I am legally Anglo-American and typically entirely unsympathetic to the regional uses to which sundry "roguish" proliferants might commit a nuclear arsenal; but still I am troubled by the ethnocentrism that suffuses the idea of a nuclear taboo. I have no difficulty whatsoever understanding, even applauding, policy decisions for a putatively permanent *nuclear* future for *my* polities. It follows that I have no difficulty comprehending why Iraqis, Iranians, North Koreans, and Libyans expect to register worthwhile security benefits from nuclear acquisition. If the Western-authored hypothesis of a nuclear taboo impairs our (Western) ability to empathize with non-Western incentives to acquire NBC weapons, it will have done us poor service.

I have striven to avoid writing scenarios of nuclear use in this book. One of the more important reasons this chapter attaches importance to BMD—and indeed to all variants of counterforce, offensive and defensive—is that I believe this age may well register an actual regional nuclear war. Whether or not there is a global nuclear taboo against the use of nuclear weapons is a question of no great interest. What is of interest is whether or not nuclear-armed, nuclear-threshold (almost-nuclear-armed), or opaquely nuclear-armed security communities would sanction nuclear threats or employment. Given that the eight currently declared nuclear weapons states have no difficulty answering that question in the affirmative, what plausible confidence can repose in the hypothesis that a nuclear taboo can severely modify the answer? Thus is the nuclear taboo revealed as a toothless proscription; somewhat true, but not true enough.

Because the theory of the nuclear (and BC) weapons taboo is neither wholly correct nor incorrect, it is exceptionally difficult to provide fair judgment upon the writings of the handful of scholars who have pursued this idea to date. Since it may well be impossible for me to do full justice to the nuanced views of those scholars, I can at least be clear in the presentation of my own views. The recognition that nuclear weapons provide cause *usefully* to be stigmatized by a taboo is, in my opinion, a fallacy because although there is a very widespread taboo that stigmatizes nuclear weapons—possession, threat, and use—that normative proscription cannot handle arguments and assertions of security necessity. Recognition, let alone celebration, of the undoubted fact of this widespread taboo helps disarm us psychologically, politically, and militarily, so that we are less able to cope with WMD realities than we might be in the absence of notice of this taboo.

In addition to the logic I have advanced that is critical of the taboo theory, two more general complaints also need airing. First, "nuclear tabooists," if I may call them such, have yet to demonstrate that they have thought very deeply about the true scope of normative influences upon political and strategic behavior. In other words, the nuclear taboo as a normative proscription is apt to be offset in its impact upon political behavior by the impulse not only of security necessity but also of competing norms. Second, as one who has ventured into the perilous waters of theory about "strategic culture," I must attest to some uneasiness about the open-ended influence allowed nuclear (and other) tabooist, or "culturalist," explanations, especially of nuclear *non*events.

CONCLUSION

Most of the discussion in this chapter has been devoted only to the analysis of nuclear, among NBC, issues. Generally, though not invariably, such problems as have been identified for Western society as likely to flow from nuclear proliferation are considerably worse when treated in the context of chemical and biological perils. BC weaponry is harder to isolate and detect than is nuclear (for example, many insecticides are nerve agents)[63] but is probably tactically easier to deliver—though not to deliver in a condition of reliable lethality. The only good news of strategic importance is that BC, and especially biological, weaponry can be difficult to employ to useful effect as weapons.

Although the exploration of a second nuclear age is far from completed by the discussion here, four "working conclusions" command attention at this juncture. First, there can be no serious dispute about the assumption that the nuclear era is with us forever. This point, though apparently obvious, nonetheless meets with resistance. One could say that the nuclear discovery of 1945 settled the matter for all time. Nuclear use may be deterred, evaded, putatively defeated, or otherwise sidelined, but it cannot be removed from the board of world politics. The contemporary literature on nuclear abolition needs augmentation by the reminder that what has been abolished could, after a while, be reassembled (with no need for reinvention).

Second, nuclear nonproliferation, antiproliferation, and counterproliferation ultimately will not work. Policy approaches that address the supply side to profound matters of security invariably fail. One could moderate this negative judgment, in praise of the additional multidimensional costs (including loss of time) that the NPT regime and adjunct measures often can impose on would-be proliferants, but one should not blur the issue and risk misleading people. Eliot Cohen is correct when he writes: "Of course it makes sense to pursue marginal remedies [fundamental remedies for proliferation being unavailable] as energetically as possible. . . . But both technically and politically they can achieve only limited success."[64] The regional security demand for some WMD offset to contemporary U.S. conventional prowess, the diffusion of nuclear (and biological and chemical) knowledge, and the post-Soviet relative ease of access to necessary technologies and skills all add up to mission impossible for nonproliferation. Sensible defense planners certainly should buy such time as they are able at a reasonable cost before an Iraq or an Iran acquires an "Islamic bomb" to add to BC arsenals; but the challenge for the future is more to learn how to cope with proliferation, and especially how to defeat the more malign of its possible consequences, than to devise new (and futile) ways to stem or reverse it.

The third conclusion is that the United States and its friends and allies are unlikely to be persuaded by anything short of the dread event of actual WMD use to take the problems of WMD security really seriously in this second nuclear age. The U.S. defense community appears still so hoist with self-regard for the presumed success of its deterrence policy during the Cold War that it has yet to notice that it has adopted no policy or strategy to date likely radically to alleviate, let alone resolve, the principal military security challenges of the early twenty-first century. Deterrence is wonderful, if achievable. Although many leaders of newly proliferant polities are likely to be as risk-averse as Waltz and Quinlan affirm *all* nuclear-menaced folk to be,[65] only an irresponsible optimist would extrapolate from the decades of the Cold War an uncritical paean to the all-purpose marvels of deterrence. It would take only one leader who was not as nuclear risk-averse as textbooks on nuclear deterrence say he or she ought to be, or only one policy decision that erroneously was believed to be prudent but transpired to be otherwise, for the second nuclear age to register a "small" nuclear war.

The fourth working conclusion to these chapters on proliferation is that the unreliability of deterrence, in a political context where the United States continues to act as the sheriff for regional order around the world, mandates rapid acquisition of active missile and extended air defenses as components integral to a multilayered "war-fighting" approach to regional NBC challenges. Admittedly, BMD will have an impossible task against truly short-range threats, and extremely low-flying NBC-armed vehicles also will stress defensive competence. There is no single magical solution to all the military threats that proliferant polities and extra-state groups technically could pose. Moreover, no matter how multitiered is the U.S. answer to proliferation and the peril of hostile NBC use in war, Stanley Baldwin's somewhat accurate claim that "the bomber will always get through" should be assumed to be a probable strategic truth for our NBC future. "Zero tolerance" of tactical, operational, strategic, and political failure is the right attitude, the correct vision with which to approach nuclear and BC threats, but it should not be the authoritative expectation. Furthermore, the typically defense-inattentive general publics in democracies, reared on official faith in deterrence, probably excessive confidence in U.S. military power, and deep incredulity about WMD disaster, most likely would be shocked into panic reactions by the utterly unexpected arrival of a "small" regional doomsday. If that oxymoronically modest doomsday were to engulf a Western expeditionary force, then truly would we see a policy and strategy debate on this subject of how to live prudently in a nuclear era that we cannot annul.

NOTES

1. For example, see Gray: "Nuclear Strategy: The Case for a Theory of Victory;" (with Payne) "Victory Is Possible"; "War Fighting for Deterrence"; "Moscow Is Cheating"; *House of Cards.*

2. Quinlan, *Thinking About Nuclear Weapons,* p. 28.

3. Morgan, *Deterrence,* ch. 2.

4. One telling indication of this political and military fact is the cumulative demotion of "Strategic Nuclear Forces" in the *Annual Reports* of the secretary of defense to the point where, in 1998, those forces appear under Chapter 5, following chapters on conventional and special operations forces. William Cohen, *Annual Report,* ch. 5. This admittedly somewhat "Kremlinological" point is checkable for accuracy with the relative positioning of the chapter-length discussion of the strategic nuclear forces in the *Annual Reports* for, say, 1990 and 1991.

5. See Sagan and Turco, *Path Where No Man Thought,* p. 54.

6. Price and Tannenwald, "Norms and Deterrence" (pp. 140–141), argue that "the drive to create 'smart' bombs and other high-tech options *so that* leaders will not have to resort to nuclear weapons is indicative of the special status of nuclear weapons." Emphasis added. The causal connection asserted by Price and Tannenwald is rather too simple and direct for my taste.

7. For discussion of this matter in a period classic with some lasting merit, see Lewis Dunn, *Controlling the Bomb,* ch. 3.

8. Mitchell Reiss, *Bridled Ambition.*

9. I equivocate a little here because the explosion of criminal and intertribal violence in the new South Africa has led to a marked deterioration in the personal security of all citizens.

10. Creveld, "New Wars for Old," p. 91.

11. Quinlan, *Thinking About Nuclear Weapons,* p. 1.

12. A strong argument for "marginalization" is advanced in Freedman, "Nuclear Weapons."

13. Sun Tzu, *Art of War,* esp. p. 177.

14. Davidson, "Secret Weapon of Byzantium."

15. Mazarr, "Virtual Nuclear Arsenals" and *Nuclear Weapons in a Transformed World.*

16. Lavoy, "Nuclear Myths and the Causes of Nuclear Proliferation," esp. p. 206, n. 7.

17. Abolitionist, eliminationist aspirations are demolished in Freedman, "Nuclear Weapons"; Quinlan, *Thinking About Nuclear Weapons;* and Payne, *Case Against Nuclear Abolition.* Also, there is some enduring merit in Garrity, "Depreciation of Nuclear Weapons in International Politics." Garrity concludes his lengthy review of nuclear matters by suggesting that "it is possible to argue that officials and scholars have hitherto been overly fascinated with thinking about nuclear weapons, as opposed to understanding other outstanding political and military issues that are now coming to the forefront. Whatever the merits of this viewpoint, we should perhaps now be concerned that in the future there will be too little official academic interest in things nuclear. Nuclear weapons may now seem to be increasingly anachronistic and irrelevant. But if this attitude prevails, or if traditional concepts are applied unthinkingly to new circumstances, nuclear weapons could re-emerge on the scene in unexpected and dangerous ways" (p. 501). Those are words of wisdom.

18. Haslam, *Soviet Union and the Politics of Nuclear Weapons in Europe;* Heuser, *NATO, Britain, France and the FRG: Nuclear Strategies and Forces for Europe.*

19. For a brief sample of an extensive literature, abolitionist sentiment may be located in the following: Schell, *Abolition* and *Gift of Time;* Regina Cowen Karp, *Security Without Nuclear Weapons;* Rotblat, Steinberger, and Udgaonkar, *Nuclear-Weapon-Free World;* Canberra Commission, *Report;* Goodpaster and Butler, "National Press Club Luncheon Address"; Butler, "Stimson Center Award Remarks"; National Academy of Sciences, *Future of U.S. Nuclear Weapons Policy.*

20. Mazarr, "Virtual Nuclear Arsenals" and "Notion of Virtual Arsenals."

21. Mazarr, "Virtual Nuclear Arsenals," p. 14.

22. Ibid.

23. Gray, *House of Cards,* ch. 6, provides detailed justification for this claim.

24. Schelling, *Strategy of Conflict,* ch. 8.

25. David Dunn, *Politics of Threat,* ch. 8.

26. Clausewitz, *On War,* p. 178.

27. Payne, *Deterrence in the Second Nuclear Age,* p. 17.

28. Quinlan, *Thinking About Nuclear Weapons,* p. 16.

29. For reasons explained admirably in Watts, *Clausewitzian Friction and Future War.*

30. Iklé, "Second Coming of the Nuclear Age," is thoughtfully skeptical about our record of success with deterrence during the Cold War. Iklé is nothing if not consistent; see his articles "Can Nuclear Deterrence Last Out the Century?" and "Nuclear Strategy." In the growing library of post–Cold War histories of the first nuclear age, the following are prominent among those works that merit close attention: Andrew and Gordievsky, *Instructions from the Centre;* Trachtenberg, *History and Strategy;* Nathan, *Cuban Missile Crisis Revisited;* Leffler, *Preponderance of Power;* Scott Sagan, *Limits of Safety;* Lebow and Stein, *We All Lost the Cold War;* Holloway, *Stalin and the Bomb;* Zubok and Pleshakov, *Inside the Kremlin's Cold War;* Haftendorn, *NATO and the Nuclear Revolution;* Dockrill, *Eisenhower's New-Look National Security Policy;* Mastny, *Cold War and Soviet Insecurity;* Gaddis, *We Now Know;* Fursenko and Naftali, *"One Hell of a Gamble";* May and Zelikow, *Kennedy Tapes;* and Fischer, *Cold War Conundrum.*

31. Stein, "Deterrence and Compellence in the Gulf," is excellent.

32. Howard, "Lessons of the Cold War."

33. Quinlan, *Thinking About Nuclear Weapons,* p. 16. Emphasis added.

34. Notwithstanding his focus upon irregular warriors, Ralph Peters offers a superb essay on the power of human motivation in "Our New Old Enemies."

35. For some arguably relevant theory, see James, *Chaos Theory.*

36. Peters, "Our New Old Enemies."

37. Suffice it for now to record that for centuries to come scholars will be arguing about "the decline and fall of the Soviet empire." At the present time there is a shortlist of contending major explanations (most are predominantly deterministic, as scholars fall into the trap of rationalizing what was substantially highly contingent), but there is no dominant theory that commands near universal respect.

38. In addition to James, *Chaos Theory,* see Ruelle, *Chance and Chaos;* Kellert, *In the Wake of Chaos;* and Beaumont, *War, Chaos, and History.*

39. See Hall, *Weapons and Warfare in Renaissance Italy,* esp. ch. 2.

40. Mandelbaum, "Lessons of the Next Nuclear War."

41. Freedman, "Nuclear Weapons," p. 39. Emphasis added.

42. Sagan and Waltz, *Spread of Nuclear Weapons,* p. 17.

43. On taboo issues, see Paul, "Nuclear Taboo and War Initiation in Regional Conflicts"; and Price and Tannenwald, "Norms and Deterrence."

44. Many of the most pertinent issues are discussed usefully in Wilkening and Watman, *Nuclear Deterrence in a Regional Context.*

45. Keegan, *Face of Battle.*

46. Krepon, "Are Missile Defenses MAD?"; Payne, *Deterrence in the Second Nuclear Age,* pp. 142–152.

47. The following sample from the large literature available covers all points of view: Carter and Schwartz, *Ballistic Missile Defense;* Payne, *Strategic Defense;* Brzezinski, *Promise or Peril;* York, *Does Strategic Defense Breed Offense?;* Marshall Institute, *Concept of Defensive Deterrence;* Chayes and Doty, *Defending Deterrence;* Payne, *Missile Defense in the 21st Century;* Baucom, *Origins of SDI;* and Edward Reiss, *Strategic Defense Initiative.*

48. On 10 November 1932, British Prime Minister Stanley Baldwin told the House of Commons in a phrase that has become cliché that "the bomber will always get through." For the context see Bialer, *Shadow of the Bomber,* ch. 1 (Baldwin's claim is quoted on p. 14).

49. White House Press Release. For the full political, legal, and strategic contexts, see Lambakis and Gray, *Political and Legal Restrictions on U.S. Military Space Activities.*

50. Appropriately scathing comment upon this unfortunate and strategically imprudent development is provided by David Smith, "Missile Defense After Helsinki."

51. It is the logic of asymmetrical strategy. See Matthews, *Challenging the United States Symmetrically and Asymmetrically.*

52. Ballistic missiles are the most militarily attractive delivery vehicles for nuclear weapons; they are good enough—though not ideal—for delivery of chemical agents that require carefully controlled dispersal if they are to be suitably and promptly lethal; but they are far from ideal for exact delivery of the delicate living organisms that are the agents of biological warfare. See U.S. Congress, *Proliferation of Weapons of Mass Destruction,* pp. 50–52, and *Technologies Underlying Weapons of Mass Destruction,* esp. pp. 32–36, 94–99.

53. Blair, *Logic of Accidental Nuclear War;* Scott Sagan, *Limits of Safety;* Fischer, *Cold War Conundrum.*

54. See Wilkening and Watman, *Nuclear Deterrence in a Regional Context;* and Arquilla, "Bound to Fail."

55. On the basics, see Panofsky, "The Mutual Hostage Relationship Between America and Russia."

56. Price and Tannenwald, "Norms and Deterrence," p. 140.

57. For example, we recognize taboos against incest and cannibalism; in addition, there is a taboo against remaining seated during the playing of the national anthem.

58. Lewis Dunn, *Containing Nuclear Proliferation,* pp. 69, 70. Emphasis added.

59. Ibid., p. 70.

60. Mueller, *Retreat from Doomsday.*

61. Quoted in Walzer, *Just and Unjust Wars,* p. 240. The chancellor's actual words were, "Necessity knows no law."

62. Clausewitz, *On War,* p. 605.

63. Crone, *Banning Chemical Weapons,* is helpful, as is Utgoff, *Challenge of Chemical Weapons.*

64. Eliot Cohen, one among "Three Comments," p. 37.

65. Waltz in Sagan and Waltz, *Spread of Nuclear Weapons,* pp. 21, 22, 24; Quinlan, *Thinking About Nuclear Weapons,* p. 16.

5

Nuclear Strategy

From the somewhat negative analysis of nuclear fallacies in Chapter 4, the discussion now moves into a positive vein. Unpopular though nuclear forces and nuclear strategy are to many people today, I brave the perils of political incorrectness and inquire how the United States should approach questions of nuclear strategy. This chapter argues the merit in adopting a strategic perspective for the consideration of nuclear arms, it proceeds to express reservations about the astrategic journey that is the START enterprise,[1] and it identifies and explains five strategic missions for U.S. nuclear forces in the second nuclear age. The discussion closes with consideration of the more vital of the similarities and dissimilarities between the first and second nuclear ages, a presentation that leads directly to providing general principles for the guidance of U.S. nuclear strategy and nuclear force planning.

A STRATEGIC PERSPECTIVE

To argue the corner of nuclear strategy as we approach the end of the twentieth century is to risk being bracketed with those who continue to deny any proven connection between smoking and ill health. In the United States, at least, nuclear weapons are not popular. Unfortunately, there are several conclusively persuasive reasons that the United States is obliged to remain a nuclear power:

1. As principal, indeed occasionally as the only practicable, guardian of international order, it must be at least as well armed as any would-be revolutionary polity.

115

2. It is the last line of its own, as well as everyone else's, security in a world that continues to operate in an only semidisciplined, essentially anarchical self-help mode.
3. The nuclear discovery is a permanent strategic fact, derived from science and technology, which yields knowledge that cannot be forgotten.[2]

I am substantially unfriendly to the idea of either minimal but existential or of virtual and postexistential nuclear weapons arsenals. The former idea is judged here to be merely imprudent, and the latter combines impracticality with a folly that could assume proportions amounting to criminal neglect of the polity's prime duty to the safety of the citizen.

A so-called minimum (would-be) deterrent of, say, a couple of hundred weapons must be an exceedingly, and in the U.S. case a needlessly, blunt strategic instrument. Moreover, again in the U.S. case, a minimum nuclear arsenal would not only ill-fit a foreign policy of global engagement that included extended deterrent duties, it could prove dangerous. Low numbers on the U.S. part (deployed on how many platforms?) could fuel competitive fires abroad and gratuitously invite technical and military-operational vulnerabilities. These thoughts may point to anxieties that should not be well founded, but given that nuclear arms will remain the *ultima ratio regum,* why would a prudently governed polity ever consider taking needless risks in this area?

The idea of virtual nuclear arsenals—or postexistential nuclear arsenals for readers who delight in abstruse jargon—is basically unsound.[3] Virtuality for nuclear arms is a poor idea because (1) a global disarmament regime mandating that nuclear arms be virtual at most could not be monitored, verified, or enforced; (2) cheating, even on a small scale, could have catastrophic consequences—and, alas, assuredly it would not be the United States or Britain that cheated; (3) even if all parties to a treaty for the "virtualization" of nuclear arms were to adhere to its terms scrupulously—which they would not—what the treaty regime would preprogram would be the certainty in the future of a massively dangerous nuclear rearmament competition under the pressure of crisis or war; and (4) a nuclear arsenal operationally ready for strategic prime time cannot just be created overnight and then promptly switched on to do its pre- or intrawar deterrent or denial jobs—Western democracies might lose a nuclear rearmament competition or lose in non-nuclear conflict before they could reassemble the "great deterrent." Fortunately, the idea of virtual nuclear arsenals is such a bad one that even many among the Western opinion leaders who routinely will endorse propositions for policy that staple together disarmament, antinuclear action, and clever-sounding theory are unlikely to be seduced.

This chapter on nuclear strategy opened by offering some body blows to the respectively poor and appallingly poor ideas of a minimum deterrent and a "virtual deterrent"—a concept that says it all, one suspects: Would one settle for "virtual love" or "virtual wealth"? The purpose of this discussion is to provide a useful contrast with a genuinely strategic approach to nuclear arms.

The mission of the chapter is somewhat daunting. Notwithstanding the disappearance, temporary removal at least, of a nuclear-armed peer competitor to the United States—politically the most necessary defining parameter of this second nuclear age—and the moderately plausible emergence of the United States as a supercombatant in non-nuclear information-led warfare, I argue here for the importance of nuclear strategy.

In common with every middle-aged strategic theorist and commentator, I have had to interrogate my Cold War–trained strategic toolkit in light of what appears to be happening in this second nuclear age. As a person reared on the thoughts of Bernard Brodie, Albert Wohlstetter, Henry Kissinger, Thomas Schelling, and Herman Kahn,[4] among others, how much and which items of my strategic nuclear "knowledge"—intellectual working capital perhaps—remains reliable? Leaving aside the now blessedly retired question of who is (was) correct about Cold War nuclear strategy, the uncomfortable fact remains that most of our ideas on nuclear strategy are between thirty and forty years old. Not only has the technology of war changed radically over the past two decades, but—more challenging still—the revolution in political context has altered foreign policy demand for (extended) nuclear deterrence beyond Cold War recognition. These are tough times indeed for the nuclear strategist. U.S. nuclear strategists now have no worthy foe (except perhaps for U.S. antinuclear strategists) and are challenged in their relevance by the claim for supercompetence in information-led warfare that derives from expectations of routine U.S. achievement of dominant battlespace knowledge.[5] By the close of the decade of the 1990s, though, the U.S. theory of information-led war had been battered by Balkan realities, much as U.S. limited-war theory was humbled in Vietnam.

A leading text on nuclear strategy argues for the political utility of nuclear armament, even though military merit to nuclear options is denied.[6] Robert Jervis believes that "Nuclear Superiority Doesn't Matter"—admittedly in the context of superpower Cold War—because nuclear catastrophe is nuclear catastrophe.[7] The question now, however, is whether the shift in political context from first to second nuclear age erases what previously was standard wisdom about nuclear superiority. What apparently was strategically true with respect to U.S.-Soviet relations in the 1970s and 1980s may not be true for U.S.-Iranian or U.S.-Chinese relations in the twenty-first century.

This chapter has the following difficulties to overcome: (1) to persuade readers that there is a continuing military need for nuclear strategy; (2) to suggest persuasively that politically the United States will find a policy demand for nuclear support; and (3) to argue that wonderful though it is, and more wonderful though it will become, U.S. prowess in I-led warfare, or in I-(cyber)war itself, cannot meet all strategic demands. If an I-led RMA is the future for strategy, what need can there be for discussion of nuclear (or BC) weapons beyond the pressing merit alleged by some in their abolition?

AN ASIDE ON ARMS CONTROL

Force planning today for nuclear arms is challenged fundamentally by the unfamiliarity (to the United States in this century) of the condition of absence of an "organizing threat."[8] START constraints—actual, pending, and possible—raise the kind of astrategic, even antistrategic, problems that arms control regimes are wont to raise. The arms control literature on strategic offensive weapons remains wedded to the foolish, or strategically irrelevant, pursuit of a "technological peace."[9] The numbers negotiated in START I and START II, and subsequently bandied about for a START III, have no strategically accessible meaning. This is not the occasion on which I should express my strategic disdain for arms control processes yet again.[10] The whole of this book really is about the control of arms, and particularly of arms commonly termed WMD. Beyond the control of arms, the subject reduces to the policy challenge to prevent war—especially wars wherein WMD figure catastrophically—on terms tolerable for prudent definition of security.

My views on the START process in particular, and indeed on negotiated arms control in general, are without significance for the argument here. The nuclear force levels licensed by START I, and even by START II, present no obviously severe difficulties for U.S. nuclear strategy.[11] If the START process is not likely to give birth to a treaty regime that would require the United States to reduce its inventory of strategic nuclear weapons to the low hundreds, then one can be relaxed about the matter. Since focus should be upon the prevention of war on terms consistent with security, and upon the control of WMD (inter alia) to that end, it would be a mistake to key discussion of future U.S. nuclear strategy to negotiated arms limitation.

To readers who may be wondering why a chapter on nuclear strategy is indulging in an aside on arms control, the reasons are that some people see START as a threat to an intelligent nuclear strategy (if that is not an oxymoron), and others see strategy as a threat to START; both views are wrong. The START process is not very interesting for international security today and tomorrow. As a minor though practical support for the formal commitment to disarmament of the nuclear weapons states under the terms of the NPT, START has some merit. As an organizing framework for the nuclear disarmament of the non–Russian Federation nuclear-armed legatees of the USSR, again START has merit—though the merit is strategically more contestable, in this case because of the needs of balance-of-power politics. The problem with the START process fundamentally is political. The United States and Russia are neither allies nor friends, but assuredly they are not enemies. If the exploration of the political context provided in Chapter 2 carries conviction, then bilateral Russian-U.S. arms limitation agreements are likely to be regarded by the strategic historians of the twenty-first century much as today we regard the earnest endeavors of Britain and the United States to curtail each other's naval power in the 1920s and early 1930s.[12] Looking to the future, Russia and the United States are more likely to be allies than foes. Although Russia has an irredentist agenda vis-à-vis the "near abroad" in Europe and central Asia, it can anticipate none too fancifully the medium-term emergence of genuine menace from a China already rising in Asia. Hostility toward the United States should be an unaffordable luxury for a Russia insecure in central Asia, Siberia, and the Far East.

Arms control processes often address yesterday's strategic problems and address them poorly at that; START is but one example of this repeated phenomenon.

STRATEGIC MISSIONS FOR U.S. NUCLEAR FORCES _____

Strategically, what does the United States require of its nuclear-armed forces? In contrast to the answers provided in the 1980s,[13] I cannot assume that anything is understood beyond need for explanation and justification. When the United States appears so potent a conventionally armed power and when there is no single dominant threat, what can be the roles for U.S. nuclear forces? I suggest five strategic missions.

1. Represent, on an appropriately superior scale, the extraordinary standing of *the* global superpower or hegemon.
2. Provide insurance against the capabilities/threat that may be posed by the rise of a peer competitor.
3. Extend deterrence to protect distant friends and allies (i) from NBC threats; (ii) from overwhelming conventional threats; (iii) who might themselves move to acquire WMD (were it not for U.S. nuclear protection).
4. Provide "niche" war-fighting denial options against very hard, elusive, or dispersed targets.
5. Hedge against the degradation or failure of U.S. conventional (I-led) forces.

Everyone is to a degree a prisoner of his or her own expertise. Whereas many analysts and other commentators see nuclear weapons preponderantly as a threat to public safety, certainly to public health, I confess to regarding these weapons predominantly as a threat to the strategical faculties. To my mind, at least, the potential awfulness of nuclear weapons is a given, but so also is the literal impossibility of revoking the nuclear discovery. Since that discovery is irrevocable, the only issue is how best to cope with nuclear facts. We are morally obliged to think strategically about nuclear arms.[14]

None of the five missions for U.S. nuclear forces identified and discussed here are particularly novel or really even controversial.

The reason this presentation may seem unusual is that the rationale for U.S. nuclear armament typically is not presented as holistically or directly as this. There are elements in this explanation of U.S. nuclear strategy that the U.S. government cannot comfortably make explicit.

The Nuclear Arsenal of a Superpower

The United States requires a scale and quality of nuclear armament appropriate to its standing as the global superpower. As potentially the last, and sometimes even the first, line of deterrence and defense for regional security around the world, the United States dare not appear less capable than any possible foe in the category at least of nuclear WMD. The general idea behind this first mission is as clear as its force-planning referents are opaque. The gold standard for adequate performance has to be the requirement for U.S. nuclear forces to be, and appear to be, "second to none" by any plausible test. This is not, at least not quite, a requirement for U.S. nuclear forces to be able to win wars militarily; such a task may be beyond their ability, even when the nuclear forces of a regional power are small in number and light in technical sophistication. Nonetheless, given the decreasing reliability of deterrence mechanisms, it would be exceedingly desirable were the global ordering polity, the currently hegemonic United States, able to impose military defeat on disturbers of regional peace at tolerable cost to itself, its forward-deployed forces, and its friends and allies.

The policy logic behind this mission essentially is the logic of Patrick Morgan's "general deterrence;"[15] it is also the policy logic described by Thucydides as motivating Athens to maintain a very large fleet. Edward N. Luttwak's interpretation of Thucydides is worth quoting at some length.

> The Athenians have in particular left us a detailed record of their imaginative exercise of naval suasion. The trireme fleet was kept in service in "peacetime" from the time of Themistocles to the beginning of the Peloponnesian War; its commanders were political appointees rather than specialists; and the political dimension of naval power was well understood. In particular, it was realized that the size of the fleet (200 boats) reflected the level of Alliance resources and the scope of Athenian ambitions, rather than a response to the scale of perceived enemy threats. Athenians would not have thought it wise to reduce the size of their fleet merely because the Persian/Phoenician or Corinthian

threat waned. Their deployment strategy was not responsive, but rather intended to provide the means needed for a positive affirmation of Athenian political goals. When war came, however, this "political" fleet fought, and by all accounts, it fought well.[16]

At present, U.S. nuclear forces are sized—in the process of being downsized, that is—to meet START (I and eventually perhaps II) criteria that were negotiated to effect some essential equivalence with the long-range nuclear forces of Russia, yesterday's foe. This is not a particularly intelligent way in which to approach the problem of nuclear force planning, but probably it is good enough. Some 3,000–6,000 strategic nuclear weapons, the active inventory zone of the START I to START II regimes (should START II ever be ratified and implemented by Russia) are quantitatively more than adequate, pro tem at least, to meet plausible U.S. strategic requirements. What matters is not that the United States' nuclear forces should settle for no less than some mindless mathematical parity for its nuclear forces with those of Russia, but only that the world at large—given the theme of general deterrence—should not judge or even wonder whether Russian nuclear forces enjoyed a politically exploitable superiority. One should recall the wise words of Robert Jervis, a scholar not overinclined to theorize enthusiastically in praise of nuclear arms, when he wrote at the tail end of the Cold War that "although *military* victory is impossible, victory is not: nuclear weapons can help reach many political goals."[17] Nuclear weapons may or may not be military weapons— we would be well advised to retain open minds on that—but assuredly they are political weapons. Not only are they political weapons, they are political weapons that can trump other weapons, including effectively upsetting the game table of strategy and statecraft as previously arranged.

Many people would like to believe that prestige today attaches primarily to demonstrated prowess with precisely usable conventional forces, not to WMD. One can argue readily that poison gas and viruses lack a heroic timbre, and indeed that they have a most odious reputation because of both their inherent character and their historical association. Even nuclear WMD may have lost some of their political magic, but one should not not rush to negative judgment on their prospective political utility. One should beware of being too quick on the draw in developing strategic arguments out of the widespread disgust—expressed, for example, in "taboos"—at the options for BC warfare. Prestige can rest upon fear, notoriety, and a respect for ruthlessly amoral ambition and behavior. This is not the prestige the United States craves or needs, but for some regional polities it may be the only prestige available. Perhaps political and strategic necessity knows no taboos.

The United States needs to conduct its global ordering duties with eminently usable, precise conventional arms under the top cover provided by the general, and occasionally the immediate, deterrent effect yielded by nuclear armament. As a general deterrent, U.S. nuclear arms are not threats with addressee labels; rather they are a general menace "to whom it may concern."[18] For all the understandable excitement of the 1980s and 1990s about the emerging high potency of information-led conventional arms, it would be a grave mistake to undervalue nuclear arms. Nuclear weapons are WMD in ways that many people, including some defense professionals, may be in peril of forgetting.[19] As suggested in Chapter 4, the wake-up call of a small nuclear war in some troubled region of Eurasia would remind U.S. defense experts belatedly that their (conventional) weapons of choice were not the weapons of choice for all of the world's belligerents.[20] A U.S. society that, though domestically violent, today recoils in horror from the prospect of suffering *or inflicting* almost any casualties in war will find itself politically, emotionally, and morally ill prepared to respond rationally to the body count from a real nuclear conflict.

Discourage, or Offset, the Nuclear Armament of an Emerging Peer Competitor

It is unlikely that the United States will face a reinvigorated Russian superpower in the twenty-first century. However, in some ways the current Russian reluctance to move expeditiously down the START II and III road toward a low scale in nuclear arsenals inadvertently serves well the interest of international security. Given that the nuclear era is here to stay, that there is no strong strategic (or other) virtue in very low levels of nuclear armament, and that Russia is not the prime candidate for "foe of the early century" after 2000, making haste only slowly in START has obvious attractions.

In the calculations and emotions of any regional power, the United States will probably long remain *the* security problem. Any country virtually anywhere in the world that seeks to become regional hegemon has to anticipate that the key opponent of that ambition will be the United States. Regional foes might just elect to try to balance the most rapidly rising polity of their own region, but they will be more likely to look extraregionally for help from the only operationally plausible source of such help, the United States.

The details of the U.S. strategic nuclear arsenal will not be of great interest to an emerging regional hegemon with extra-regional interests and ambitions, because it is highly improbable that the precepts of classical strategy would rule. In other words, the regional challenger would not anticipate being able to fight U.S. nuclear forces directly in quest of a favorable military decision.[21] Nonetheless, a regional foe seeking to challenge the United States to gain greater influence will be daunted if the United States has a huge advantage in nuclear weapons.

There are several reasons the United States is going to continue to have difficulty achieving adequate levels of deterrent effect in regional crises; the problem, however, does not stop there. Within several would-be regional hegemons there lurk the possibilities of great powers almost peer-competitive with the United States. Much after the fashion of imperial expansion, one need not postulate exceptionally roguish ambitions in order to identify the growth of supraregional challenges to the U.S.-led international order. As an empire acquires additional holdings, or options on holdings to secure what it has already, so a rising hegemon could hardly be secure in its recently achieved regional prominence if it did not seek security through an extraregional balance-of-power policy designed to offset the influence of the United States.

There is not much that the United States can do effectively to dampen the ambition, especially the prudentially rational ambition, of would-be regional hegemons to ascend the slope from great power to superpower. But what can be done should be done, and that category of intended countervailing behavior includes U.S. retention of a nuclear arsenal incomparably greater than any that a still regional hegemon could acquire for many years. Beyond this logic, however, resides the need to recognize the strong probability that one day the United States will indeed be confronted by what amounts to a genuinely peer competitor. One must say "what amounts to," because it is important to discourage an inclination to assume that the return in a third nuclear age to a dominant international axis of hostility would be a close replay of the great Soviet-U.S. contest of the Cold War. A Chinese peer competitor, for an example selected not entirely at random, would pose geopolitical and geostrategic—and an absence of ideological—challenges radically different from those familiar from the course of strategic history from 1945 to 1989.

Although deterrence always is more or less unreliable, the emergence of a superpower rival in China or—less likely—the resurgence of a superpower Russia could find the United States rather complacent about the dynamics of nuclear deterrence and strategy. Much as the U.S. defense community has had no little difficulty adjusting to a second nuclear age bereft of a dominant threat, so that community is in danger of allowing itself to be trained by and for this second age in accordance with terms and conditions that will be only transitory. Historians have noticed, for example, that England no sooner had learned which grand strategy to apply in order to beat the Dutch in the seventeenth century than the enemy changed—to France—and yesterday's strategic assumptions no longer worked.[22] This familiar problem of the need to adapt to a changing strategic context is compounded when previous conflicts were concluded successfully. It can be hard to innovate both in a void of current threat and against the backdrop of recent victory.[23]

When the United States approaches the task of planning for regional conflicts, even major theater wars, there ought to be several healthily redundant paths to success. For example, in 1991 Iraq could have been defeated more exclusively by Coalition airpower, much more exclusively by Coalition landpower and amphibious power, or even—politically improbably—by selective nuclear strikes. Major theater wars will not always play out as relatively cheap and easy military enterprises for the United States, but an expectation that several paths to victory will be available can become a near habitual expectation for a superpower. The United States is in peril of mistraining itself strategically against a second-rate or lower class of opponent. The British army looked invincible in December 1940 when it routed the Italians in Libya; it appeared much less invincible in March–April 1941 when it unexpectedly ran into Erwin Rommel and the Afrika Corps.

It is something of a paradox that relatively easy though it should be for the United States to defeat a regional power in war—though an NBC-equipped regional power could be a different matter (see below)—experience and logic advise us that deterrence is exceptionally unreliable in the asymmetrical strategic relations between a superpower and a regional power. The good news is that the United States ought to be able to win virtually any conflict against a regional power. The bad news is that the United States is quite likely to actually have to win such military conflicts because deterrence will fail. The huge disparity in physical strength between the United States and an Iraq, Iran, or North

Korea is all but beside the point when there is perceived to be a no less huge disparity (to the disfavor of the United States) in intensity of national interest at stake. Moreover, the hegemonic qualities of the contemporary United States, married to popular classification of that country as the exemplar of Western civilization, themselves offer hope for diplomatic leverage, jiujitsu fashion, by ambitious regional powers. In 1990–1991, Iraq could not use international resentment of U.S. hegemony to sufficient diplomatic effect; other regional polities may well perform strategically better in that regard in the future.

A peer, at least more than strictly regional, rival to the United States could decide that nuclear capability is the path to fame and global fortune. Even a long U.S. lead in strategic nuclear arms— hovering, say, in the START II completion zone of 3,000–3,500 weapons—may appear more catchable than will the conventional power of U.S. information-led forces. If current trends continue, START-blessed U.S. strategic nuclear forces are going to be long in the tooth by the second and third decade of the twenty-first century.[24] It is as certain as anything can be in world politics that eventually a rival will arise to challenge the United States. As noted already, at present the leading nominee for the role of emerging peer competitor has to be China,[25] but it is worth recalling that at the beginning of the 1990s Japan was the leading candidate. An emerging (or reemerging) peer, be it China, Russia, "Europe," an Islamic coalition, or other, most likely would have some or all of the following characteristics relevant to this discussion of U.S. nuclear strategy:

1. Strong conventional forces, with particular emphasis upon naval assets in the Chinese or Japanese cases, which could be "nichely" competitive with U.S. conventional forces in geostrategically restricted contexts. (By analogy, on paper Geronimo's handfuls of Chiricahua Apaches were absurdly overmatched by the U.S. Army in the 1880s—but in the Sierra Madre, that overmatching was often nominal and tactically irrelevant.)

2. Strong capabilities to conduct warfare unconventionally, which might enable the peer to evade, offset, or even defeat U.S. high-technology *regular* forces by means of asymmetrical methods of war.[26]

3. Strong, even formidable capability to wage "cyberwar" politically, strategically, operationally, and tactically so as to assault the digitized center of gravity of the U.S. Revolution in Military Affairs (RMA) in suitable "niche" ways.

4. Strong international support, because—by definition—the emerging peer competitor would be building an anti-U.S. team that some polities would be powerfully motivated, opportunistically, to join. The appearance of a superpower-looking China, Russia, Japan, "Islam," or "Europe" would create a transfer market for political support. If the next great power struggle is not colored significantly with the kind of ideological baggage that helped shape the Cold War, then alliance agility could well become fashionable again.

5. Strong nuclear forces, to help negate the U.S. I-led RMA, to epitomize and register newly claimed, or reclaimed, superpower status, and to counter the potential deterrent effect of U.S. nuclear forces.[27]

Deterrent effect is not, of course, a matter reducible simply to the menace in large nuclear forces. If that were the case, then we should have been much more secure than I believe we were in times of crisis during the Cold War, and Saddam Hussein should never have dared invade Kuwait or launch Scud missiles at Israel. Furthermore, suspicion of some future deficit in deterrent effect cannot reliably be answered by the elementary expedient of procuring larger forces. In addition, one cannot just extrapolate merrily from the strategic experience of the Cold War the basic rules for promotion of reliable deterrence and expect as a consequence that peace with security assuredly must ensue.

To know how to deter—if truly one does—is important and should be useful. That knowledge, however, is not synonymous with success in deterrence. As Clausewitz was at pains to explain, the theory of war can educate the commander, but it cannot deliver battlefield success.[28] The reasons that the United States predictably will have difficulty deterring an emerging peer competitor are likely to owe nothing of deep significance to any deficiency in the extant *theory* of deterrence. If the United States fails, the failure will reside in efforts to *practice* deterrence.

The challenge to U.S. nuclear strategy posed by an emerging would-be superstate rival is to be compared only in part with the strategic conditions in the early Cold War years. If, for example, China is the emerging peer rival, consider how different that rivalry must be from the context of the Cold War, in which the United States learned its deterrence lore.

1. The United States understands Chinese political and strategic culture much less confidently than it did the strategic culture of the USSR.

2. The United States understands the political and strategic culture of its allies and friends in Asia much less confidently than it did the culture of its security dependents in Europe.

3. It cannot possibly be clear to either side—established but extra-regional U.S. superpower, or "emerging China"—just where they should agree their spheres of preponderant influence ought to meet. Presumably, "emerging China" will push until it meets firm resistance. The geostrategic fact that Sino-U.S. rivalry is bound to be substantially maritime is cause for both relief and anxiety. It is cause for relief in that the receiving of offense at sea is more easily borne than is the receiving of offense on land, where people live. It is cause for anxiety in that there is a lack of geopolitical definition to the open sea, which fails to yield guidance to prudent behavior.

An emerging peer rival to the United States—probably, but not necessarily, China—would be likely to place severe pressure on the U.S. ability to deter. The United States could not be sure either just what the rival would be seeking to achieve or what the current U.S. "ordered" security structure might concede safely. The most appropriate historical analogy for the rise of a peer competitor to the United States is not really the USSR of Cold War fame, but rather the imperial Germany that sought its place in the sun in the 1890s and 1900s. The inability of the European balance-of-power system to cope adequately with the geostrategic fact of a rising, and then returning rising, Germany is a vital part of the explanation of why the twentieth century witnessed the waging of two world wars. A like inability of the now global political system to cope adequately with the geostrategic fact of a rising China (or Russia, or "Europe," or Japan, or "Islam," and so forth) all too plausibly could shape strategic history toward a notable World War III.

The point is not only that by definition the emergence of a peer competitor to the United States would mean the emergence of a physically very strong power. Scarcely less important is the prediction that that very strong, emergent power genuinely would not know which actions would, and which actions would not, enrage the United States as the superstate hegemon in situ. One does not need to postulate awesomely villainous leaders of unquestionably rogue states in order to set the stage for large-scale conflict.

Extend Deterrence in
Aid of Distant Friends and Allies

If the preceding analysis appeared to be focused unduly upon the strategic problems of tomorrow—those that would attend the emergence of a peer competitor—here one returns foursquare to the challenges extant, or immediately probable, today. U.S. strategic commentators understandably, even commendably, vectored toward damaging the foes of the republic occasionally need to be reminded that the protection of friends is strategically more important than is the punishing of foes—which is not to deny that the two tasks are related intimately.

The protection of friends and allies is a process of deterrence, of defense or denial, and of reassurance. A protecting power such as the United States today seeks influence over both the foes of its friends and its friends themselves. In few realms of statecraft is this latter point more salient than with reference to U.S. nuclear strategy. The analysis that follows considers the missions of U.S. nuclear forces and strategy with respect to three aspects of extended protection: threats to friends and allies from NBC-armed foes; threats to those friends and allies from powerfully conventionally armed foes; and the value of U.S.-provided deterrence and reassurance to help discourage friends and allies from proceeding down the path of self-help toward national nuclear arsenals.

Counter NBC threats to friends and allies. With the rapid contemporary proliferation of ballistic and cruise missiles, the slow but eventually inexorable if modest-scale spread of nuclear weapon capabilities, and the quite expeditious dissemination of the more readily accessible BC assets, NBC menaces to U.S. friends and allies are certain to grow. Although no arms control regime should be assumed to be sacrosanct in time of war, and although international law can be held to allow at least some right of reprisal,[29] it is improbable that the United States and its NATO allies will be interested in acquiring—or reacquiring in some cases—the kind of offensive chemical, let alone biological, weapons that could be dedicated to efforts at symmetrical deterrence of BC threats. For political, strategic, and ethical reasons, the United States will seek to extend deterrence of BC use on behalf of regional order in general and selected valued friends and allies in particular by virtually any means other than a military response-in-kind. Should an Iraq or an Iran use chemical, toxin, or biological weapons against U.S. allies in the Middle East, or against U.S. forces deployed forward into that region, the military answer would take the form of a precisely devastating conventional air (including cruise missile) campaign; or, if the injury suffered were truly chronic, the answer would be distinctly limited nuclear action. Obviously, the United States would be exceedingly reluctant to use nuclear weapons. Not only would a hugely squeamish U.S. society—and U.S. government sensibly fearful of the "CNN effect"—recoil in horror from U.S. employment of WMD, but U.S. policymakers rightly would anticipate that such nuclear employment would inflict massive political damage upon the global nonproliferation regime (an "own goal" or "safety").

Notwithstanding the points just registered, international order, which in this second nuclear age preeminently means U.S. guardianship, requires that the leading ordering power pose at least residual nuclear threats in order to deter, counter, or punish potential rogues who consider the merit in NBC statecraft and strategy. Regional nuclear threats, or use, at least provide an obvious license for the U.S. would-be protecting power to respond in kind; BC threats or use poses a tougher challenge, since, as just noted, they require strategically asymmetrical treatment. However, the challenge to U.S. strategy is less severe in practice than it may appear in principle, rather like NATO's wonderfully opaque doctrine of flexible response during the later decades of the Cold War. To try to deter BC use, the United States would be obliged to have recourse to somewhat veiled nuclear menace, as it (and Israel) did in 1990–1991. In the dire event that BC weaponry actually inflicted heavy losses on U.S. troops, or on the soldiers or civilians of regional allies, then the United States might well elect not to respond with nuclear use, though controlling the nuclear options of a BC-damaged ally—Israel, say—would be quite another matter.

As long as the BC, let alone nuclear, peril remains strictly latent—at least insofar as the United States directly is concerned—one can speculate with some ease about the strong likelihood that veiled U.S. threats of a nuclear response to hostile BC use are one thing and are eminently sensible for their putative deterrent effect; but an actual U.S. nuclear response to BC use would be something else entirely. The United States would be the only power to have used nuclear weapons, *again;* and again those weapons most probably would be used against a non-Western polity and society.

It is important, however, that analysis occasionally should dare transcend the boundary of the politically correct consensus on WMD. The United States hypothesized at this juncture is not the awesomely casualty-averse, NPT regime–oriented United States of today. Instead, one is considering U.S. grand and military strategy following the use of NBC weapons against U.S. citizens and the peoples of U.S. allies. In some respects, commendably, the United States does not want to kill, or even risk killing, innocent Iraqis or Serbs as a consequence of coercive air strikes intended to make a diplomatic point. But, how would the United States feel about its willingness to be responsible for, say, thousands (or more) of "enemy" (guilty and innocent alike) deaths had they just suffered NBC attacks that caused possibly tens of thousands of "friendly" casualties? The contemporary U.S. public mood, which appears to insist upon resort to war and coercion only if it can be effected without pain, would—one can predict—swing massively toward demands for punishment of the perpetrators of NBC horrors.

U.S. policy intended to maximize the prospect for the deterrence of NBC use against friends and allies must cope with harassment from a currently inalienable paradox. In order to extend protection of friends and allies against menace from WMD-armed foes, the United States must emphasize the political, strategic, and even perhaps military merit in its nuclear arsenal. U.S. nuclear deterrence on behalf of distant security dependents thus risks undercutting the global NPT regime. No matter what the United States says in criticism of WMD, U.S. actions in praise of the strategic effect of nuclear weapons for deterrence speak louder than words. This is not a criticism of extended nuclear deterrence; it is simply a reminder that national and international security requirements can pull policy simultaneously in apparently opposite directions.

Counter potentially overwhelming conventional threats to friends and allies. It is in part because of the incredibility of U.S. nuclear use to protect friends and allies against large conventional threats that several of those friends and allies have seen the merit in developing national nuclear arsenals. Although very few U.S. security dependents have proceeded to the actual nuclear threshold (or beyond) preponderantly for this reason—Britain, France, Israel, and Pakistan are more or less cases in point, though Taiwan and South Korea have flirted seriously with the idea—the strategic logic for nuclear acquisition thus motivated is distinctly powerful.

Strictly speaking, there are no "nuclear guarantees" either written into, or glued on, the NATO Treaty.[30] Nonetheless, during the years of the Cold War it was always NATO strategic doctrine, as encapsulated in the evolving strategic concept, that the Alliance would be prepared to have resort to nuclear weapons rather than acquiesce in defeat in a conventional war. The periodically renewed public debate, then and now, about "no first use (NFU)" of nuclear weapons, though foolish because no NFU declaration possibly could be worth the paper it was written on, nonetheless did refer to a topic that had symbolic political meaning.[31] Whatever the probable reality of military behavior under the pressure of a hot war, interest in NFU on the part of the United States was always likely to be interpreted by ever nervous and insecure allies as U.S. willingness to tolerate the conventional conquest of an ally or two rather than have resort to any level of nuclear employment. No first use may or may not have been the political reality of U.S. policy in some years of the Cold War; we can never know for certain.

So confident is the United States today in its information-led conventional military prowess that even the idea of nuclear deterrence of, let alone nuclear response to, regional conventional menace seems as inappropriate as it is contrary to the (American) spirit of the age. In contemporary U.S. debate about the extended deterrence mission, even the notion of U.S. nuclear use initiatives is deemed all but obscene. It should be self-evident to all right-thinking folk, not to mention military experts now well schooled in the ways in which the "U.S. RMA" must yield strategic advantage through "dominant battlespace knowledge,"[32] that the only strategically necessary and politically legitimate role of U.S. nuclear weapons is to act as a counterdeterrent or response to the WMD of regional rogues. As a strategic result of nuclear counterdeterrence, the regional ring can be kept square for decisive U.S. exercise of its precisely navigated conventional muscle. This is an attractive strategic vision. Moreover, it is an attractive strategic vision that is politically and militarily quite plausible.

On the military side, there should be few regular-style, which is to say tolerably symmetrical, military challenges that the United States could not defeat, or at least thwart, with its information edge enforced by formidable conventional forces. Of course, those U.S. forces might be busy elsewhere, but let us not muddy the waters unduly by raising doubts about the prospective adequacy of the size of the U.S. military establishment.[33] On the political side, surely one is right to be skeptical of the strategic relevance of nuclear options, because it is difficult to imagine the United States choosing to have resort to nuclear arms as a desperation move to alter the course of a regional conflict. The United States of today, notwithstanding the singularity of its superpower standing, does not exactly resemble the kind of country likely to choose nuclear war rather than condone the conventional defeat of a friend or ally. Whether or not that suspicion is well founded, the strategic calculation would differ significantly were large numbers of U.S. soldiers being engulfed in some regional conventional disaster. We shall return to this possibility under a separate heading below. Suffice it to note for now that the future is open-ended, and war, even conventional war in this information age, is a roll of the iron dice.[34] It may not seem likely that the United States would seriously consider employing nuclear weapons in a conventional war, but not all among the enemies of the United States in the future are going to be as militarily inept as was Saddam Hussein in 1991.

Reassure friends and allies, thereby demotivating them from the pursuit of a national nuclear option. Because of the potential liability to the would-be nuclear extended deterrer, nuclear guarantees worthy of the name are more difficult to extract from NPT-licensed nuclear weapons states than is water from desert sands. To be a nuclear protector, in the sense that one extends protection over distant countries against nuclear menaces, is by definition to risk the suffering of nuclear damage on behalf of others. The protection business is very much what being a great power has always been about, but the incurring of risk of damage *by WMD* on behalf of foreigners is something else entirely. As Karl Marx insisted, quantity changes quality. To fight, even to fight bloodily in a protracted conflict for the protection of an ally whose fate is significant for your national security is one matter; knowingly to hazard one's forces and one's country itself with the risk of nuclear catastrophe is a different matter entirely. NATO-Europeans during the Cold War were not as understanding as they should have been of the historically unprecedented character of risk that the United States willingly ran in part on their behalf.[35]

Potential nuclear proliferants long have sought security guarantees as a price for adherence to the formally discriminatory NPT regime. As a general rule, the best promise they could extract took the undersatisfactory form of negative security assurances. Specifically, non-nuclear weapon adherents to the NPT regime are assured that they will not be the victims of nuclear

threats or attacks. This kind of assurance is of a class with promises of NFU and for detargeting by nuclear-armed missiles. The
problem is that the negative security assurance is worthless because it has no operational authority. Unfortunately, the kind of
security assurance, or reassurance, that potential nuclear proliferants seek is not confined to the thwarting of threats by WMD. The
Pakistani nuclear program, for example, is not driven solely by the
need to provide a counterdeterrent to Indian nuclear weapons; if
that were the case, the subcontinent would be rendered reasonably safe for the conduct of yet another conventional war. Understandably enough, Pakistan has judged that a national nuclear
arsenal must help deter both nuclear intimidation by, and conventional attack from, India.

Forward deployment of U.S. armed forces can create that
credible commitment to a distant friend that the words alone of
foreign policy are unable to effect. For example, the United States
cannot promise credibly to wage nuclear war on behalf of, say, Taiwan, South Korea, or Japan. But it is all but self-evident that the
United States would employ whatever weapons were necessary to
protect its own forces deployed in defense of those countries. It
would be difficult to exaggerate the strategic significance of the
reassurance that such U.S. support can provide.

Admittedly it is difficult, probably to the point of impossibility,
to distinguish among the United States as the global superpower,
the United States as militarily the most potent power on earth, and
the United States as a nuclear-armed polity. The overwhelming reason the countries of East-Central Europe want to join
NATO is that the Alliance, uniquely, is seen as the security club
whose members are guaranteed in their enjoyment of their most
vital interests by the U.S. superpower. Such would-be NATO members as Romania and Lithuania are not interested in the detail of
their potential security nexus to the United States; what counts,
what really counts, is that the United States is the superpower. U.S.
nuclear armament is but one, albeit one significant and necessary,
element of that currently unique superstate classification. The
point is that the other players in world politics, including potential player-victims, naturally subsume nuclear armaments as a dimension of U.S. power writ large. Most emphatically, this does not
mean that U.S. nuclear armament is a trivial matter in the context
of U.S. strength overall. Information-rich U.S. armed forces, able
to strike precisely and conventionally against located targets—one
day even against located and moving targets in bad weather—

worldwide, could be rendered strategically irrelevant by the "knight's move" of plausible nuclear threats. Counterdeterrence by U.S. nuclear arms might not work in a regional context where there was a huge disparity in intensity of interest between the superpower and its regional foe.

As a general rule, the greater the willingness of the United States to protect potentially embattled friends and allies *à outrance*, the less likely is it that those embattled friends and allies will be moved to proceed decisively toward (or beyond) nuclear-threshold status. There are, alas, two emerging strategic challenges to the practical authority of this political logic. First, in a second nuclear age in which there is no globally dominant hostile relationship, the United States is acutely short of popularly powerful reasons for accepting exceedingly high risks on behalf of others. U.S. vital—let alone survival—interests are not obviously engaged in regional disputes around Eurasia today. Second, just as the intensity of U.S. interest has diminished, so the intensity of risk to U.S. forces, and eventually even to the U.S. homeland, is in the process of increasing exponentially. Americans may well have been willing enough to risk their all on behalf of NATO-Europe and Western Civilization in the great Cold War, but how do they feel about knowingly placing themselves at NBC risk on behalf of only "major"—not vital, and certainly not survival-level—national interests at stake in regional conflicts in this second nuclear age?[36]

It is only responsible to emphasize the perils in extended (nuclear) deterrence. Those perils can be reduced, though one should hesitate to add controlled, both by military defensive and offensive preparation and by considerable care in policy. All of that properly granted, still it is an important mission for the U.S. nuclear arsenal to stand between potentially menaced regional friends and allies and their foes. Regional friends and allies who feel confident enough in the dissuasive authority of U.S. nuclear-backed diplomatic support are friends and allies who should have the political and military arguments necessary to defeat domestic pressures for nuclear acquisition.

Provide war-fighting options against high-priority very hard or elusive targets. It is a commonplace belief today that the military effects of nuclear weapons can be achieved by precisely targeted conventional weaponry. Commonplace or not, this belief is unfounded. It is true that accuracy in targeting is more important than energy yield in consequence for lethal effect, but that mathematical physical relationship does not mean that circular error probable (CEP) is everything.[37] Although nuclear weapons by their energy yield can offset some intelligence uncertainties about target coordinates, those weapons also can apply unmatchable destructive effect against targets that are superhardened or otherwise elusive or difficult to destroy with conclusive assurance. For example, and notwithstanding what cinema audiences were told in the movie *The Rock,* VX nerve gas and many other chemical, toxin, and even biological agents (which, of course, tend to be fragile as living organisms) are extremely difficult to destroy definitively, as opposed merely to disperse, except by means of the extraordinary heat generated by nuclear explosives. This is not to claim that counterforce action against BC weapons has to take a nuclear form to be effective. But the reliable forcible elimination of BC weapons and stockpiled agents is a military niche of growing strategic importance for which mission nuclear arms are uniquely well suited.[38]

As this second nuclear age settles somewhat uncomfortably into an inter-war zone between post–Cold War and pre–next great contest,[39] it is all too easy to assume that the unique military virtues of nuclear weapons have no place in satisfaction of future security needs. Preeminently, it has become commonplace to acknowledge no role for nuclear weapons beyond that of deterrence of threat or use of WMD by rogue polities.[40] But what if an enemy has military forces or military production facilities—for example, a chemical weapons factory (more likely a chemical weapons factory masquerading as an insecticide plant[41])—of cardinal strategic significance that cannot be targeted for thoroughly reliable total destruction either by U.S. special operations forces or by information-led conventional weapons (even with warheads designed for deep penetration)? Truly superhard underground targets generally can be destroyed or reliably sealed off only by nuclear weapons. This is not strategically fanciful. Deep underground basing of key military assets was practiced by Germany and Britain in World War II, was a feature of Soviet and Chinese military construction during the Cold War, is a feature of the Libyan and North Korean WMD factory complexes today, and—frankly—is military common sense. Moreover, as stated above, the problem with the targeting of BC weapons is not confined strictly to penetration of their physical defensive barriers of rock and concrete, but also pertains to reliable elimination of agents that can be lethal even in very small doses.

A similar military logic applies to mobile, and some other forms of elusive military, deployment of unusually important assets. Superhardening and mobility are both atypical and unwelcome because they are extraordinarily expensive to organize, build, and operate. The point is not that some U.S. nuclear weapons should be custom designed to menace superhard and mobile targets just because those targets may exist. In a context wherein several regional powers are likely to seek to protect their strategic and political "crown jewels" (WMD, delivery vehicles, political leaders, and key staff) by means of physical barriers or positional uncertainty, U.S. policy should recognize that its nuclear arsenal might well be uniquely capable of offsetting such efforts for survivability. Given that the stakes at issue could be the vulnerability of U.S. and allied forces, and homelands, to assault by NBC weapons, one should not be too hasty in recoiling in politically correct horror from the possibility of U.S. first use of nuclear weapons for "niche" war-fighting purposes.

Hedge against the large-scale degradation or outright failure of conventional fighting power. At this point some readers, because they are not professional strategic theorists and commentators, will complain that I am worried about something very implausible: a conventional-level U.S. military defeat.

Several answers to such a complaint beg for attention. First, the professional strategic commentator who has read Clausewitz and studied military history knows that friction rules; things go wrong "on the night." Second, the professional strategic commentator has read Luttwak on the paradoxical logic of conflict[42] and is likely to assume an intelligent enemy. In practice, future strategic foes of the United States may prove to be ineducably strategically stupid, or wise in understanding and decision but hopelessly inept in strategic behavior. All things are possible, but as hypothetical defense planners, how should we bet? Can we safely assume that U.S. foes will stand up conveniently in open terrain to be "Desert Stormed"? For example, what if a rising regional polity, whose collective strategy IQ-equivalent reaches triple digits, should notice U.S. dependence upon space systems for military effectiveness? More to the point, what if such a perceptive polity were able to contest, not necessarily win, space control?[43] U.S. information-led military power might find itself at least temporarily deprived of much of the information that derives from space systems upon which its combat lethality depends. A United States deeply wedded to the conduct of network-centric warfare would be profoundly embarrassed militarily if its network "went down" ungracefully.

Having failed to deter war, U.S. conventional forces also could fail to deliver the necessary strategic effectiveness in war. Should that occur, a United States sensibly, as well as legally, bereft of offensive BC options would face a straight choice between accepting military defeat in conventional war or using nuclear weapons. One cannot predict how a U.S. president would choose, especially since no particular scenario dominates this strategic logic—unlike the former Cold War context with its leading edge comprising NATO's Central Front along the border of the then West German Federal Republic. Nonetheless, one can predict that there could be cases wherein a president would prefer nuclear first use to nonnuclear defeat. That general prediction gains authority if one postulates large-scale loss of U.S. life in the unsuccessful conduct of a regional war.

The strategic logic that argues the salience of this mission for nuclear forces—to serve as a hedge against the failure of conventional forces—works both ways. Actual or persuasively imminent U.S. defeat in regional conventional combat must licence U.S. policymakers to conduct urgent examination of nuclear options. But the alternative generic scenario of great U.S. conventional success in a regional conflict also raises the nuclear specter, though this time initially in the form of desperation options for the regional power that is facing non-nuclear defeat. In this second case, the mission for U.S. nuclear strategy, though probably not the burden on U.S. decisionmakers, is likely to be almost as heroically difficult to perform successfully as was true for the first case. To recap, in a regional conflict that has the United States pitted against a rising regional power, conventional defeat *for either side* could, indeed must, fuel policy interest in the prompt use of nuclear (and BC, though particularly chemical and toxin weapons on the regional power's side) weapons to offset conventional failure. Underpinning this argument is the fairly plausible assumption that in the future one must presume that any power able to be militarily at least somewhat competitive with the United States in a regional conventional conflict also would have the resources, and certainly the motivation, to acquire real NBC options. It is true that biological weapons must lack the promptness in effect that renders chemical, toxin, and nuclear arms so militarily attractive, but the military deficiencies of BW may well find ample compensation in the terror that their menace would engender.

I am not predicting that U.S. conventional forces will be defeated by some rising regional power, and neither am I asserting that either the United States or a regional foe assuredly would prefer to escalate the military character of a war into the nuclear zone rather than acquiesce in defeat. U.S. conventional military prowess is today, and will be tomorrow, incontestably impressive. There are some caveats, however, that a professional strategic commentator is obliged to note.

* * *

The understandable warm glow of self-satisfaction with which one regards Western triumphs in the Cold War and the Gulf War should not induce blindness toward less happy episodes in U.S. strategic history. The fact that these famous victories are recent is a source of concern at least as much as a source of confidence. The U.S. armed forces able to see off the late and unlamented USSR and dance operational arabesques around the static, unimaginatively commanded, and then literally paralyzed forces of Saddam Hussein plainly had military virtues that, though possibly a wasting asset, nonetheless should retain a notable half-life. But history teaches us that victory in war is far inferior an educator than is failure. German armies in 1940–1941, and Japanese in 1941–1942, both suffered ultimately fatally from "victory disease." Rephrased, one begins to believe in one's own invincibility—a malady with symptoms that include a pathological inability to assess risks prudently. Polities that "win big"—as, for instance, the United States in the Cold War and the Gulf—are prone to believe that the normal lore of statecraft and strategy does not apply to them because they are blessed, sanctioned, and enabled by some variant upon History's Purpose or Divine Will. By analogy, a gambler on a winning streak comes to believe that Luck, not a truly randomly working chance, is with him or her. The possibility of catastrophic failure fades from the consciousness. How many Germans could conceive, let alone tentatively predict, in midsummer 1940 that their Third Reich would overreach itself fatally within only two years and suffer one of history's more complete defeats within only five?

It is hard to imagine defeat when every strategic project appears to prosper. The United States should recall, however, that its strategic history shows a pattern of defeat early in war, because that peace-loving democracy is systemically inclined to respond late to security challenge.[44] The United States eventually may well win every armed conflict in which it engages for the next half century. But as a general rule, which is to say unlike the Gulf War of 1991, the U.S. armed forces will not be donated the strategic and operational initiative. An intelligent foe, able over a number of years to study and plan against particular U.S. military capabilities and able to select the time and place for initial hostilities, could inflict substantial damage on U.S. forces. Moreover, that damage need not necessarily be imposed by NBC weaponry. Any regional power that plans and is able to impose a large scale of loss, up to and including a level that translates as outright defeat, upon the U.S. armed forces is very likely to have bought itself NBC counterdeterrent "cover" to dissuade the United States from nuclear escalation.

This speculative commentary and theory appears less fanciful when one makes the effort to frame the immediate strategic historical context with a wide-angle lens. All but inconceivable though it may be to people whose strategic memories are challenged by reference to events prior to 1989 and the fall of the Berlin Wall, it is not long ago that the U.S. armed forces quite widely were regarded as "the gang that could not shoot straight." Remember Vietnam? Remember Desert One (the abortive Iranian hostage rescue mission of 1980)? Remember Beirut and the Marine Corps barracks in 1983? Remember Grenada in 1983? Somewhat more controversially, even Panama 1989 and Somalia 1993–1994 were less than exemplars of immaculate military performance. This short history should remind any readers in need of reminding that friction rules in war and U.S. soldiers, just causes or not, are not guaranteed by History to perform immaculately. The rapid demise of the Soviet empire, closely succeeded by a kind of victory in the Gulf, appears to yield evidence of one's strategic— not to say political and ethical—superiority of a kind and on a scale that discourages a strategically healthy self-doubt. I am inclined to predict that the mixture of (1) success in the Cold War, (2) campaign victory over Iraq in 1991, and (3) confidence in U.S. exploitation of information technologies will combine to produce a United States perilously vulnerable to intelligently planned military initiatives by a nuclear (and BC)-armed (for counterdeterrence) regional foe who is a niche peer competitor even in conventional ways of war.

* * *

The potential value for public policy in this analysis of the strategic missions for U.S. nuclear forces depends almost entirely upon the spirit in which the analysis is approached. The purpose here is that of the policy scientist, meaning the person who explains the structure of the relevant problem area. This chapter presents a full-frontal array of arguments that should guide the future development of U.S. nuclear strategy. The missions identified and analyzed are not popular, they are not self-evidently necessary of performance today, and they cannot reliably be projected as dominant concerns tomorrow; they are, nonetheless, the ones the United States will need performed. Recall the problem of defense comprehension in a democracy: the more successfully U.S. nuclear forces perform deterrent missions, the more difficult is it to demonstrate the need for performance of those missions. The fourth and fifth missions, to provide war-fighting options against high-priority superhard and other elusive targets and to serve as a military "hedge" against conventional defeat, are, of course, missions whose successful performance could be assessed readily.

U.S. NUCLEAR FORCES FOR THE SECOND NUCLEAR AGE AND BEYOND: PRINCIPLES FOR GUIDANCE

I must confess to a prejudice of a methodological kind that may be less-than-universally shared. I am inclined to believe that once one has explained the structure of an issue area—in this case the strategic missions for U.S. nuclear forces—the details follow naturally and logically. It seems to me that the nuclear strategy and forces required by the United States follow from the analysis in the previous section without much scope for contentious argument. Furthermore, different though the second nuclear age certainly is from the first, the relevant lore for the guidance of nuclear force planning appears none too distinctive from that familiar from the late 1940s to 1989.[45]

It is important to pay genuine homage to the question of the continuing working validity of the leading principles and assumptions that came, by the mid-1960s at the latest, to govern planning for and understanding of the structure and scale of U.S. nuclear forces. In the early 1990s, it was prudent and at least casually plausible to assume that the nuclear lore of the Cold War might no longer be valid. Just how valid U.S. nuclear lore of Cold War vintage actually had been, even for peace with security in the Cold War, is, of course, an unfinished story.

Scholars, and even a few among the more cerebral of policymakers, have speculated that our "knowledge" of nuclear strategy has been consigned to the garbage pail of history by the abrupt demise of the USSR.[46] As the United States switched grand strategic focus from global Cold War to regional conflicts, and as U.S. conventional military prowess—especially as packaged intellectually as an RMA—waxed and dominated, so nuclear strategy looked more and more like yesterday's solution to yesterday's problem. All that appeared to remain valid from yesterday's estimate of the strategic merit in nuclear-armed forces was the prudential thought that our nuclear capability would offset, by a reliable deterrence, the putative strategic effect of the nuclear (and possibly the biological and chemical) capabilities of others. This is one of those cases wherein everyone is right, up to a point.

1. The second nuclear age is radically different in political and strategic structure from the first nuclear age; this fact has important military operational and tactical implications.
2. But the quantity and quality of nuclear-armed forces required for the United States in a second nuclear age are not difficult to derive from long-standing analyses of nuclear-relevant strategic scenarios.
3. Much of the strategic enlightenment generated by modern strategic studies to guide nuclear force development in the Cold War remains sensible for the different context of this second nuclear age.

The largest problem for the U.S. nuclear force posture, excluding hypothetical and heroically challenging further START regimes, is the need to accommodate genuinely *strategic* rationales. When one considers nuclear-armed forces strategically, one discovers that the roles and missions for those forces today and for tomorrow look distinctly familiar. It should be recalled that U.S. nuclear-armed forces today need to be able to perform five strategic missions: (1) represent the nuclear force posture perceived as appropriate for a (or *the*) superpower, for general deterrent effect; (2) discourage or offset the nuclear arms of a would-be "peer" competitor; (3) extend nuclear deterrence to protect friends and allies; (4) provide specialized, "niche," war-fighting capabilities against high-priority superhard or otherwise elusive targets; and (5) serve as a hedge, or insurance, against the military failure of U.S., or U.S.-allied, conventional forces. Notwithstanding the radical restructuring of the distribution of power in world politics effected by the demise of the USSR, those five strategic missions for U.S. nuclear forces look familiar.

During the Cold War, the United States had to procure and maintain nuclear-armed forces that not only were at or beyond parity with their Soviet counterparts but also looked as if they were such. In addition to appearing in general ways appropriate for the support of U.S. policy globally, nuclear forces in the Cold War were sized and shaped to deter, and if need be to fight, a USSR that after the early 1960s was believed to be very much a worthy peer competitor. The need to extend nuclear deterrence to protect far-flung friends and allies perennially was the major driving force behind the evolution of U.S. nuclear doctrine and nuclear force planning. In the Cold War, as today and tomorrow, U.S. friends and allies could be menaced by NBC perils, certainly were threatened by overwhelming conventional power, and generally could be discouraged from pursuing national solutions to problems of security by U.S. policy for extended nuclear deterrence. The United States developed a cumulatively large target list that included many hard, superhard, or otherwise elusive (or dispersed) Soviet targets that could be effectively threatened or struck plausibly only by nuclear weapons.[47] Finally, the failure of U.S. and U.S.-allied conventional forces in the defense of NATO-Europe was not only possible but expected and, to some degree, even preprogrammed and welcomed as necessarily raising in Soviet minds the credibility of nuclear escalation under what became after 1967 NATO's doctrine of flexible response.[48]

None of the points just registered undermines the broad pattern of argument of this book about the emergence of a second nuclear age noticeably different from the first nuclear age of Cold War. The issue at this juncture, however, is not whether the strategic context for U.S. nuclear forces has altered massively over the past decade; such a question does not merit even an article-length reply. Rather the question is whether the principles that guided U.S. nuclear forces and doctrine in the latter years of the Cold War retain strategic vitality for the different conditions that now obtain. Given the emphasis on continuity rather than discontinuity in the preceding paragraphs, it is important to record those leading differences between the first and second nuclear ages that might have implications for the U.S. nuclear force posture and the implications of those differences.

1. Deterrence is less reliable than it was during the Cold War. Regional foes are apt to be more highly motivated to take risks for possible gain or to avert otherwise anticipated losses than typically was the case for the USSR. The United States thus must operate as the leading protecting power for a context wherein some foes are less risk-averse than the United States is used to and wherein the credibility of U.S. extended deterrence commitments generally is not intrinsically high. In contrast with the Cold War context, therefore, today the risks of deterrence failure have increased, the regional consequences have become more dire with growing NBC and missile dissemination, and the security benefits to the United States of regional risk-running are less easy to specify than used to be the case when most conflicts had some bearing on the course of the central East-West struggle.

Implications: Deterrence will fail, or fail to apply, more often in the second, than it did in the first, nuclear age.

2. *There is at present no "peer" nuclear threat to the United States.* Notwithstanding the alarming analyses of some expert commentators on the perils of continuing high alert rates by U.S. and Russian nuclear forces,[49] effectively enough there is an all but (admittedly not) zero possibility of a nuclear World War III occurring today or in the near future. There is, of course, residual momentum in the watchfulness of Russian and U.S. strategic nuclear forces toward each other, but truly there is no strategic relationship, persuasively even of latent threat, in Russian-U.S. relations. Needless to add, perhaps, this benign political condition could change; and the aging of Russian equipment for command and control, in the context of an eminently contestable political succession, provides grounds for concern. It is, however, less in anticipation of a return to political relevance of the Russian-U.S. strategic balance than in expectation of the burgeoning of Chinese strategic forces that I include the discouragement or thwarting of a rising peer competitor among the strategic missions for U.S. nuclear forces.

Implications: The excellent news that the United States faces no plausible near-term prospect of a gallop to nuclear Armageddon is offset somewhat by two political facts. First, extended deterrence becomes more problematic in the absence of a central architecture of threat in world politics. Second, this condition of absent menace of World War III will not endure. Because major weapon systems can require fifteen or more years to proceed from the status of idea to that of operational equipment, the United States should be thinking hard today about the nuclear (and other) force posture they may need—START permitting—for the second and third decades of the twenty-first century.

3. *The United States has acquired the most potent conventional forces in the world.* To people—like myself—reared on the military and

strategic logic that derived from the putative conventional mismatch between NATO and the Warsaw Pact in Central Europe, it is still a little startling to recognize just how radically the terms and conditions of the U.S. strategic context have changed since the mid-1980s. Unfortunately, U.S. conventional military excellence, real enough though it is, does not quite translate into the usable power that could be so beneficial for extended deterrence, or defense, on behalf of world and regional order. Non-nuclear excellence motivates foes to try to find effective asymmetric forms of war (e.g., political, NBC, irregular). Furthermore, genuinely "magic swords" are in short supply, even if the United States enjoys the military benefits of some approximation to dominant battle-space knowledge.[50] Above all else, even an awesomely competent, conventionally armed U.S. military machine can only be as strategically effective as the American people and their commander-in-chief allow.

Implications: The still-rising net military effectiveness of U.S. conventional forces should yield to U.S. high policy an all but surgical, historically unprecedented ability to apply force for worthy ends at extremely low human cost to friend *and even foe* alike. In practice, though, the implications of "America's Information Edge" are likely to prove less traumatic for the foes of "order" than one might think.[51] NBC and/or irregular—including plainly terroristic—warfare, married to an only modest level of intensity of U.S. political interest in many cases, renders the awesome conventionally armed forces of the United States rather less awesome than prediction of probable tactical performance alone can indicate.

4. The feasibility of counterforce. After the early 1960s there was no realistic possibility—though, in practice, who knows?—of either Cold War superpower being able forcibly to disarm the other comprehensively of its nuclear arsenal. That persisting condition of secure second-strike capabilities, of mutual invulnerability in weaponry was, however, not a product of the laws of physics, let alone of strategic history. Both superpowers worked hard to ensure the strike-back integrity of their strategic nuclear forces. In this second nuclear age, by way of major contrast, none of the United States' plausibly prospective foes—which probably is to disallow the new Russia—has to be conceded assurance in its ability to strike second, let alone first, with NBC weapons. By a mix of offensive and defensive counterforce (as well as some passive measures—for example, mass inoculation against particular BC agents), embracing non-nuclear as well as possibly nuclear forces, the United States can develop the military ability to defeat the NBC arsenals of regional enemies; in a phrase, the job generally is doable. Small (relative to Cold War superpower nuclear) and probably quite primitive NBC-armed forces should be acutely vulnerable both before and (especially) after launch to a multilayered array of U.S. (and some U.S.-allied) special operations, offensive conventional strikes, air and missile defenses, and electronic warfare. There can never be guarantees in war. As Clausewitz reminds us about war, "No other human activity is so continuously or universally bound up with chance." Even though an Iranian or North Korean nuclear-armed missile force should be vulnerable to forward-deployed U.S. TMD and, one day, to defeat even by a "thin" U.S. NMD deployment, friction still may rule. No bonus points will be awarded to readers who notice that the placing of additional and novel legal restrictions on BMD options could prove exceedingly costly in the coin of strategic risk.

Implications: Because missiles must be the agent of choice for the delivery of NBC weapons (especially cruise missiles for the dispatch of BC agents that must work in aerosol form), because the United States intends to continue with a policy of global engagement in protection of order and other civilized values, and because proliferant polities can acquire arsenals that are only modest in scale and sophistication, counterforce often could be effective to neutralize such menaces. This situation is hugely different from the strategic condition of nuclear standoff in the Cold War that came to be described poignantly as mutual assured destruction (MAD). There is strictly no need for the United States to tolerate a condition of MAD vis-à-vis any regional power in the future. Furthermore, even with respect to a rising peer competitor, a United States that begins the competition notably ahead in relative war-fighting prowess should be a United States well able to remain ahead at bearable cost.[52]

From the analysis in this chapter, it is possible to derive a short list of principles for the guidance of U.S. nuclear forces and doctrines: I suggest eight.

First, U.S. nuclear forces should risk erring on the side of being too large rather than too small. Although there is no need to plan to return from the START I–III zone of numbers to anything remotely resembling the scale of arsenal acquired by the 1970s and early 1980s, still there is everything to be said in favor of an arsenal that is too large to be overwhelmed on short order, perceptually or actually in war-fighting terms, by some rising polity.

Second, the United States should continue to attend carefully to the operational survivability of its nuclear forces. Some Western theorists have persuaded themselves that strategic metastability is the rule in a heavily nuclear-armed era. That belief may or may not be well founded. We have no way of knowing in detail how a would-be aggressor will choose to calculate and compare probable risks and costs with possible gains. By all means, relax from readiness for near-instant action (de-alerting) but not by such means that a putative aggressor discerns the dazzling eponymous prospect of "Pearl Harbor" possibilities. Diversity of nuclear-armed delivery agents—ballistic and cruise missiles, manned aircraft, land and sea basing—may be an expensive luxury for a metastable context, but insurance is prudent for the last line of deterrence and defense.

Third, it is essential that U.S. nuclear forces should enjoy secure connectivity with the National Command Authorities (NCA). Indeed, the machinery for essential strategic command and control needs to be as survivable as the forces that it is supposed to command. Nothing in this second nuclear age suggests any diminution in the significance of security of minimum essential command and control, even though the military threat to that security is in abeyance pending reemergence of a strategic peer, or even just emergence of a regional but potently niche competitor.

Fourth, for the reassurance of U.S. policymakers, as well as possibly (though only possibly) for the optimum deterrence of regional rogues, the United States' contemporary "post-heroic" society requires as much precision in discriminating nuclear strike capabilities as can be devised.[53] The deterrent clout of nuclear arms, such as it may be, really resides in the fact that they are weapons of *mass destruction,* but the U.S. defense community cannot bring itself to think that way today. The United States has no visible notion of "bonus damage" attaching to its nuclear arsenal. Of course, it does not much matter how politically correct the United States strives to be when talking about discrimination and avoidance of unwanted collateral damage with reference to its nuclear arsenal. The potential enemies of the United States know that nuclear weapons, whether or not applied with great care and discrimination, are entirely in a class of their own as reliably predictable prompt WMD.

Fifth, U.S. nuclear-armed forces should be flexible and adaptable to fleeting strategic contexts. If imperial Germany's Schlieffen Plan (1906–1914),[54] or the U.S. SIOP through much of the

1960s and 1970s,[55] was the epitome of preplanned rigidity—tied to an arguably admirable fixity of purpose—then nuclear force planning for the future should be substantially real-time adaptable and flexible. What General Sir Archibald Wavell called "the mechanism of war," and what Clausewitz called war's "grammar,"[56] must work to inhibit adaptability, but nonetheless one can strive for flexibility. Given the modest scale of target list that the United States' regional nuclear- (and BC-)armed foes will present, the case for great flexibility all but makes itself.

Sixth, self-evidently the United States should not operate its nuclear-armed forces in a manner likely to render them prone either to technical accident or to missassessment of political intent by intended deterrees. It should be the case that the most secure nuclear arsenal is the least nuclear arsenal, but in practice so powerful are the reasons for choosing a more than minimal nuclear force posture that arsenal reduction cannot be the highest priority goal for policy.

Seventh, the United States should develop and acquire nuclear forces tailored not to ravage wide areas, but rather to effect the kind of damage to targets that other U.S. forces cannot impose reliably. Enemy military or political assets that are deep underground, whose position, though generally known, is not known precisely, or biological, toxin, and chemical agents that need to be vaporized should be at risk to U.S. nuclear weapons designed to penetrate the ground or to disable equipment over a wide area.

Eighth, and finally, by way of sharp contrast with U.S. policy in the Cold War, notwithstanding the praiseworthy flirtation of the Reagan administration after 1983 with the Strategic Defense Initiative (SDI), the United States requires nuclear-armed forces sustained in tandem with multilayered TMD and NMD (which would include space-based as well as as only space-cued BMD weapons). If regional foes, let alone a rising peer competitor, are not to "deter our [nuclear] deterrent,"[57] and if the United States is to discourage first use of most kinds of NBC weapons, it needs to build active defenses as part of a national military strategy that looks with favor upon denial options.

NOTES

1. START is scarcely less "strategic" than was SALT. See Gray, *House of Cards,* ch. 5.

2. Unanswerably persuasive statement of this central point is provided in Quinlan, *Thinking About Nuclear Weapons*, ch. 1.

3. Mazarr, "Virtual Nuclear Arsenals" and *Nuclear Weapons in a Transformed World.*

4. Baylis and Garnett, *Makers of Nuclear Strategy*, is uniquely useful.

5. Perry, "Defense in an Age of Hope."

6. Jervis, *Meaning of the Nuclear Revolution*, p. 22.

7. Jervis, "Why Nuclear Superiority Doesn't Matter"; Waltz, "Nuclear Myths and Nuclear Realities."

8. Gray, "Defense Planning for the Mystery Tour." Khalilzad and Ochmanek, *Strategic Appraisal 1997*, reviews the whole subject intelligently.

9. An idea that surfaces usefully in Booth, "Teaching Strategy."

10. Gray, *House of Cards.*

11. START I, which entered into force on 4 December 1994, allows each side 6,000 "accountable warheads" on 1,600 strategic offensive delivery vehicles (no more that 4,900 of the "accountable warheads" may be carried by ballistic missiles [ICBMs and SLBMs]). START II, if ratified, would constrain each party to 3,000–3,500 warheads on their strategic offensive forces and would prohibit all ICBMs with multiple independently targetable reentry vehicles (MIRVs).

12. Brodie, *Sea Power in the Machine Age*, p. 336, makes this point sardonically.

13. For my answer, see Gray, *Nuclear Strategy and National Style*, esp. ch. 9.

14. Gray, "On Strategic Performance."

15. Morgan, *Deterrence*, ch. 2.

16. Luttwak, *Political Uses of Sea Power*, pp. 71–72, n. 31.

17. Jervis, *Meaning of the Nuclear Revolution*, p. 22. Emphasis in original.

18. Quinlan, *Thinking About Nuclear Weapons*, p. 28.

19. See Gray, "Nuclear Weapons and the Revolution in Military Affairs."

20. Freedman, *Revolution in Strategic Affairs*, ch. 3, "Asymmetric Wars."

21. "Classical strategy" has become a term of art that refers to the requirement to defeat the military forces of the foe. Nuclear arms have been a challenge to classical strategy because their absolute quality translates strategically as the ability to defeat the enemy without first defeating the enemy's armed forces. The probable fact that the enemy also could defy the precepts of classical strategy and defeat you by way of unopposable nuclear retaliation has understandably served to limit the appeal of this particular argument.

22. Jones, "Limitations of British Sea Power in the French Wars," p. 35.

23. But see Rosen, *Winning the Next War*, and especially Murray and Millett, *Military Innovation in the Interwar Period.*

24. Cambone and Gray, "Role of Nuclear Forces in U.S. National Security Strategy," esp. pp. 7–8. We note in this article that, for example, "the B-52s will be almost 65 years old in 2025," p. 8.

25. Pilsbury, *Chinese Views of Future Warfare*, merits close attention.

26. Matthews, *Challenging the United States Symmetrically and Asymmetically.*
27. See Betts, "What Will It Take to Deter the United States?"
28. Clausewitz, *On War,* p. 161.
29. Walzer, *Just and Unjust Wars,* ch. 13; Brownlie, *Principles of Public International Law,* pp. 466, 509–510.
30. Although NATO membership—and there is only one class of member—is widely regarded as the gold standard of national security in a superpower protection system, there is nothing in the NATO Treaty that strictly obliges the United States actually to do anything in particular on behalf of fellow members. Article 5 of the treaty does state that "the Parties agree that an armed attack against one or more of them in Europe or North America shall be considered an attack against them all." But each party is obliged only to take "such action as it deems necessary" by way of assistance to its allies. North Atlantic Treaty Organization, *NATO Handbook,* p. 232.
31. Quinlan, *Thinking About Nuclear Weapons,* pp. 50–54, sinks the NFU concept without a trace. For the leading statement of the NFU case, see Bundy et al., "Nuclear Weapons and the Atlantic Alliance." Gompert, Watman, and Wilkening, "Nuclear First Use Revisited," recommends a declaratory policy of NFU except for cases of response to attack by WMD other than nuclear weapons.
32. Nye and Owens, "America's Information Edge"; Perry, "Defense in an Age of Hope"; Joint Chiefs of Staff, "Joint Vision 2010."
33. For example, the U.S. Navy (USN) currently has programmed a decline in the number of its principal surface combatants from 138 to approximately 116. The USN of 2020, as a surface fleet, will comprise totally technologically high-end combatants. Predictably, the USN will find itself acutely short of numbers of hulls of low-end warships.
34. The great man said it all, as usual. Clausewitz, *On War,* p. 85. "No other human activity is so continuously or universally bound up with chance."
35. Schwartz, *NATO's Nuclear Dilemmas;* Haftendorn, *NATO and the Nuclear Revolution;* Heuser, *NATO, Britain, France and the FRG.*
36. On the distinctions among different levels of intensity of national interest, see Gray, *Explorations in Strategy,* pp. 116, 200–206.
37. CEP is a measure of accuracy expressed with reference to the rule that 50 percent of the ordnance will strike within a target circle of a given radius.
38. Starr, "USA Conventionally Challenged by Saddam's Hidden Weapons," reports accurately enough on the counter-BC limitations of the current U.S. conventional arsenal but does not discuss nuclear options.
39. Admittedly, this interwar categorization is distinctly parochial. Many people outside the G8 world are trying to survive in a period of conflict and even war—certainly a period characterized by much savage violence.
40. See Johnson, *Niche Threat.*
41. To be specific in the example, Libya's chemical weapons production facility beneath a mountain at Tarhunal.
42. Luttwak, *Strategy.*
43. Lambakis, "Space Control in Desert Storm and Beyond," and, by inference at least, Friedman and Friedman, *Future of War,* Part 3.

44. Heller and Stofft, *America's First Battles.*

45. See Gray, "Nuclear Strategy" and "Strategy in the Nuclear Age," esp. pp. 601–610. Garrity, "Depreciation of Nuclear Weapons in International Politics," also reviews nuclear lore.

46. Booth, *New Thinking About Strategy and International Security;* van den Bergh, *Nuclear Revolution and the End of the Cold War;* Regina Cowen Karp, *Security Without Nuclear Weapons;* Gjelstad and Njolstad, *Nuclear Rivalry and International Order.*

47. Ball and Richelson, *Strategic Nuclear Targeting;* Martel and Savage, *Strategic Nuclear War.*

48. See Duffield, *Power Rules.*

49. For example, Blair, Feiverson, and von Hippel, "Taking Nuclear Weapons Off Hair-Trigger Alert"; Blair, "Plight of the Russian Military and Nuclear Control." Pry, *War Scare,* is alarming if not necessarily alarmist.

50. Johnson and Libicki, *Dominant Battlespace Knowledge.*

51. Nye and Owens, "America's Information Edge."

52. The hazards to a persisting condition of military superiority are highlighted in Sumida, "Technological Innovation and Twentieth-Century Naval Force Structure."

53. Luttwak, "Toward Post-Heroic Warfare."

54. Ritter, *Schlieffen Plan.*

55. Ball, " Development of the SIOP"; Blair, *Logic of Accidental Nuclear War,* ch. 3.

56. Wavell, *Generals and Generalship,* p. 10; Clausewitz, *On War,* p. 605.

57. With thanks to Nitze, "Deterring Our Deterrent," for the phrasing of the problem.

6

Coping with
a Nuclear Future

As an organizing concept, the hypothesis of a second nuclear age can be tested only for its plausible explanatory merit; it cannot be demonstrated to be either true or false. As the inventor of the concept of a second nuclear age—in that formulation, at least—I need to be cautious lest I become overenamored of my own creation. This book develops an apparent paradox. On the one hand, the analysis shows how substantially different is the political context for nuclear strategy in the second, as contrasted with the first, nuclear age. With no nostalgia for Cold War certitudes and simplicities, the argument here registers the emergence of a transient second nuclear age wherein there is no single dominant axis of threat in world politics. On the other hand, the analysis shows both how generally sensible were the leading principles and practices adopted to govern the U.S. nuclear force posture and nuclear strategy in the Cold War and how useful those principles and practices should continue to be in the future. It is at least an apparent paradox that the dramatic shift of "nuclear ages," from Cold War to a diffusion of menace in a political context bereft of a super menace, should not require a dramatically different approach to nuclear questions. Probably the closest to an identifiable requirement for a major shift in U.S. policy and strategy is the need today for the declining reliability of deterrence to be offset by a new emphasis upon military denial by offensive, *and especially defensive,* counterforce. The contemporary necessity for such a shift of U.S. strategic emphasis is as clear as much of the detail of future NBC peril remains opaque.

Some important segments of this book are likely to be deemed strongly controversial. Three broad arguments that find much favor here are particularly apt to spur widespread unease.

First, many people will be uncomfortable with the argument (in Chapter 5) that, overall, the U.S. approach to nuclear force planning and strategy during the Cold War retains solid merit for the future also. By way of caveats, I would like to see the United States devote serious attention to air defense and to BMD and to be more flexibly adaptable in its war planning. Nonetheless, the nuclear strategic enlightenment of the 1950s, 1960s, and 1970s continues to appear to have been emphatically correct on the basics of nuclear lore.

Second, most probably there will be some significant unease among readers about the political analysis that informs the hypothesis of a second nuclear age and that fuels the argument that deterrence is becoming ever less reliable. Given that I have suggested that deterrence has never been reliable, readers could be excused for concluding that I anticipate strategic conditions wherein deterrence cannot function (save by accident). Those readers would be correct. The argument is that deterrence, even nuclear deterrence, is inherently unreliable and that as a consequence the prudent U.S. policymaker should choose to acquire denial/defense capabilities as a crucial backstop to ever more uncertain efforts at dissuasion.

Third, it is entirely predictable that some readers will be offended, at the least surprised, by my apparent strategic demotion of the obvious military potential of information superiority. In fact, my only moderate enthusiasm for the several RMAs that may be in process today derives from a respect for the whole realm of strategy—in its many dimensions—and especially from respect for the strategic potential of even modestly intelligent defense planning for asymmetric combat by foes of the United States.

* * *

The argument developed in this book around the organizing concept of a second nuclear age does not rest upon any great conceptual or empirical discovery. In some ways, the very familiarity of the detail of the subject impedes understanding. The postulate of nuclear ages, rather like RMAs, helps organize possible evidence and guides the theorist, for good or ill. It is possible to make sense of a period of strategic history even though there is no dominant item of argument that would warrant a shout of "eureka." So it is here. Everything considered here has been considered elsewhere. However, everything considered here has not been considered all together elsewhere, nor has it been considered from the perspective of strategy. While alert to change—witness the hypothesis of a succession of nuclear ages of which the current one is by no means the last—I am more impressed by continuities than by discontinuities in strategic history. Although history will not repeat itself in its fine print, this second nuclear age is but one way, albeit obviously an important one, to characterize yet another span of years of an inter(great)war kind.

It would be emotionally, if not intellectually, satisfying to be able to compress the diverse strands of argument in this book into some single, marvelously reductionist aphorism. If only some equivalent to "never divide the fleet," "peace now," or even "no more nukes" could fit the bill. Unfortunately, our NBC-related security condition is complex and does not lend itself to bumper-sticker treatment; that being so, there is no alternative other than to present the findings as they are, not reduced to some master cure (or band-aid). Each of these findings has been well flagged in the body of the book. Should any of these major points occasion great surprise, there would have to be something seriously wrong with the narrative trajectory of the whole of this enterprise. *The Second Nuclear Age* is not a dramatic production wherein an entirely unpredictable plot twist in the closing scene of the final act resolves all dilemmas and enables all parties to live happily ever after.

1. The nuclear fact is a condition, not a problem. The nuclear fact refers to the strategic consequences of the nuclear discovery. None of the contemporary or predicted political, military, technological, or other trends discussed in this book will rescind the nuclear era. Neither narrowly—in the form of military and civil technologies, via an information-led RMA or in the form of chemical and biological weapons—nor broadly, because of an evaporation of policy demand for the strategic effect that nuclear weapons can produce, are agents appearing that will consign nuclear weapons to the museum of strategic history.

This finding, also identified as a theme in Chapter 1, will come as no grand revelation. It is, however, perhaps close to a revelation to appreciate how little impact new information-led military capabilities, new developments in BC weaponry, and the political restructuring of world politics after the Cold War are having upon the strategic salience of nuclear arsenals. The contemporary U.S. antinuclear preference is as understandable in light of the country's "information edge" as it is either irrelevant or even likely to prove self-negating. If foreign and defense policy were a game of solitaire, then the strong U.S. preference for a postnuclear world order would be of major interest and indeed would be feasible. If anything, the strength of the U.S. non-nuclear preference—more precisely, the reasons for that preference—must fuel interest elsewhere in the search for an equalizer to U.S. conventional advantage. One does not require a Ph.D. in strategic studies to applaud the logic expressed by Gennadiy K. Khromov when he writes: "Liquidating existing nuclear arsenals, along with the transition to virtual nuclear arsenals, will benefit those countries with the most powerful conventional forces. Potential signatories of such a treaty would only be interested in it if conventional weapons were similarly restricted."[1] As we saw in the extensive discussion of nuclear fallacies in Chapter 4, the difficulties with virtual nuclear arsenals would far exceed that identified by Khromov (its unfairness to polities who find themselves conventionally disadvantaged), but he does signal usefully a massive structural problem for any great scheme of multinational nuclear deemphasis or outright abolition (from the active weapons inventory, at least).

Much of the better RMA analysis, for example as reported by Williamson A. Murray, suggests persuasively that RMAs overlie each other,[2] meaning that yesterday's RMA (or RMAs) can persist into today and beyond, that today's mega-RMA might comprise a cluster of quasi-independent—and somewhat interdependent—RMAs, or that today there are several RMAs jostling simultaneously for authority. A somewhat more radical idea than those entertained by Murray is the possibility that the contemporary RMA, or RMAs, do not constitute a great change with clearly knowable parts and consequences but rather yield hugely contestable evidence that lends itself to some notably rival interpretations. But no matter what edifice of theory one erects to help understand and explain what is going on in contemporary strategic history, there is an enduring necessity to take account of the unique strategic value that policymakers of different cultures find in the actual, or prospective, acquisition of a national nuclear arsenal.

The nuclear revolution arguably is different from other RMAs in that it offers a long-term resting place for polities unable or unwilling to compete for advantage in later RMAs. An appropriate analogy might be with a belligerent who rejects conventional resistance in favor of irregular warfare (including terrorism). Thinking "arrow-like" about the course of strategic history, one is apt to assume that the military prowess achievable from exploitation of today's accessible RMA must trump the prowess that derives from exploitation of yesterday's RMA.[3] Indeed, one of the more popular definitions of a "military revolution," offered by Andrew F. Krepinevich, points explicitly to a nonlinear increase in military effectiveness.

> What is a military revolution? It is what occurs when the application of new technologies into a significant number of military systems combines with innovative operational concepts and organizational adaptations in a way that fundamentally alters the character and conduct of conflict. It does so by producing *a dramatic increase—often an order of magnitude or greater—in the combat potential and military effectiveness of armed forces.*[4]

As a general rule, as Krepinevich emphasizes, exploitation of an RMA brings major strategic advantage. But the absolute quality to nuclear weapons about which Bernard Brodie and his collaborators wrote so eloquently in 1946[5] means that an information-led RMA might be trumped by the "old reliable" equalizer of a nuclear arsenal. In practice, that may not prove easy to effect. An information-dominant United States, supreme in space, air, and cyberspace, should be well equipped to wage conventional (and even some unconventional) warfare against a nuclear-armed enemy, and by prompt offensive and defensive counterforce defeat that enemy's nuclear-armed forces militarily. Nonetheless, no matter how competent multilayered protection ought to be, it is a safe prediction that nuclear-armed forces, even if small and unsophisticated, would equalize well enough with state-of-the-art conventional arms. Rephrased, yesterday's RMA—the nuclear revolution—will not be strategically eclipsed by the late-model conventional weaponry of information-age America.

2. Deterrence is wonderful, when it works. Time and again I have exceeded the empirical evidence when I have propounded the theme that deterrence is unreliable. The reason this theme, argument, or finding is so important is that its implications for the practical realm of strategy and statecraft could be literally devastating. It stands to reason, as the formula has it, that nuclear-armed states should conduct their mutual strategic relations with historically unusual caution. However, everything that a professional strategic analyst—at least *this* professional strategic analyst—understands about the structure and functioning of strategy screams beware of complacency about the reliability of deterrence.

To write in praise of deterrence is as undemanding as often it is necessary; it is not, however, sufficient to pass the test of strategic prudence. After the fashion of Payne's path-breaking study *Deterrence in the Second Nuclear Age,*[6] my examination of the second nuclear age leads me to be skeptical of the reliability of deterrence, not to be critical of the concept, or even the theory, of deterrence itself. Unlike arms control theory, the theory of deterrence does not suffer from a fatal internal contradiction. The only problem with deterrence is that it can be difficult, and on occasions impossible, to achieve. The criticism is not of deterrence the theory, the policy, or the strategy, but rather of any inclination to believe that the success of deterrence somehow can be assured. Admittedly, there is no historical evidence of the failure of nuclear deterrence; if anything, the record of the "long nuclear peace" of the Cold War suggests that nuclear deterrence does work reliably.[7]

The problems that most impress me are (1) the abundant historical evidence of failure of "conventional deterrence"; (2) the structural and ultimately indeterminate human element in all putative deterrence relationships; (3) the necessarily voluntary, if coerced, character of deterrence; (4) the lack of conclusively persuasive evidence of any kind demonstrating that nuclear threats deterred war between East and West from the late 1940s to the late 1980s; and (5) appreciation that even a single failure of nuclear deterrence might ruin our country, our region, and possibly our planet (just one failure could have catastrophic consequences).

The preceding paragraph is not intended to form the basis for an indictment of deterrence as concept, theory, policy, or strategy. Quite to the contrary, as the title of this subsection (and "finding") affirms, deterrence is wonderful, when it works. Arms control literally cannot work in the toughest of tough cases when it is really required because of the paradox that the enemies who need to cooperate cannot cooperate because they are enemies—at least they cannot cooperate through arms control. Deterrence, however, can work when one really needs it. The difficulty is that it can never be relied upon to work with the kind of assurance that we would like when under nuclear menace. Reliable deterrence can neither be bought by calculable threats that can translate into determinate force-building plans nor be assured by immaculate execution of strategic theory. Intended deterrees simply may fail to "get the message," they may get the message but choose to discount it, they may not be able to control their country's military machine, or they may be drunk, otherwise incapacitated, or willing to suffer a collective martyr's death for what to them seems a great and worthy cause. One cannot predict that any of these dire conditions will obtain between nuclear-armed adversaries, but such a possibility surely is more probable than is the postulate of a perfect, repeat perfect, performance of nuclear deterrence *forever*.[8]

For this second nuclear age, and perhaps beyond, the appropriately prudent conclusion to draw about a policy of deterrence is that it is necessary, but it cannot possibly be sufficient for public safety. With respect to nuclear peril, we in our current condition may well be not unlike those Europeans who in late July 1914—and ignorant of the decision for war already taken in Vienna and Berlin[9]—reasonably could find comfort in the undeniable fact that the general European peace had held despite a series of alarms since 1905 (the First Morocco Crisis). A quarter century on, Fred Charles Iklé's 1973 article "Can Nuclear Deterrence Last Out the Century?" still appears to be focused on the most pressing question of modern times.[10] The all but historical fact, as of this writing, that Iklé's question is answered in the affirmative does not, at least should not, engender dismissive contempt for that question. Whether we have been more clever than lucky, or vice versa, over the years of the nuclear era to date, one can hardly deny the possibility that the margin of safety against the failure of nuclear deterrence could be frighteningly slim and fragile.

3. Nuclear weapons are weapons; nuclear strategy is strategy. One can argue, not unreasonably, that the effectively open-ended scale of damage that nuclear weapons might inflict has had the result that "strategy hits a dead end."[11] In one sense, at least, such an idea undeniably is correct. Nuclear weapons could be used in ways, and on a scale, such as to void any relevance to strategic considerations: so much is not in doubt. The challenge, however—at least as these matters are regarded here—is to craft approaches for coping well enough with the permanent nuclear fact. To tell policymakers and professional military people that nuclear arsenals, if unleashed, could make a mockery of any and every strategic aspiration is, one suspects, to risk telling them what they know already. It is improbable that policymakers anywhere need to be educated as to the extraordinary qualities, and quantities, of nuclear armament. But once one has registered politically correctly the awesome awfulness of nuclear (let alone BC) armament, what next? This is a nuclear age plainly distinguishable in political structure from the decades of the East-West Cold War, and the nuclear thread continues to weave in and out of matters of regional and global security. Once one reads that strategy hits a dead end because of the nuclear fact, what does one say about our, and others', nuclear arsenals and strategies? More to the point, which working hypotheses can best help explain and understand how nuclear weapons could influence international security?

I have long believed that recognition of the possibility of nuclear catastrophe should not be allowed to paralyze the strategic imagination. Moreover, given the permanence of the nuclear fact, intellectual or policy resignation in the face of undeniably awful nuclear possibilities appears most imprudent.

Nuclear problems are not entirely generic. Because the United States of 1980s vintage could not with high assurance have defeated Soviet nuclear arms in a classic military sense, it does not follow that the United States of the early twenty-first century could not defeat the nuclear arms of an Iraq, Libya, Iran, or North Korea—or, dare one suggest, of a China also. Much of that putative defeat could be inflicted by U.S. conventional forces operating offensively and defensively to achieve multilayered counterforce effect. But most likely there would be some nuclear (and BC) arms buried deep underground or deployed with an agility that would thwart precise conventional firepower.

Nuclear weapons would not usually engage other nuclear weapons in a classic military clash of armed forces, though such a role most probably would predominate in the U.S. case. It does not follow as a consequence, however, that nuclear arms would not be weapons and that nuclear strategy would be something other than strategy. Terror can be a weapon and form the basis for strategy, to cite the leading practicable option for newly nuclear-proliferant polities. In point of fact, whenever one inquires at all rigorously how strategy and statecraft can exploit the unique strategic properties of nuclear armament, one finds answers readily enough. It is unfortunate for clarity of useful focus in public debate that in this second nuclear age there exists very little prudent discussion of nuclear weapons in strategic perspective. More often than not, nuclear arms simply are disdained as an embarassing military artifact of the Cold War that cannot be wished away definitively because of the nuclear discovery. At worst, nuclear weapons are not really treated as weapons at all but rather as antihuman devilish devices urgently in need of exorcism. Even typically realistic—and "classic realist"—strategic commentators incline to the view that the leading purpose suitable for approaching nuclear armament should be a desire to secure their "marginalization."[12] The problem with marginalization pertains not to its desirability but rather to its political feasibility and even its military wisdom.

With regard to military roles for nuclear arms, it is interesting to note that the leading Western historian of nuclear strategy, Lawrence Freedman, has written that "*however questionable their military purposes,* then, nuclear arsenals can serve a variety of political goals—from holding together alliances, to gaining international attention, to deterrence and intimidation."[13] The argument in Chapter 5 did not emphasize military purposes for nuclear arms; on the contrary, the analysis was very much along the lines that Freedman's words suggest, but neither did it shy away from specifying both specialized niche and more general war-fighting roles. The public debate over nuclear arms thus continues in this second nuclear age in the context of what amounts to a conspiracy of silence over the military uses of those weapons for strategic effect, a conspiracy also noticeable in the years of the Cold War. Nuclear "employment" as threat and as diplomatic message indicating (intending to indicate, perhaps) willingness to escalate both fall within the realm of strategy, though not within the realm of military strategy.[14]

Few if any would-be nuclear proliferants will seek nuclear arms with a view to securing military victory by the actual use of those weapons. Nuclear weapons status, even nuclear-weapons threshold status, instead will be seen as a vital means for achieving strategic effect directly upon foes' policymaking processes, rather than indirectly via the imposition of damage in battle. Nonetheless, nuclear weapons are weapons, and nuclear strategy is strategy. Whether the immediate focus is military or political consequences, recognition of the common currency of strategic effect alerts us to the authority of strategy.

4. Ethnocentricity can mislead. Ethnocentric judgment can take different forms and is pervasive in Western strategic literature. I use ethnocentrism "as a term to describe feelings of group centrality and superiority."[15] "Culture-bound" strategic commentators have long been susceptible to being overimpressed with their own genius and rectitude at the expense of recognizing the role played by their particular interests. The most salient connection between these thoughts and the thrust of this book is the all but "trained incapacity" of some Western experts on NBC non- (counter- and anti-)proliferation to take sufficiently seriously the motives of local and regional "rogues."[16] Readers may recall that earlier in this text

I offered a public security warning against uncritical reference to "rogue" polities. Notwithstanding the no less perilous path of an uncritical relativism—for example, the use of poison gas is just the Iraqi way of telling Iranians and Kurds that they mean business—frequent reference to "rogues" can promote a creeping self-deception.

Such thoughtful and well-respected theorists as Waltz and Martin van Creveld, for example, in an important sense write ethnocentrically as Western analysts even when they appear to write in a contrary mode. Both theorists have argued forcefully that there is no evidence that new nuclear proliferants, or nuclear-threshold states, in the developing world either have behaved, or are likely to behave, other than with extreme caution in their management and employment of a nuclear arsenal.[17] One is moved to comment, a little cynically, that that position bears some family resemblance to solemn judgments from the late 1930s to the effect that there was no proof that Adolf Hitler wanted either to begin a European war or to kill all the Jews in Europe. The line between a strictly true, and a true but deeply misleading, claim can be a fine one.

The argument here as the fourth finding is not entirely cultural by reference or in content. Even though WMD command universal respect for reason of the *MD* in the WMD, it is the genuine insecurity context of proliferant polities and groups that will loosen the bonds of policy restraint, just as it provided a leading motive for proliferation in the first place. Moreover, the content of strategic culture is not universal. A near-universal respect for WMD, and especially for nuclear weapons, need not translate through the social action of culture into a command for "utility [only] in nonuse."[18] U.S. professors of politics may not be encultured readily to appreciate feelings of desperation about national security, a deeply un-American attitude of policy resignation in the face of what appears to be the will of God (or Allah), let alone to endorse an all but unthinkable enthusiasm to wield WMD as an instrument for achieving change.

A difficulty with the essentially ethnocentric—if in many ways worthy—view that there is a global strategic (and political and moral) enlightenment about WMD is that that view does not have to be much in error in order to be catastrophically wrong. Waltz and van Creveld are plausible in their optimism about new nuclear proliferants, *on the evidence to date,* for what that is worth. It is not worth much of policy relevance to the United States, because the golden rule of prudence in national and international security obliges us to consider what may happen as well as what has happened. History tells us that all weapons eventually are used, that accidents happen, that policymakers miscalculate, and that friction can rule.

Ethnocentrism can have at least two serious negative consequences for security. First, its operation disinclines us to treat with due seriousness the scale and velocity of local motivation to acquire WMD for reasons that are locally compelling. (One should not forget how useful the extant nuclear weapons states continue to find their nuclear arms.) Second, with minds and hearts worthily keyed to questions of arms control, and at worst to matters of political semiotics, we may be culturally incapable of empathizing with polities who are prepared *actually to use* NBC, but especially nuclear, weapons in war.

5. *Nuclear war(s) can happen.* It is tempting to subsume this fifth theme or argument under the rubric of the Clausewitzian admonition that friction rules, but to do that would be to succumb to the ethnocentric error discussed above. U.S. strategists today can scarcely conceive of the purposeful first use of nuclear weapons, let alone the resort to a classic first strike. It follows in such U.S. perspective that a nuclear war would have to be the product of some variants of friction. Inadvertence, accident, miscalculation—these are the stuff of which nonpurposeful nuclear conflict would be made. The granting of validity to that view, however, should not blind us to the possibility—and if one looks far enough, the strong probability even—of (small) nuclear wars waged by belligerents who fully intended to wage them (if with aspirations for one-sided nuclear operations, of course).

It would be agreeable to be able to report that the absence of nuclear war since 1945 proves, indeed demonstrates, the extreme unlikelihood of nuclear war conducted by anyone over any issue. Unfortunately, scholars do not really know how to interpret that absence of nuclear use. One can talk now of a tradition of nonuse of nuclear weapons, even of a taboo against nuclear use, but that is only talk. The tradition or taboo in question is just one detonation away from being exposed as a wishful thought. Alternatively, to be fair, the tradition or taboo-breaking nuclear explosion could be the shocking exception that would reinforce and somehow lock in the taboo against nuclear use. As of now we do not, and cannot, know which judgment is the more correct.

Initially, at least, the unique event of a (hopefully small) nuclear war cannot be predicted statistically. We are entirely in the realm of guesswork when we pass judgment on the prospects for continuation of the long nuclear peace.

    6. Biological and chemical weapons pose some unique challenges. The U.S. defense community that ultimately delivered, at least safeguarded, the historic political victory of the late 1980s over the Evil Empire of the heirs of Lenin spent more than forty years analyzing and overanalyzing nuclear weapons. That defense community did not much study the strategic implications of old and new biological, toxin, and chemical weaponry. That is a fact rather than a criticism. Notwithstanding the offensive and defensive BC weapons research and production programs of *both* sides in the Cold War (until late 1969, with reference to the U.S. offensive BW program, illegally into the 1990s for the Soviet program), the range of BC menace literally was dwarfed in strategic significance by nuclear threats. Nuclear weapons reliably deliverable over transoceanic distances by missile or aircraft were much more obviously militarily useful—though not necessarily ultimately more controllable—than were BC weapons with their effects heavily dependent on the weather, on precise mechanical dispersal of lethal aerosols, on the most careful storage, and (for biological agents) on the elapse of considerable time (for incubation). A military assault upon the United States by designer viruses or clouds of poison gas, even if such weapons performed their dastardly missions as intended, could not disarm U.S. nuclear-armed forces of the ability most promptly to write *finis* to the Soviet experiment. When planning for a great military contest, BC weaponry, especially of the necessarily non–promptly fatal biological kind, cannot begin to compete with nuclear arms for the honor of attempting a disarming first strike, or even a strike that should limit the damage likely to be suffered in immediate retaliation. For this reason, preeminently, BC weaponry generally was as technically underdeveloped as were the concepts, policy, and strategy for its employment.[19]

    The reality of the situation just described is that until very recently Western strategic thought and defense planning have viewed the BC tranches in the NBC basket largely as terra incognita. Both superpowers developed and deployed biological and chemical weapons in the Cold War. However, in good part for the reasons provided in the preceding paragraph, there is effectively no strategic theory of, or doctrine for, biological or chemical warfare (though there is a large literature on the tactical employment of chemical weapons). The first major work of theory worthy of the name has yet to be written, at least published, on "strategy for biological warfare." We should probably be grateful for this ne-glect. Readers should be aware that the BC realm is not alone in being avoided by Western strategic theorists; there exists no major work on "strategy for space warfare" either.

The absence of a strategic theoretical literature on BC warfare does not mean that polities and substate groups will not figure out strategically effective ways to use BC agents for coercion in peace-time and success in war. England had an effective navy centuries before Alfred Thayer Mahan told that navy about "seapower," and the United States today exercises "spacepower" even though it does not really understand the concept very well (but see the dis-cussion below, under the eighth finding).

When a community of security experts does not know how to treat a category of difficulty, it is apt to retreat into conditions of denial or wishful thinking. A common response to the BC chal-lenge to world security today is simply to shunt discussion toward the prospects for arms control via the current, alas pathetically in-adequate, conventions on biological and toxin and on chemical weapons. As noted earlier, biological and chemical weapons pro-grams are extraordinarily difficult to identify unambiguously in the context of pharmaceutical and chemical research facilities and industrial activity apparently geared to legal, and nonmilitary, mis-sions. For recent illustration, it is reported that Libya currently is well embarked—with help from Iraqi scientists—on developing a "biological warfare complex under the guise of a medical facil-ity."[20] Probably with self-conscious irony, Libya's General Health Laboratories near Tripoli have been acquiring such dual-use—medical research *and* biological warfare—items as freeze driers, incubators, amino acid analyzers, and toxin identification kits.

Key asymmetries in the distribution of power mean that the United States and other G8 polities are especially in need of think-ing and planning strategically about biological and chemical per-ils to their security. Whereas the late USSR reasonably could aspire to compete militarily in symmetrically regular forms of combat, most possible foes of the United States tomorrow probably will not so aspire. Of course, there are undeniable old-fashioned virtues to nuclear arms. Such arms are the ultimate in swift brutality, they are reliable in their destructive effect (if their delivery is tactically practicable, that is), and they are universally comprehended and feared. But nuclear weapons are more difficult, and certainly much more expensive, to develop, deploy, and keep operationally ready than are many of the more accessible BC weapons options.

Moreover, if—unlike the case of the superpowers in the Cold War—a polity is seeking weapons of terror for strategic effect through coercive diplomacy, the military-operational arguments against BC arms all but evaporate. If a polity plans to try to win militarily against the United States—the Soviet aspiration in the 1950s, 1960s, and 1970s—then there is no prudent choice other than to rely heavily upon the kind of armament that can strike immediately, swiftly, and reliably with a promptly lethal destructive or disabling effect, all of which conflates to a strategic and policy demand for *nuclear* weapons. But regional players, or even local groups who cannot aspire to wage war symmetrically with a superpower, could afford to be less impressed by the uniquely predictable virtues of *nuclear* arms.

7. *Counterforce is essential for antiproliferation.* Just because NBC nonproliferation in the long run is a lost cause, it does not follow that particular antiproliferation acts have to be bereft of strategic value. Because one cannot do everything, for all time, still it can be worth doing something now. To explain, I have shown how and why the nonproliferation regime keyed to the NPT of 1968 and the biological (and toxin) and chemical weapons conventions of 1972 and 1995, respectively, cannot possibly succeed—if by success one means the definitive arrest and reversal of the trend toward NBC proliferation (and the proliferation of their missile means of delivery).[21] Such a heroically ambitious definition of policy success, however, is not very interesting to the practical world of statecraft and strategy. What can be attempted in aid of nonproliferation, and if need be by way of active antiproliferation, is some mix of the following:

- Reduce demand for NBC-based security by shaping a more relaxed global context of external security.
- Offer security options alternative to national NBC arms for those cases wherein external security contexts cannot be alleviated at source. Alliance, lesser security assurances, and non-NBC armament assistance all come within this category.
- Deter whatever NBC menaces can be deterred by a mixture of symmetrical and asymmetrical threats.
- Deny political clout and tactical military feasibility to NBC threats by means of offensive and defensive counterforce. Special operations, conventional weapon strikes, and even precise nuclear assault, backstopped by several layers of air and ballistic missile defenses, should help to take the potential sting out of regional NBC menace.

Readers may recall that magic moment in the movie *The Dirty Dozen* when the scrofulous "general" Donald Sutherland asks the immaculately groomed colonel about his beautifully uniformed honor guard: "Very pretty, Colonel, but can they fight?" Today there are grounds for concern that the ever more marvelously information-rich armed forces of the United States are becoming less and less usable as an instrument of U.S. policy. U.S. readers should ask themselves how serious they wish their country to be or to become in its deeds in support of its antiproliferation policy. Of course, Americans care about the proliferation of NBC arms. But do they care sufficiently to take effective military means—of any and every kind necessary—to thwart such proliferation?

The excuses truly are legion for a U.S. preference not to have resort to literally forceful options to ensure NBC weapons control or disarmament. What is more, most of the candidate excuses will either be or be made to sound reasonable and assuredly prudent. A short list of excuses for a decision not to use force against the WMD of a proliferant polity includes the following:

- Important members of the international community will not agree to the use of force.
- Diplomatic efforts are not yet exhausted.
- Target intelligence is less than perfect.
- Innocent people may be killed.
- Other Arab (Islamic, Asiatic, African, etc.) countries will be offended.
- We risk dignifying the target country and its NBC program by the attention of such a strike (any polity in combat against the United States is elevated politically as a consequence).
- Such a strike, even if successful, cannot enforce "the end of history" for NBC proliferation. Physical harassment of nascent and junior NBC programs ultimately is an exercise in futility.
- Offensive counterforce strikes, even if not quite incompatible with the rule of law, certainly give propaganda material to those who would portray the United States as a bully and a hypocrite. On the latter charge, and notwithstanding the formal sanctions of the NPT regime, the United States would be taking more or less unilateral action against a polity for attempting to do exactly what the United States has done for itself ever since 1945—namely, protect its security with nationally owned WMD.

- The strikes could cause environmental effects that would pose severe health hazards downwind to innocent civilians.
- The military will not guarantee the complete destruction of the NBC targets.
- The candidate target polity promises to behave well in the future.

Excuses for inaction in the face of plausible evidence of NBC proliferation will never be in short supply, and the fact that very occasionally—for example, as in December 1998—forceful action will be taken does not lessen the authority of this list. An obvious implication of the short list just provided is that defensive reactive means of active counterforce, rather than anticipatory or proactive offensive means, are by far the more politically user friendly. If the leading-edge answer to regionally acquired WMD is air defense and BMD, then strictly speaking one needs to take action only in response to the launch of those weapons by the regional foe. There should be no need to emphasize the point that in aid of policy legitimation, heavy reliance upon defensive counterforce sacrifices the advantages of the initiative.

   8. Contested space control may be the United States' Achilles' heel. It may seem strange that a book on the second nuclear age that has of necessity devoted most of its attention to NBC, and especially to nuclear, weapons and their implications should need to conclude the itemization of major themes, arguments, and findings with a strong caveat on the subject of space control. The reason is that the U.S. armed forces are, and are becoming ever more, dependent upon space systems for their combat effectiveness. The information-led RMA *does not work* if the United States loses control of space. Space control refers to the ability both to use earth orbit on a predictable basis and to deny such reliable use to a foe. "The American way of modern war" will not work if a foe can contest U.S. use at will of the spaceways. The U.S. armed forces—land, sea, air, special operations, nuclear—depend upon space systems for early warning, communications, navigation/targeting, weather, geodesy, and intelligence, and—one day—for some key BMD, air defense, and terrestrial bombardment options also.

   In particular, the U.S. ability to conduct precise, which is to say precisely effective, conventional warfare is vitally dependent upon the enabling agency of space capabilities. Enemies able to harm U.S. space systems, and perhaps to use space systems (for example, by the prompt purchase of near real-time imagery from the commercial satellites of nonbelligerent polities), would have found a notable equalizer to the military effectiveness of the United States' latest RMA. If, as one can and must predict, earth orbit becomes yet another geographical environment for armed conflict,[22] it is likely as a consequence that the sharp cutting edge of U.S. information-led weaponry would be noticeably dulled. The prospect of such an eventuality must reduce confidence in the putative strategic effectiveness of those conventional forces linked to an information-led RMA. If or when the United States loses assured control of space, it will be obliged to either revise dramatically downward its foreign policy aspirations or return to a condition of higher reliance upon nuclear menace in its strategy.[23]

This is not a fine academic point; it is, rather, registration of a classic lesson of strategic experience. Any geographical environment the military exploitation of which yields significant advantage has to be an environment well worth fighting to contest. Because the U.S. information-led RMA depends critically upon information gathered by, and passed from, space systems, it is entirely certain that foes of the United States will devote great energy to exploring cost-effective ways to deny the United States strategically effective use of the spaceways. This strategic logic has been true for the use of the sea and the air; there is no reason it should not hold for outer space also.

ENVOI

This book may be deeply unsettling, not to say unsatisfactory, to some readers. Any work that determines as an effort in policy science to try to explain the structure of a problem, rather than advance a preferred solution, invites a dissatisfied readership. My approach to the subject is flagged plainly enough in my title. *The Second Nuclear Age* conveys intentionally the suggestion that strategic history must accommodate at least several nuclear "ages." To advertise the complexity of NBC security issues is good for fit with historical experience but is less good for appeal to those who already have found their single, simple, preferred solution to NBC ills.

I have argued for the proposition that we live today in a second nuclear age. In addition, I have suggested that the global political structure and policy demand for nuclear assistance in this second nuclear age are vastly different both from the first nuclear age of the great Cold War and from a forthcoming third nuclear age, which is likely to be defined most characteristically by the return of a single, dominant axis of international antagonism. Would that there were some magic wand that would render NBC-related security issues miraculously and reliably resolvable. Candidates for the magic wand include deterrence, BMD, arms control/ disarmament, and offensive counterforce keyed to an information-led RMA. Each is interesting and worth pursuing, but none—indeed not even all together—can banish NBC perils. Insecurity, including NBC insecurity, is the human condition.

NOTES

1. Khromov, Letter to the Editor. Blank, "Nuclear Strategy and Nuclear Proliferation in Russian Strategy," explains the current necessity for nuclear dependency in Russian strategy.
2. Murray, "Thinking About Revolutions in Military Affairs."
3. Gould, *Time's Arrow, Time's Cycle.*
4. Krepinevich, "Cavalry to Computer," p. 30. Emphasis added.
5. Brodie, *Absolute Weapon.*
6. Payne, *Deterrence in the Second Nuclear Age.* Also see his "Post–Cold War Requirements for U.S. Nuclear Deterrence Policy."
7. I adapt "long nuclear peace" from Edward Gibbon's reference to "this long peace," *History of the Decline and Fall of the Roman Empire,* vol. 1, p. 62.
8. See Iklé, "Second Coming of the Nuclear Age."
9. Herwig, *First World War,* chs. 1, 2.
10. Iklé, "Can Nuclear Deterrence Last Out the Century?"
11. Brodie, "Strategy Hits a Dead End."
12. Freedman, "Nuclear Weapons."
13. Ibid., p. 187. Emphasis added.
14. The classic treatment remains Schelling, *Arms and Influence.*
15. Booth, *Strategy and Ethnocentrism,* p. 14.
16. "Trained incapacity" was one of the favorite concepts of Herman Kahn. Personal discussions with Kahn.
17. Sagan and Waltz, *Spread of Nuclear Weapons,* chs. 1, 3; Creveld, *Nuclear Proliferation and the Future of Conflict,* esp. chs. 3, 4.
18. Brodie, *War and Politics,* ch. 9.
19. The extent to which times have changed is flagged in Shubik, "Terrorism, Technology, and the Socioeconomics of Death."
20. Evans, "Iraqi Scientists 'Helping Libyan Germ Warfare.'"
21. See Rumsfeld Commission, *Executive Summary.*
22. Gray, "Influence of Space Power Upon History."
23. See U.S. Space Command, *Long Range Plan;* and Gray and Sheldon, "Spacepower and the Revolution in Military Affairs."

Bibliography

Andrew, Christopher, and Oleg Gordievsky. *Instructions from the Centre: The Secret Files on KGB Foreign Operations, 1975–1985.* London: Hodder and Stoughton, 1991.

Aron, Raymond. "The Evolution of Modern Strategic Thought." In Institute for Strategic Studies (ISS), *Problems of Modern Strategy, Part One.* Adelphi Paper 54. London: ISS, February 1969, pp. 1–17.

———. *Peace and War: A Theory of International Relations.* London: Weidenfeld and Nicolson, 1967.

Arquilla, John. "Bound to Fail: Regional Deterrence After the Cold War." *Comparative Strategy* 14, no. 2 (April-June 1995), pp. 123–135.

Arquilla, John, and David Ronfeldt, eds. *In Athena's Camp: Preparing for Conflicts in the Information Age.* Santa Monica, CA: RAND, 1997.

Bailey, Jonathan. *The First World War and the Birth of the Modern Style of Warfare.* Occasional Paper 22. Camberley, UK: Joint Services Command and Staff College, Strategic and Combat Studies Institute, 1996.

Bailey, Kathleen C. *Doomsday Weapons in the Hands of Many: The Arms Control Challenge of the 90's.* Urbana: University of Illinois Press, 1991.

———. *Strengthening Nuclear Nonproliferation.* Boulder, CO: Westview, 1993.

———, ed. *Weapons of Mass Destruction: Costs Versus Benefits.* New Delhi: Manohar, 1996.

Baldwin, David A. "Security Studies and the End of the Cold War." *World Politics* 48, no. 1 (October 1995), pp. 117–141.

Ball, Desmond. "The Development of the SIOP, 1960–1983." In Desmond Ball and Jeffrey Richelson, eds., *Strategic Nuclear Targeting.* Ithaca, NY: Cornell University Press, 1986, pp. 57–83.

Ball, Desmond, and Jeffrey Richelson, eds. *Strategic Nuclear Targeting.* Ithaca, NY: Cornell University Press, 1986.

Bathurst, Robert B. *Intelligence and the Mirror: On Creating an Enemy.* London: Sage, 1993.

Baucom, Donald R. *The Origins of SDI, 1944–1983.* Lawrence: University Press of Kansas, 1992.

Baylis, John, and John Garnett, eds. *Makers of Nuclear Strategy.* New York: St. Martin's Press, 1991.

Beaumont, Roger. *War, Chaos, and History.* Westport, CT: Praeger, 1994.

Benson, Sumner. "Competing Views on Strategic Arms Reduction." *Orbis* 42, no. 4 (fall 1998), pp. 587–604.

Bernstein, Richard, and Ross H. Munro. *The Coming Conflict with China.* New York: Alfred A. Knopf, 1997.

Betts, Richard K. "The New Threat of Mass Destruction." *Foreign Affairs* 77, no. 1 (January/February 1998), pp. 26–41.

———. "Should Strategic Studies Survive?" *World Politics* 50, no. 1 (October 1997), pp. 7–33.

———. "What Will It Take to Deter the United States?" *Parameters* 25, no. 4 (winter 1995/96), pp. 70–79.

Beyerchen, Alan. "Clausewitz, Nonlinearity, and the Unpredictability of War." *International Security* 17, no. 3 (winter 1992/93), pp. 59–90.

Bialer, Uri. *The Shadow of the Bomber: The Fear of Air Attack and British Politics, 1932–1939.* London: Royal Historical Society, 1980.

Blair, Bruce G. *The Logic of Accidental Nuclear War.* Washington, DC: Brookings Institution Press, 1993.

———. "The Plight of the Russian Military and Nuclear Control." In Commission to Assess the Ballistic Missile Threat to the United States (Rumsfeld Commission), *Report. Appendix III: Unclassified Working Papers.* Washington, DC: U.S. Government Printing Office, 15 July 1998, pp. 41–55.

Blair, Bruce G., Harold A. Feiverson, and Frank von Hippel. "Taking Nuclear Weapons Off Hair-Trigger Alert." *Scientific American* (November 1997), pp. 42–49.

Blaker, James R. *Understanding the Revolution in Military Affairs: A Guide to America's 21st Century Defense.* Defense Working Paper 3. Washington, DC: Progressive Policy Institute, January 1997.

Blank, Stephen J. "Nuclear Strategy and Nuclear Proliferation in Russian Strategy." In Commission to Assess the Ballistic Missile Threat to the United States (Rumsfeld Commission). *Report. Appendix III: Unclassified Working Papers.* Washington, DC: U.S. Government Printing Office, 15 July 1998, pp. 57–77.

Booth, Ken. "Dare Not to Know: International Relations Theory Versus the Future." In Ken Booth and Steve Smith, eds., *International Relations Theory Today.* Cambridge: Polity, 1995, pp. 328–350.

———. "A Reply to Wallace." *Review of International Studies* 23, no. 3 (July 1997), pp. 371–377.

———. *Strategy and Ethnocentrism.* London: Croom, Helm, 1979.

———. "Teaching Strategy: An Introductory Questionnaire." *Survival* 16, no. 2 (March/April 1974), pp. 79–85.

———, ed. *New Thinking About Strategy and International Security.* London: HarperCollins Academic, 1991.

Brodie, Bernard. *Sea Power in the Machine Age.* Princeton: Princeton University Press, 1941.

———. "Strategy Hits a Dead End." *Harper's* 211 (October 1955), pp. 33–37.

———. *War and Politics.* New York: Macmillan, 1973.

———, ed. *The Absolute Weapon: Atomic Power and World Order.* New York: Harcourt, Brace, 1946.

Brown, Chris. *Understanding International Relations.* London: Macmillan, 1997.

Brown, Michael E., Sean M. Lynn-Jones, and Steven E. Miller, eds. *Debating the Democratic Peace: An International Security Reader.* Cambridge: MIT Press, 1996.

Brownlie, Ian. *Principles of Public International Law.* 4th ed. Oxford: Clarendon Press, 1990.

Brzezinski, Zbigniew, ed. *Promise or Peril: The Strategic Defense Initiative.* Washington, DC: Ethics and Public Policy Center, 1986.

Bull, Hedley. *The Anarchical Society: A Study of Order in World Politics.* New York: Columbia University Press, 1997.

———. "Strategic Studies and Its Critics." *World Politics* 20, no. 4 (July 1968), pp. 593–605.

Bundy, McGeorge, George F. Kennan, Robert S. McNamara, and Gerard Smith. "Nuclear Weapons and the Atlantic Alliance." *Foreign Affairs* 60, no. 4 (spring 1982), pp. 753–768.

Butler, General Lee. "Stimson Center Award Remarks." Transcript. Washington, DC: Henry L. Stimson Center, 8 January 1997.

Buzan, Barry. *People, States and Fear: An Agenda for International Security Studies in the Post–Cold War Era.* 2d ed. Boulder, CO: Lynne Rienner, 1991.

Buzan, Barry, and Eric Herring. *The Arms Dynamic in World Politics.* Boulder, CO: Lynne Rienner, 1998.

Buzzanco, Robert. *Masters of War: Military Dissent and Politics in the Vietnam Era.* Cambridge: Cambridge University Press, 1996.

Calder, Kent E. *Asia's Deadly Triangle: How Arms, Energy and Growth Threaten to Destabilize Asia-Pacific.* London: Nicholas Brealey, 1997.

Cambone, Stephen, and Colin S. Gray. "The Role of Nuclear Forces in U.S. National Security Strategy: Implications of the B-2 Bomber." *Comparative Strategy* 15, no. 3 (July-September 1996), pp. 207–231.

Canberra Commission on the Elimination of Nuclear Weapons. *Report of the Canberra Commission.* Canberra: Australian Department of Foreign Affairs and Trade, August 1996.

Carter, Ashton B., and David N. Schwartz, eds. *Ballistic Missile Defense.* Washington, DC: Brookings Institution Press, 1984.

Chayes, Antonia H., and Paul Doty, eds. *Defending Deterrence: Managing the ABM Treaty Regime into the 21st Century.* Washington, DC: Pergamon-Brassey's, 1989.

Clausewitz, Carl von. *On War.* Trans. and ed. Michael Howard and Peter Paret. Princeton: Princeton University Press, 1976.

Cohen, Eliot. "Three Comments." In Heather Wilson, "The Politics of Proliferation." *The National Interest,* no. 34 (winter 1993/94), pp. 37–38.

Cohen, William S., Secretary of Defense. *Annual Report to the President and the Congress.* Washington, DC: U.S. Government Printing Office, 1998.

———. "Report of the Quadrennial Defense Review." *Joint Force Quarterly,* no. 16 (summer 1997), pp. 8–14.

Cole, Leonard A. *The Eleventh Plague: The Politics of Biological and Chemical Warfare.* New York: W. H. Freeman, 1997.

Conrad, Joseph. *Heart of Darkness.* London: Penguin, 1994.

Creveld, Martin van. "New Wars for Old." In The Economist, *The World in 1997*. London: The Economist, 1996, p. 91.

———. *Nuclear Proliferation and the Future of Conflict*. New York: Free Press, 1993.

Crone, Hugh D. *Banning Chemical Weapons: The Scientific Background*. Cambridge: Cambridge University Press, 1992.

Dando, Malcolm. *Biological Warfare in the 21st Century: Biotechnology and the Proliferation of Biological Weapons*. New York: Macmillan, 1994.

Davidson, H. R. Ellis. "The Secret Weapon of Byzantium." *Byzantinische Zeitschrift* 66 (1973), pp. 61–74.

Davis, Zachary S., and Benjamin Frankel, eds. "The Proliferation Puzzle: Why Nuclear Weapons Spread (and What Results)." *Security Studies* 2, nos. 3/4 (spring/summer 1993).

Desch, Michael D. "Culture Clash: Assessing the Importance of Ideas in Security Studies." *International Security* 23, no. 1 (summer 1998), pp. 141–170.

Dockrill, Saki. *Eisenhower's New-Look National Security Policy, 1953–61*. London: Macmillan, 1996.

Dror, Yehezkel. *Design for Policy Science*. New York: American Elsevier, 1971.

Duffield, John S. *Power Rules: The Evolution of NATO's Conventional Force Posture*. Stanford: Stanford University Press, 1995.

Dunn, David H. *The Politics of Threat: Minuteman Vulnerability in American National Security*. London: Macmillan, 1997.

Dunn, Lewis A. *Containing Nuclear Proliferation*. Adelphi Paper 263. London: International Institute for Strategic Studies, winter 1991.

———. *Controlling the Bomb: Nuclear Proliferation in the 1980s*. New Haven: Yale University Press, 1982.

Evans, Michael. "Iraqi Scientists 'Helping Libyan Germ Warfare.'" *The Times* (London), 6 January 1998, p. 10.

Ewing, Humphrey Crum, Robin Ranger, and David Bosdet. *Ballistic Missiles: The Approaching Threat*. Bailrigg Memorandum 9. Lancaster, UK: Lancaster University, CDISS, 1994.

Ewing, Humphrey Crum, Robin Ranger, David Bosdet, and David Wiencek. *Cruise Missiles: Precision and Countermeasures*. Bailrigg Memorandum 10. Lancaster, UK: Lancaster University, CDISS, 1995.

Falkenrath, Richard A. "Confronting Nuclear, Biological and Chemical Terrorism." *Survival* 40, no. 3 (autumn 1998), pp. 43–65.

Feaver, Peter Douglas. *Guarding the Guardians: Civilian Control of Nuclear Weapons in the United States*. Ithaca, NY: Cornell University Press, 1992.

———. "Neo-optimists and the Enduring Problem of Nuclear Proliferation." *Security Studies* 6, no. 4 (summer 1997), pp. 93–125.

Fischer, Ben B. *A Cold War Conundrum: The 1983 Soviet War Scare*, CSI97-10002. Langley, VA: Center for the Study of Intelligence, Central Intelligence Agency, September 1997.

Flank, Steven. "Exploding the Black Box: The Historical Sociology of Nuclear Proliferation." *Security Studies* 3, no. 2 (winter 1993/94), pp. 259–294.

Forsberg, Randall, William Driscoll, Gregory Webb, and Jonathan Dean. *Nonproliferation Primer: Preventing the Spread of Nuclear, Chemical, and Biological Weapons*. Cambridge: MIT Press, 1995.

Frankel, Benjamin, ed. *Opaque Nuclear Proliferation*. London: Frank Cass, 1991.

Freedman, Lawrence. "Great Powers, Vital Interests and Nuclear Weapons." *Survival* 36, no. 4 (winter 1994/95), pp. 35–52.

———. "Nuclear Weapons: From Marginalisation to Elimination?" *Survival* 39, no. 1 (spring 1997), pp. 184–189.

———. *The Revolution in Strategic Affairs*. Adelphi Paper 318. London: International Institute for Strategic Studies, April 1998.

Friedman, George, and Meredith Friedman. *The Future of War: Power, Technology, and American World Dominance in the 21st Century*. New York: Crown, 1996.

Friedman, George, and Meredith Lebard. *The Coming War with Japan*. New York: St. Martin's Press, 1991.

Fukuyama, Francis. *The End of History and the Last Man*. New York: Free Press, 1992.

Fursenko, Aleksandr, and Timothy Naftali. *"One Hell of a Gamble": Khrushchev, Castro, Kennedy, and the Cuban Missile Crisis, 1958–1966*. London: John Murray, 1997.

Gaddis, John Lewis. *We Now Know: Rethinking Cold War History*. Oxford: Clarendon Press, 1997.

Gardner, Gary T. *Nuclear Nonproliferation: A Primer*. Boulder, CO: Lynne Rienner, 1994.

Garrity, Patrick J. "The Depreciation of Nuclear Weapons in International Politics: Possibilities, Limits, Uncertainties." *Journal of Strategic Studies* 14, no. 4 (December 1991), pp. 463–514.

Gibbon, Edward. *The History of the Decline and Fall of the Roman Empire*. 7 vols. Ed. J. B. Bury. London: Methuen, 1909.

Gjelstad, John, and Olav Njolstad, eds. *Nuclear Rivalry and International Order*. London: Sage, 1996.

Glaser, Charles L. "Nuclear Policy Without an Adversary: U.S. Planning for the Post-Soviet Era." *International Security* 16, no. 4 (spring 1992), pp. 34–78.

Goldman, Emily O. "Thinking About Strategy Absent the Enemy." *Security Studies* 4, no. 1 (autumn 1994), pp. 60–85.

Gompert, David, Kenneth Watman, and Dean Wilkening. "Nuclear First Use Revisited." *Survival* 37, no. 3 (autumn 1995), pp. 27–44.

Gong, Gerrit W. *The Standard of "Civilization" in International Society*. Oxford: Clarendon Press, 1984.

Goodpaster, General Andrew, and General Lee Butler. "National Press Club Luncheon Address." Transcript. Washington, DC: National Press Club, 4 December 1996.

Gould, Stephen Jay. *Time's Arrow, Time's Cycle: Myth and Metaphor in the Discovery of Geological Time*. Cambridge: Harvard University Press, 1987.

Grace, Charles S. *Nuclear Weapons: Principles, Effects and Survivability*. London: Brassey's, 1994.

Grant, Charles. "America's Ever Mightier Might." In The Economist, *The World in 1998*. London: The Economist, 1997, p. 78.

Gray, Colin S. *The American Revolution in Military Affairs: An Interim Assessment*. Occasional Paper 28. Camberley, UK: Joint Services Command and Staff College, Strategic and Combat Studies Institute, 1997.

———. "The Arms Race Phenomenon." *World Politics* 24, no. 1 (October 1971), pp. 39–79.

———. "Arms Races and Other Pathetic Fallacies: A Case for Deconstruction." *Review of International Studies* 22, no. 3 (July 1996), pp. 323–335.

———. "Defense Planning for the Mystery Tour: Principles for Guidance in a Period of Nonlinear Change." *Airpower Journal* 5, no. 2 (summer 1991), pp. 18–26.

———. *Explorations in Strategy.* Westport, CT: Greenwood Press, 1996.

———. "Fuller's Folly: Technology, Strategic Effectiveness, and the Quest for Dominant Weapons." In A. J. Bacevich and Brian R. Sullivan, eds., *The Limits of Technology in Modern War.* Forthcoming.

———. *The Geopolitics of Super Power.* Lexington: University Press of Kentucky, 1988.

———. *House of Cards: Why Arms Control Must Fail.* Ithaca, NY: Cornell University Press, 1992.

———. "The Influence of Space Power Upon History." *Comparative Strategy* 15, no. 4 (October-December 1996), pp. 293–308.

———. "Moscow Is Cheating." *Foreign Policy*, no. 56 (fall 1984), pp. 114–152.

———. *NATO and the Evolving Structure of Order in Europe: Changing Terms of the TransAtlantic Bargain.* Hull Strategy Papers 1. Hull, UK: University of Hull, Centre for Security Studies, 1997.

———. *Nuclear Strategy and National Style.* Lanham, MD: Hamilton, 1986.

———. "Nuclear Strategy: The Case for a Theory of Victory." *International Security* 4, no. 1 (summer 1979), pp. 54–87.

———. "Nuclear Strategy: What Is True, What Is False, What Is Arguable?" *Comparative Strategy* 9, no. 1 (January-March 1990), pp. 1–32.

———. "Nuclear Weapons and the Revolution in Military Affairs." In T. V. Paul, Richard Harknett, and James J. Wirtz, eds., *The Absolute Weapon Revisited: Nuclear Arms and the Emerging International Order.* Ann Arbor: University of Michigan Press, 1997, pp. 99–134.

———. "On Strategic Performance." *Joint Force Quarterly*, no. 10 (winter 1995/96), pp. 30–36.

———. "RMAs and the Dimensions of Strategy." *Joint Force Quarterly*, no. 17 (autumn/winter 1997/98), pp. 50–54.

———. *The Soviet-American Arms Race.* Lexington, MA: Lexington Books, 1976.

———. "Strategic Culture as Context: The First Generation of Theory Strikes Back." *Review of International Studies* 25, no. 1 (January 1999), pp. 49–69.

———. *Strategic Studies: A Critical Assessment.* Westport, CT: Greenwood Press, 1982.

———. "Strategy in the Nuclear Age: The United States, 1945–1991." In Williamson Murray, MacGregor Knox, and Alvin Bernstein, eds., *The Making of Strategy: Rulers, States, and War.* Cambridge: Cambridge University Press, 1994, pp. 579–613.

———. "Villains, Victims, and Sheriffs: Strategic Studies and Security for an Interwar Period." *Comparative Strategy* 13, no. 4 (October-December 1994), pp. 353–369.

———. "War Fighting for Deterrence." *Journal of Strategic Studies* 7, no. 1 (March 1984), pp. 5–28.

Gray, Colin S., and Keith B. Payne. "Victory Is Possible." *Foreign Policy*, no. 39 (summer 1980), pp. 14–27.

Gray, Colin S., and John B. Sheldon. "Spacepower and the Revolution in Military Affairs: A Glass Half-Full." Manuscript. Hull, UK: University of Hull, Centre for Security Studies, July 1998.

Grove, Hugh D. *Banning Chemical Weapons: The Scientific Background.* Cambridge: Cambridge University Press, 1992.

Haftendorn, Helga. *NATO and the Nuclear Revolution: A Crisis of Credibility, 1966–1967.* Oxford: Clarendon Press, 1996.

Hall, Bert S. *Weapons and Warfare in Renaissance Italy: Gunpowder, Technology, and Tactics.* Baltimore: Johns Hopkins University Press, 1997.

Harkavy, Robert E. "Images of the Coming International System." *Orbis* 41, no. 4 (fall 1997), pp. 569–590.

Haslam, Jonathan. *The Soviet Union and the Politics of Nuclear Weapons in Europe, 1969–87.* Ithaca, NY: Cornell University Press, 1990.

Heller, Charles E., and William A. Stofft, eds. *America's First Battles, 1776–1965.* Lawrence: University Press of Kansas, 1986.

Herwig, Holger. *The First World War: Germany and Austria-Hungary, 1914–1918.* London: Arnold, 1997.

Heuser, Beatrice. *NATO, Britain, France and the FRG: Nuclear Strategies and Forces for Europe, 1969–2000.* London: Macmillan, 1997.

Hoffmann, Stanley. *Gulliver's Troubles, Or the Setting of American Foreign Policy.* New York: McGraw-Hill, 1968.

Holloway, David. *Stalin and the Bomb: The Soviet Union and Atomic Energy, 1939–1956.* New Haven: Yale University Press, 1994.

Howard, Michael. "The Forgotten Dimensions of Strategy." *Foreign Affairs* 57, no. 5 (summer 1979), pp. 975–986.

———. "Lessons of the Cold War." *Survival* 36, no. 4 (winter 1994/95), pp. 161–166.

———. "Reassurance and Deterrence: Western Defense in the 1980's." *Foreign Affairs* 61, no. 2 (winter 1982/83), pp. 309–324.

Huntington, Samuel P. "The Clash of Civilizations." *Foreign Affairs* 72, no. 3 (summer 1993), pp. 22–49.

———. *The Clash of Civilizations and the Remaking of World Order.* New York: Simon and Schuster, 1996.

———. "Why International Primacy Matters." *International Security* 17, no. 4 (spring 1993), pp. 68–83.

Huth, Paul K. *Extended Deterrence and the Prevention of War.* New Haven: Yale University Press, 1988.

Iklé, Fred Charles. "Can Nuclear Deterrence Last Out the Century?" *Foreign Affairs* 51, no. 2 (January 1973), pp. 267–285.

———. "Nuclear Strategy: Can There Be a Happy Ending?" *Foreign Affairs* 63, no. 4 (spring 1985), pp. 810–826.

———. "The Second Coming of the Nuclear Age." *Foreign Affairs* 75, no. 1 (January/February 1996), pp. 119–128.

Ion, A. Hamish, and E. J. Errington, eds. *Great Powers and Little Wars: The Limits of Power.* Westport, CT: Praeger, 1993.

James, Glenn E. *Chaos Theory: The Essentials for Military Applications.* Newport Paper 10. Newport, RI: Naval War College, Center for Naval Warfare Studies, October 1996.

Jervis, Robert. "International Primacy: Is the Game Worth the Candle?" *International Security* 17, no. 4 (spring 1993), pp. 52–67.

———. *The Meaning of the Nuclear Revolution: Statecraft and the Prospect of Armageddon.* Ithaca, NY: Cornell University Press, 1989.

———. "Why Nuclear Superiority Doesn't Matter." *Political Science Quarterly* 94, no. 4 (fall 1979), pp. 617–633.

Joffe, Joseph. "'Bismarck' or 'Britain'? Toward an American Grand Strategy After Bipolarity." *International Security* 19, no. 4 (spring 1995), pp. 94–117.

———. "How America Does It." *Foreign Affairs* 76, no. 5 (September/October 1997), pp. 13–27.

Johnson, Stuart E., ed. *The Niche Threat: Deterring the Use of Chemical and Biological Weapons.* Washington, DC: National Defense University Press, 1997.

Johnson, Stuart E., and Martin C. Libicki, eds. *Dominant Battlespace Knowledge.* Washington, DC: National Defense University, Institute for National Strategic Studies, April 1996.

Johnston, Alastair Iain. *Cultural Realism: Strategic Culture and Grand Strategy in Chinese History.* Princeton: Princeton University Press, 1995.

———. "Thinking About Strategic Culture." *International Security* 19, no. 4 (spring 1995), pp. 32–64.

Joint Chiefs of Staff. "Joint Vision 2010: America's Military—Preparing for Tomorrow." *Joint Force Quarterly*, no. 12 (summer 1996), pp. 34–49.

Jones, J. R. "Limitations of British Sea Power in the French Wars, 1689–1815." In Jeremy Black and Philip Woodfine, eds., *The British Navy and the Use of Naval Power in the Eighteenth Century.* Leicester, UK: Leicester University Press, 1988, pp. 33–49.

Jurist, A. (Pseud. for F. J. P. Veale). *Advance to Barbarism.* London: Thames and Smith, 1948.

Kagan, Donald. *On the Origins of War and the Preservation of Peace.* New York: Doubleday, 1995.

Kahn, Herman. *On Thermonuclear War.* Princeton: Princeton University Press, 1960.

Kane, Tomas M. "Sins of Omission: The Quadrennial Defense Review as Grand Strategy." *Comparative Strategy* 17, no. 3 (July-September 1998), pp. 279–289.

Kaplan, Robert D. "The Coming Anarchy." *Atlantic Monthly* (February 1994), pp. 44–76.

Karl, David J. "Proliferation Pessimism and Emerging Nuclear Powers." *International Security* 21, no. 3 (winter 1996/97), pp. 89–119.

Karp, Aaron. *Ballistic Missile Proliferation: The Politics and Technics.* Oxford: Oxford University Press, 1996.

Karp, Regina Cowen, ed. *Security Without Nuclear Weapons: Different Perspectives on Non-Nuclear Security.* Oxford: Oxford University Press, 1992.

Kaufmann, William W. "The Requirements of Deterrence." In William W. Kaufmann, ed. *Military Policy and National Security.* Princeton: Princeton University Press, 1956, pp. 12–38.

Kay, David A. "Denial and Deception Practices of WMD Proliferators: Iraq and Beyond." *Washington Quarterly* 18, no. 1 (winter 1995), pp. 85–105.

Keegan, John. *The Face of Battle*. London: Johathan Cape, 1976.
————. *A History of Warfare*. London: Hutchinson, 1993.
Kellert, Stephen H. *In the Wake of Chaos: Unpredictable Order in Dynamical Systems*. Chicago: University of Chicago Press, 1993.
Kennedy, Paul. *The Rise and Fall of the Great Powers: Economic Change and Military Conflict from 1500 to 2000*. New York: Random House, 1987.
Khalilzad, Zalmay M., and David A. Ochmanek, eds. *Strategic Appraisal 1997: Strategy and Defense Planning for the 21st Century*. Santa Monica, CA: RAND, 1997.
Khromov, Gennadiy K. Letter to the Editor. *Survival* 39, no. 1 (spring 1997), p. 206.
Kissinger, Henry. *Diplomacy*. New York: Simon and Schuster, 1994.
Klare, Michael. *Rogue States and Nuclear Outlaws: America's Search for a New Foreign Policy*. New York: Hill and Wang, 1995.
Knox, MacGregor. "Conclusion: Continuity and Revolution in the Making of Strategy." In Williamson Murray, MacGregor Knox, and Alvin Bernstein, eds., *The Making of Strategy: Rulers, States, and War*. Cambridge: Cambridge University Press, 1994, pp. 614–645.
Krepinevich, Andrew F. "Cavalry to Computer: The Pattern of Military Revolutions." *The National Interest*, no. 37 (fall 1994), pp. 30–42.
Krepon, Michael. "Are Missile Defenses MAD? Combining Defenses with Arms Control." *Foreign Affairs* 74, no. 1 (January/February 1995), pp. 19–24.
Lambakis, Steven J. "Space Control in Desert Storm and Beyond." *Orbis* 39, no. 3 (summer 1995), pp. 417–433.
Lambakis, Steven J., and Colin S. Gray. *Political and Legal Restrictions on U.S. Military Space Activities*. Fairfax, VA: National Institute for Public Policy, December 1997.
Lasswell, Harold D. "The Policy Orientation." In Daniel Lerner and Harold D. Lasswell, eds., *The Policy Sciences*. Stanford: Stanford University Press, 1951, pp. 3–15.
Lavoy, Peter R. "Nuclear Myths and the Causes of Nuclear Proliferation." In Zachary S. Davis and Benjamin Frankel, eds., "The Proliferation Puzzle: Why Nuclear Weapons Spread (and What Results)." *Security Studies* 2, nos. 3/4 (spring/summer 1993), pp. 192–212.
Layne, Christopher. "The Unipolar Illusion: Why New Great Powers Will Rise." *International Security* 17, no. 4 (spring 1993), pp. 5–51.
Lebow, Richard Ned, and Janice Gross Stein. *We All Lost the Cold War*. Princeton: Princeton University Press, 1994.
Leffler, Melvyn P. *A Preponderance of Power: National Security, the Truman Administration, and the Cold War*. Stanford: Stanford University Press, 1992.
Luttwak, Edward N. *The Endangered American Dream*. New York: Simon and Schuster, 1993.
————. "From Geopolitics to Geo-Economics: Logic of Conflict, Grammar of Commerce." *The National Interest*, no. 20 (summer 1990), pp. 17–23.
————. *The Political Uses of Sea Power*. Baltimore: Johns Hopkins University Press, 1974.
————. *Strategy: The Logic of War and Peace*. Cambridge: Harvard University Press, 1987.

————. "Toward Post-Heroic Warfare." *Foreign Affairs* 74, no. 3 (May/June 1995), pp. 109–122.

Mandelbaum, Michael. "Lessons of the Next Nuclear War." Foreign Affairs 74, no. 2 (March/April 1995), pp. 22–37.

Marshall, George C., Institute. *The Concept of Defensive Deterrence: Strategic and Technical Dimensions of Missile Defense.* Washington, DC: George C. Marshall Institute, 1988.

Martel, William C., and Paul L. Savage, eds. *Strategic Nuclear War: What the Superpowers Target and Why.* Westport, CT: Greenwood Press, 1986.

Mastanduno, Michael. "Preserving the Unipolar Moment: Realist Theories and U.S. Grand Strategy After the Cold War." *International Security* 21, no. 3 (spring 1997), pp. 49–88.

Mastny, Vojtech. *The Cold War and Soviet Insecurity: The Stalin* Years. New York: Oxford University Press, 1996.

Matthews, Lloyd J., ed. *Challenging the United States Symmetrically and Asymmetrically: Can America Be Defeated?* Carlisle Barracks, PA: U.S. Army War College, Strategic Studies Institute, July 1998.

May, Ernest R., and Philip D. Zilikow, eds. *The Kennedy Tapes: Inside the White House During the Cuban Missile Crisis.* Cambridge: Harvard University Press, 1997.

Mazarr, Michael J. "The Notion of Virtual Arsenals." In Michael J. Mazarr, ed., *Nuclear Weapons in a Transformed World: The Challenge of Virtual Nuclear* Arsenals. London: Macmillan, 1997, pp. 3–29.

————. "Virtual Nuclear Arsenals." *Survival* 37, no. 3 (autumn 1995), pp. 7–26.

————, ed. *Nuclear Weapons in a Transformed World: The Challenge of Virtual Nuclear Arsenals.* London: Macmillan, 1997.

Mearsheimer, John. "Back to the Future: Instability in Europe After the Cold War." *International Security* 15, no. 1 (summer 1990), pp. 5–56.

Morgan, Patrick M. *Deterrence: A Conceptual Analysis.* Beverly Hills, CA: Sage, 1977.

Morgenthau, Hans J. *Politics Among Nations: The Struggle for Power and Peace.* 6th ed. Revised by Kenneth W. Thompson. New York: McGraw-Hill, 1985.

Mueller, John. *Retreat from Doomsday: The Obsolescence of Major War.* New York: Basic Books, 1989.

Murray, Williamson A. "Thinking About Revolutions in Military Affairs." *Joint Force Quarterly,* no. 16 (summer 1997), pp. 69–76.

Murray, Williamson A., and Mark Grimsley. "Introduction: On Strategy." In Williamson A. Murray, MacGregor Knox, and Alvin Bernstein, eds., *The Making of Strategy: Rulers, States, and War.* Cambridge: Cambridge University Press, 1994, pp. 1–23.

Murray, Williamson A., and Allan R. Millett, eds. *Military Innovation in the Interwar Period.* Cambridge: Cambridge University Press, 1996.

Nandy, Ashis. *The Tao of Cricket: On Games of Destiny and the Destiny of Games.* London: Penguin, 1989.

Nathan, James A., ed. *The Cuban Missile Crisis Revisited.* New York: St. Martin's Press, 1992.

National Academy of Sciences, Committee on International Security and Arms Control. *The Future of U.S. Nuclear Weapons Policy.* Washington, DC: National Academy Press, 1997.

Nitze, Paul. "Deterring Our Deterrent." *Foreign Policy*, no. 25 (winter 1976/ 77), pp. 195–210.

Nolan, Janne E. *Trappings of Power: Ballistic Missiles in the Third World.* Washington, DC: Brookings Institution Press, 1991.

———, ed. *Global Engagement: Cooperation and Society in the 21st Century.* Washington, DC: Brookings Institution Press, 1994.

North Atlantic Treaty Organization. *NATO Handbook.* Brussels: NATO Office of Information and Press, 1995.

Nye, Joseph S. *Bound to Lead: The Changing Nature of American Power.* New York: Basic Books, 1990.

———. "China's Re-emergence and the Future of the Asia-Pacific." *Survival* 39, no. 4 (winter 1997/98), pp. 65–79.

Nye, Joseph S., and William A. Owens. "America's Information Edge." *Foreign Affairs* 75, no. 2 (March/April 1996), pp. 20–36.

Owens, William A. "The Emerging System of Systems." U.S. Naval Institute *Proceedings* 121, no. 5 (May 1995), pp. 35–39.

Panofsky, Wolfgang K. H. "The Mutual Hostage Relationship Between America and Russia." *Foreign Affairs* 52, no. 1 (October 1973), pp. 109–118.

Paul, T. V. "Nuclear Taboo and War Initiation in Regional Conflicts." *Journal of Conflict Resolution* 39, no. 4 (December 1995), pp. 696–717.

Paul, T. V., Richard Harknett, and James J. Wirtz, eds. *The Absolute Weapon Revisited: Nuclear Arms and the Emerging International Order.* Ann Arbor: University of Michigan Press, 1998.

Payne, Keith B. *The Case Against Nuclear Abolition and for Nuclear Deterrence.* Fairfax, VA: National Institute for Public Policy, December 1997.

———. *Deterrence in the Second Nuclear Age.* Lexington: University Press of Kentucky, 1996.

———. *Missile Defense in the 21st Century: Protection Against Limited Threats, Including Lessons from the Gulf War.* Boulder, CO: Westview, 1991.

———. "Post–Cold War Requirements for U.S. Nuclear Deterrence Policy." *Comparative Strategy* 17, no. 3 (July-September 1998), pp. 227–277.

———. *Strategic Defense: "Star Wars" in Perspective.* Lanham, MD: Hamilton, 1986.

Perry, William J. "Defense in an Age of Hope." *Foreign Affairs* 75, no. 6 (November/December 1996), pp. 64–79.

Peters, Ralph. "Constant Conflict." *Parameters* 27, no. 2 (summer 1997), pp. 4–14.

———. "The Culture of Future Conflict." *Parameters* 25, no. 4 (winter 1995–96), pp. 18–27.

———. "The New Warrior Class." *Parameters* 24, no. 2 (summer 1994), pp. 16–26.

———. "Our New Old Enemies." In Lloyd J. Matthers, ed., *Challenging the United States Symmetrically and Asymmetrically: Can America Be Defeated?* Carlisle Barracks, PA: U.S. Army War College, Strategic Studies Institute, July 1998, pp. 215–238.

———. "Our Soldiers, Their Cities." *Parameters* 26, no. 1 (spring 1996), pp. 43–50.

Pilsbury, Michael, ed. *Chinese Views of Future Warfare.* Washington, DC: National Defense University Press, 1997.

Posen, Barry R. "U.S. Security Policy in a Nuclear-Armed World, Or: What If Iraq Had Had Nuclear Weapons?" *Security Studies* 6, no. 3 (spring 1997), pp. 1–31.

Posen, Barry R., and Andrew L. Ross. "Competing Visions for U.S. Grand Strategy." *International Security* 21, no. 3 (winter 1996/97), pp. 5–53.

Price, Richard, and Nina Tannenwald. "Norms and Deterrence: The Nuclear and Chemical Weapons Taboos." In Peter J. Katzenstein, ed., *The Culture of National Security: Norms and Identity in World Politics*. New York: Columbia University Press, 1996, pp. 114–152.

Pry, Peter V. *War Scare: Nuclear Countdown After the Soviet Fall*. Atlanta, GA: Turner Publishing, 1997.

Quinlan, Michael. *Thinking About Nuclear Weapons*. London: Royal United Services Institute for Defence Studies, 1997.

Ranger, Robin, ed. *The Devil's Brews I: Chemical and Biological Weapons and Their Delivery Systems*. Bailrigg Memorandum 16. Lancaster, UK: Lancaster University, CDISS, 1996.

Reiss, Edward. *The Strategic Defense Initiative*. Cambridge: Cambridge University Press, 1992.

Reiss, Mitchell. *Bridled Ambition—Why Countries Constrain Their Nuclear Capabilities*. Washington, DC: Woodrow Wilson Center, 1995.

Ritter, Gerhard. *The Schlieffen Plan: Critique of a Myth*. London: Oswald Wolff, 1958.

Rohwer, Jim. *Asia Rising: How History's Biggest Middle Class Will Change the World*. London: Nicholas Brealey, 1996.

Rosen, Stephen Peter. *Winning the Next War: Innovation and the Modern Military*. Ithaca, NY: Cornell University Press, 1991.

Rotblat, Joseph, Jack Steinberger, and Bhalchandra Udgaonkar, eds. *A Nuclear-Weapon-Free World: Desirable? Feasible?* Boulder, CO: Westview, 1993.

Ruelle, David. *Chance and Chaos*. London: Penguin, 1993.

Rumsfeld [Donald H.] Commission. Commission to Assess the Ballistic Missile Threat to the United States. *Executive Summary*. Washington, DC: U.S. Government Printing Office, 15 July 1998.

Sagan, Carl, and Richard Turco. *A Path Where No Man Thought: Nuclear Winter and the End of the Arms Race*. London: Century, 1990.

Sagan, Scott D. *The Limits of Safety: Organizations, Accidents, and Nuclear Weapons*. Princeton: Princeton University Press, 1993.

———. "Why Do States Build Nuclear Weapons? Three Models in Search of a Bomb." *International Security* 21, no. 3 (winter 1996/97), pp. 54–86.

Sagan, Scott D., and Kenneth N. Waltz. *The Spread of Nuclear Weapons: A Debate*. New York: W. W. Norton, 1995.

Schell, Johathan. *The Abolition*. New York: Alfred A. Knopf, 1986.

———. *The Gift of Time*. London: Granta, 1998.

Schelling, Thomas C. *Arms and Influence*. New Haven: Yale University Press, 1960.

———. *The Strategy of Conflict*. Cambridge: Harvard University Press, 1960.

Schwartz, David N. *NATO's Nuclear Dilemmas*. Washington, DC: Brookings Institution Press, 1983.

Segal, Gerald. "How Insecure Is Pacific Asia?" *International Affairs* 73, no. 2 (April 1997), pp. 235–249.

Seng, Jordan. "Less Is More: Command and Control Advantage of Minor Nuclear States." *Security Studies* 6, no. 4 (summer 1997), pp. 50–92.

———. "Optimism in the Balance: A Response." *Security Studies* 6, no. 4 (summer 1997), pp. 126–136.

Shambaugh, David. "Containment or Engagement of China? Calculating Beijing's Responses." *International Security* 21, no. 2 (fall 1996), pp. 180–209.

Sheehan, Michael. *The Balance of Power: History and Theory.* London: Routledge, 1996.

———. "Chinese Hegemony over East Asia by 2015?" *Korean Journal of Defense Analysis* 9, no. 1 (summer 1997), pp. 7–28.

Shubik, Martin. "Terrorism, Technology, and the Socioeconomics of Death." *Comparative Strategy* 16, no. 4 (October-December 1997), pp. 399–414.

Singer, Max, and Aaron Wildavsky. *The Real World Order.* Chatham, NJ: Chatham House, 1993.

Smith, David J. "Missile Defense After Helsinki." *Comparative Strategy* 16, no. 4 (October-December 1997), pp. 369–376.

Smith, Steve, and John Baylis. "Introduction." In Steve Smith and John Baylis, eds., *The Globalization of World Politics: An Introduction to International Relations.* Oxford: Oxford University Press, 1997, pp. 1–11.

Solingen, Etel. "The Political Economy of Nuclear Restraint." *International Security* 19, no. 2 (fall 1994), pp. 126–169.

Speier, Hans. "Magic Geography." *Social Research* (September 1941), pp. 310–330.

Spiers, Edward M. *Chemical and Biological Weapons: A Study of Proliferation.* London: Macmillan, 1994.

———. *Chemical Warfare.* London: Macmillan, 1986.

Spykman, Nicholas. *The Geography of the Peace.* New York: Harcourt, Brace, 1944.

Starr, Barbara. "USA Conventionally Challenged by Saddam's Hidden Weapons." *Jane's Defence Weekly* (19 November 1997), p. 19.

Stein, Janice Gross. "Deterrence and Compellence in the Gulf, 1990–91: A Failed or Impossible Task?" *International Security* 17, no. 2 (fall 1992), pp. 147–179.

Strassler, Robert B., ed. *The Landmark Thucydides: A Comprehensive Guide to The Peloponnesian War.* Trans. Richard Crawley. New York: Free Press, 1996.

Stumpf, Waldo. "South Africa's Nuclear Weapons Programme." In Kathleen C. Bailey, ed., *Weapons of Mass Destruction: Costs Versus Benefits.* New Delhi: Manohar, 1996, pp. 63–81.

Suganami, Hidemi. *On the Causes of War.* Oxford: Clarendon Press, 1996.

Sumida, Jon Tetsuro. "Technological Innovation and Twentieth-Century Naval Force Structure: Alternative Perspectives and Their Implications." In Andrew J. Bacevich and Brian R. Sullivan, eds., *The Limits of Technology in Modern War.* Forthcoming.

Sun Tzu. *The Art of War.* Trans. and ed. Ralph D. Sawyer. Boulder, CO: Westview, 1994.

Thayer, Bradley A. "The Risk of Nuclear Inadvertence: A Review Essay." *Security Studies* 3, no. 3 (spring 1994), pp. 428–493.

"The Kenneth Waltz–Scott Sagan Debate. The Spread of Nuclear Weapons: Good or Bad?" *Security Studies* 4, no. 4 (summer 1995), pp. 693–810.

"The Kenneth Waltz–Scott Sagan Debate II." *Security Studies* 5, no. 1 (autumn 1995), pp. 149–170.

Trachtenberg, Marc. *History and Strategy.* Princeton: Princeton University Press, 1991.

Trevan, Tim. *Saddam's Secrets: The Hunt for Iraq's Hidden Weapons.* London: HarperCollins, 1999.

Tucker, Robert W., and David C. Hendrickson. *The Imperial Temptation: The New World Order and America's Purpose.* New York: Council on Foreign Relations, 1992.

U.S. Congress, Office of Technology Assessment (OTA). *Proliferation of Weapons of Mass Destruction: Assessing the Risks.* OTA-ISC-559. Washington, DC: U.S. Government Printing Office, August 1993.

———. *Technologies Underlying Weapons of Mass Destruction.* OTA-BP-1115. Washington, DC: U.S. Government Printing Office, December 1993.

U.S. Space Command. *Long Range Plan.* Peterson AFB, CO: U.S. Space Command, March 1998.

Utgoff, Victor A. *The Challenge of Chemical Weapons: An American Perspective.* New York: St. Martin's Press, 1991.

van den Bergh, Godfried van Benthem. *The Nuclear Revolution and the End of the Cold War.* London: Macmillan, 1992.

Wallace, William. "Truth and Power, Monks and Technocrats: Theory and Practice in International Relations." *Review of International Studies* 22, no. 3 (July 1996), pp. 301–321.

Waltz, Kenneth N. "Nuclear Myths and Nuclear Realities." *American Political Science Review* 84, no. 3 (September 1990), pp. 731–745.

———. *The Spread of Nuclear Weapons: More May Be Better.* Adelphi Paper 171. London: International Institute for Strategic Studies, 1981.

———. *Theory of International Politics.* Reading, MA: Addison-Wesley, 1979.

Walzer, Michael. *Just and Unjust Wars: A Moral Argument with Historical Illustrations.* New York: Basic Books, 1977.

Watts, Barry D. *Clausewitzian Friction and Future War.* McNair Paper 52. Washington, DC: National Defense University, Institute for National Strategic Studies, October 1996.

Wavell, Archibald. *Generals and Generalship.* New York: Macmillan, 1943.

Weaver, Ole, Barry Buzan, Morten Kelstrup, and Pierre Lemaitre. *Identity, Migration and the New Security Agenda in Europe.* London: Pinter, 1993.

White House Press Release. "Joint Statement Concerning the Anti-Ballistic Missile Treaty, Helsinki Summit, March 21 1997." Reprinted in *Comparative Strategy* 16, no. 4 (October-December 1997), pp. 415–416.

Whittow, Mark. *The Making of Orthodox Byzantium, 600–1025.* London: Macmillan, 1996.

Wilkening, Dean A. "The Future of Russia's Strategic Nuclear Force." *Survival* 40, no. 3 (autumn 1998), pp. 89–111.

Wilkening, Dean, and Kenneth Watman. *Nuclear Deterrence in a Regional Context.* Santa Monica, CA: RAND, Arroyo Center, 1994.

Williams, Raymond. "The Analysis of Culture." In John Storey, ed., *Cultural Theory and Popular Culture: A Reader.* Hemel Hempstead, UK: Harvester Wheatsheaf, 1994, pp. 56–64.

Wright, Susan, ed. *Preventing a Biological Arms Race*. Cambridge: MIT Press, 1990.

York, Herbert. *Does Strategic Defense Breed Offense?* Cambridge: Harvard University, Center for Science and International Affairs, 1987.

Zubok, Vladislav, and Constantine Pleshakov. *Inside the Kremlin's Cold War: From Stalin to Khrushchev*. Cambridge: Harvard University Press, 1996.

Index

ABM Treaty, 99–100, 103
Adversarial relationships, 13
American Century theory, 29–30
Arms control, 58–60, 98, 118–120, 122, 158; paradox, 58
Aron, Raymond, 41
Arsenals, 22–24, 41, 146; minimum, 116, 148; virtual, 83, 85–88, 116–117

Balance of power. *See* Bipolar political system
Baldwin, Stanley, 110
Balkans, 48
Ballistic missile defense (BMD), 97–103; deterrence and, 100–101; merits of, 101–103
Bethmann Hollweg, Theobald von, 65, 106
Betts, Richard, 28
Biological and chemical (BC) weapons, 10, 11, 72–74, 96, 130, 136, 164–166. *See also* Nuclear, biological, and chemical weapons
Biological and Toxin Weapons Convention of 1972, 72, 166
Biological weapons (BW), 10, 11, 72–74, 138
Bipolar political system, 71, 98; hegemony and, 29, 33, 37, 124; second nuclear age and, 14, 20, 22, 25; third nuclear age and, 39–40

Bismarck, Otto von, 31
Blair, Tony, 61
BMD. *See* Ballistic missile defense
Booth, Ken, 26
Britain, 53, 54–55, 61, 76(n12), 96–97, 125
Brodie, Bernard, 157
Brown, Chris, 3
BW. *See* Biological weapons

"Can Nuclear Deterrence Last Out the Century?" (Iklé), 159
Chaos theory, 93
Chemical weapons (CW). *See* Biological and chemical weapons
Chemical Weapons Convention of 1995, 72, 166
China, 7–8, 10, 29, 71, 80, 91; arms control and, 119; defense issues and, 98–99, 101–102; as peer rival, 32–34, 38–40, 127–128, 144
Clash of civilizations theory, 37
Clausewitz, Carl von, 3, 19, 23, 68, 69, 88, 127, 137, 146, 148
Coalition, 125
Cohen, Eliot A., 109
Cold War, 1, 8, 14, 25, 138; BC weapons and, 164–165; deterrence theory and, 89, 90, 101; nuclear strategy, 143–144
Command and control, 147
Commonwealth of Independent States (CIS), 63

187

Continuity, 12, 20–24, 155
Conventional warfare, 3, 8–9;
    countering, 131–133; nuclear
    strategy and, 137–139, 144–145;
    RMA and, 156–157; targeting,
    135–137
Counterforce, 129–131, 145–146,
    153–154, 166–168; RMA and,
    132, 157–158
Counterproliferation policy, 70–71,
    166–168. *See also* Proliferation
Creveld, Martin van, 82, 162
Cuban missile crisis, 18

Delegitimization, 37
Demand-side forces, 58–61
Denial, 59, 97
Deterrence, 12, 24, 41, 71, 81; BMD
    and, 100–101; Cold War and, 89,
    90, 101; general, 80, 121, 123;
    RMA and, 132, 157–158; stability
    of, 91–93; Type I and Type II, 62;
    unreliability, 88–91, 101,
    109–110, 143–144, 154, 157–159
Deterrence in the Second Nuclear Age
    (Payne), 158
Disarmament, 58–60
Domestic politics, 54, 65–66
Drug problem, 60
Dunn, Lewis A., 105

East Asia, 33, 71, 75(n2)
East-Central Europe, 6, 92
Economic issues, 41, 42
Endist theories, 42–43
Engagement policy, 38
Ethnocentricity, 107, 161–163
EU-Europe, 34
Evidence, 17–20
Exceptionalism, 51–53
External threat, 61–63

Fallacies: antinuclear taboos,
    103–108; defense issues, 97–103;
    feasibility of abolition, 82–85;
    post-nuclear era, 80–82;
    reliability of deterrence, 88–91;
    small nuclear wars, 93–97, 110;
    virtual arsenals, 83, 85–88
First nuclear age (1945–1989), 5–6.

    See also Cold War
Flexibility, 10, 147–148
France, 62, 70
Freedman, Lawrence, 49, 50, 96,
    161
Friction, concept of, 13–14, 50,
    137, 146, 163

G8, 68, 102
General deterrence, 80, 121, 123
General Health Laboratories
    (Libya), 165
Germany, 22, 93, 96–97, 128, 139,
    147
Globalization of World Politics, The,
    35
Global security environment,
    29–32, 34–36
Gorbachev, Mikhail, 92, 93
Great power rivalry, 31–33, 37–38
Gulf War, 139

Hegemony, 31–32, 37–39, 91,
    98–99; regional, 38, 49, 123–
    126
Helsinki Summit meeting (1997),
    99
Hitler, Adolf, 70, 162
Holocaust, 4, 21
Honor, 66–68, 122–123
*House of Cards: Why Arms Control
    Must Fail* (Gray), 58
Huntington, Samuel P., 37
Hussein, Saddam, 89, 133

Iklé, Fred Charles, 159
India, 24, 71, 85, 104, 134
Information age, 8, 12–13, 23–24,
    117–118. *See also* Revolution in
    military affairs
Intermediate-Range Nuclear
    Forces (INF), 84
International relations theory,
    53–54
Iran, 64, 67, 71
Iraq, 64, 65, 71, 74, 89, 125, 126,
    165
Israel, 71, 74, 85, 104

Japan, 33–34, 38, 41, 93, 126

Jervis, Robert, 118, 122
Joffe, Joseph, 31
Just War theory, 105

Kahn, Herman, 62
Kennedy, Paul, 29
Khromov, Gennadiy K., 156
Knowledge, 18, 117, 141–142
Korea, 67
Krepinevich, Andrew F., 157

Launch after attack (LAA), 64
Lavoy, Peter R., 75, 83
Law of the Instrument, 56
Libya, 165
Local culture, self-delusion and, 12–13
Luttwak, Edward N., 121–122, 137

Madariaga, Salvador de, 59–60
Mahan, Alfred Thayer, 165
Manhattan Project, 84
Marginalization, nuclear, 83, 85–86, 160–161
Military security, 40–41, 51
Millennium, 3, 37
Minimalist theory, 25
Morgan, Patrick, 121
Murray, Williamson A., 156
Mutual assured destruction (MAD), 146

National Command Authorities (NCA), 147
Nationalism, 23–24
National missile defense (NMD), 102
NATO. *See* North Atlantic Treaty Organization
NBC. *See* Nuclear, biological, and chemical weapons
Neorealism, 39, 41–42
New security environment, 24–26
No first use (NFU), 132
North Atlantic Treaty Organization (NATO), 3, 38, 41, 150(n30); defense doctrine, 62, 84–85, 130, 132
NPT. *See* Nuclear Nonproliferation Treaty

NPT regime, 66–68, 77(n20), 81–82, 166; importance of, 95, 104; reassurance and, 133–134
Nuclear abolition, 2, 59, 82–85
Nuclear acquisition, 59; Security I motivations, 61–63, 64; Security II motivations, 61, 64–65
Nuclear, biological, and chemical (NBC) weapons, 11, 96, 102, 108–110, 164–166; counterforce and, 145–146; countering threats, 129–131
Nuclear condition, 2, 4, 8–9, 51, 69, 155–157
Nuclear discovery, 82–83, 84, 120, 155
Nuclear fallacies. *See* Fallacies
Nuclear Nonproliferation Treaty (NPT), 24, 63, 66–67, 80–81, 106, 166. *See also* NPT regime
Nuclear proliferation. *See* Proliferation
Nuclear strategy, 2, 82–83, 115–118; aid of distant friends and allies, 129–131; arms control, 118–120; Cold War, 143–144; conventional warfare and, 137–139, 144–145; counterforce and, 145–146; countering conventional threats to allies, 131–133; countering NBC threats to allies, 129–131; discouragement of competitors, 123–128; failure of conventional warfare and, 137–139; flexibility, 147–148; peer rivalry and, 144; political context, 39–42; principles for guidance, 141–148; reassurance of friends and allies, 133–135; scholars, 13–14; strategic missions, 120–121, 142–143; superpower status and, 121–123; targeting and, 135–137, 148. *See also* Ballistic missile defense; Deterrence; Strategic history
Nuclear threshold states, 63, 70–71, 81
Nuclear war: consequences, 96–97;

possibility of, 163–164; small-scale, 93–97, 110
Nuclear weapons, 3; political goals and, 159–161; reductions, 24, 81; reliability of, 71–74; RMA and, 8–9; as useful, 69–70
Nuclear weapons states (NWS), 53, 54, 63, 66, 81

On War (von Clausewitz), 3
Opaque proliferation, 66, 85

Pakistan, 24, 71, 85, 104, 134
Payne, Keith B., 88, 158
Peer rivals, 127–128, 144
Peloponnesian War, The (Thucydides), 54
Periodization, 21–22
Policy science, 42
Political context: bipolar balance of power and, 39–42; domestic politics, 54, 65–66; global security environment, 29–32, 34–36
Political correctness, 147, 159
Political history, 98
Post–Cold War period, 14, 20, 23, 32–33. *See also* Second nuclear age
Post-nuclear era, 80–82
Price, Richard, 104–105
Proliferation, 4–5; analysis, 47–48; domestic politics and, 54, 65–66; honor and, 66–68; importance of, 49–51; opaque, 66, 85; optimism and pessimism, 68–69; regionalism and, 49, 50, 162–163; security environment and, 58–61; Security I motivations, 61–63, 64; Security II motivations, 61, 64–65
Proliferation study industry, 47–48; blind alleys, 55–56; expertise and, 56–57; local diversity and, 53–56; U.S. self-concept and, 51–53; Western attitudes and, 57–58
Prudence, 43, 54–55, 162–163

Quinlan, Michael, 62, 80, 88–89, 90

Realism, 26, 39, 41–42
Reassurance of friends and allies, 133–135
Regionalism, 32, 39–40, 109–110; hegemony and, 123–126; proliferation and, 49, 50, 162–163; U.S. as guardian, 49, 110, 130, 134–135
Revolution in military affairs (RMA), 8–9, 12, 24, 28, 126, 154; counterdeterrence and, 132, 157–158; failures, 137–138; space systems and, 168–169; U.S., 34–35, 118
Rise and Fall of the Great Powers, The (Kennedy), 29
RMA. *See* Revolution in military affairs
Rogue states, 12–13, 52, 53, 67, 91, 161–162
Russia, 25, 38, 41, 80, 144; arms control and, 119–120, 122; defense issues and, 98–99; security concerns, 32–34. *See also* USSR
Russian-U.S. agreement (1997), 99

Sagan, Scott D., 55, 61, 65
Schelling, Thomas C., 87
Schlieffen Plan, 147
Scholar's Fallacy, 51, 53
Scholarship, 13–14, 25–26. *See also* Proliferation study industry
Second nuclear age, 1, 8, 20, 153, 169–170; as construct, 5; evidence, hypothesis, and argument, 17–20, 27; transition to, 12
Security environment, 23–26, 170; global, 29–32, 34–36; military security, 40–41, 51; proliferation and, 58–61
Security I, 61–63, 64
Security II, 61, 64–65
Security space, 64, 77(n32)
Security theory, 2
Self-delusion, 12–13, 139–140, 162
Shubik, Martin, 10
Single Integrated Operational Plan (SIOP), 41, 147

Soviet Union. *See* USSR
Space systems, 137, 168–169
START. *See* Strategic Arms
　Reduction Talks
States: globalization and, 34–35;
　interstate conflicts, 36–37. *See*
　also NPT regime; Nuclear
　threshold states; Nuclear
　weapons states; Rogue states
Strategic Arms Reduction Talks
　(START), 54, 98, 115, 118–120,
　122, 126
Strategic Defense Initiative (SDI),
　148
Strategic history: continuity and,
　12, 20–24, 155; deterrence and,
　89, 91–92; future course, 13–14,
　18; periodization, 21–22;
　permanent nuclear condition,
　8–9; political history and, 98; of
　United States, 139–140. *See also*
　Nuclear
　strategy
Strategic studies, 28
Superpower status, 121–123,
　134–135; characteristics, 126–127
Supply-side policies, 58–61, 109

Taboos, antinuclear, 93–95,
　103–108, 122–123
Taiwan, 10, 101
Tannenwald, Nina, 104–105
Targeting, 135–137, 148
Technological peace, 26, 118
Theater missile defense (TMD),
　99–100, 102, 148
Theory, 2–3, 25–28, 127. *See also*
　individual theories
Third nuclear age, 6–8, 25, 39–40,
　169–170
Thucydides, 54, 57, 66, 121–122
TMD. *See* Theater missile defense
Toxin weapons (TW), 10, 11
Turkish Empire, 92
Type I deterrence, 62

Type II deterrence, 62

Uncertainty, 74–75
Unipolar moment, 30–32, 37–39,
　45(n31)
United Nations, 107
United States, 7, 62, 83; American
　Century theory, 29–30;
　antinuclear stance, 13, 115–116,
　155–156; exceptionalism, 51–53;
　hegemony, 31–32, 37–39, 91,
　98–99; nuclear arsenal, 22–24, 41,
　146; as regional guardian, 49,
　110, 130, 134–135; self-concept,
　12–13, 51–52, 139–140; strategic
　history, 139–140; theorists, 28–29;
　unipolar moment, 30–32, 37–39,
　45(n31)
U.S.-Japan Mutual Security Treaty,
　33, 38
USSR, 6, 22, 25, 92–93. *See also*
　Russia

Vietnam, 48, 75(n2)
Virtual nuclear arsenals, 83, 85–88,
　116–117

Waltz, Kenneth N., 10, 55, 61, 94,
　162
Walzer, Michael, 4
War convention, 4
War crimes, 4
Wavell, Archibald, 148
Weapons of mass destruction
　(WMD), 1, 10–12, 36; delivery,
　73–74, 75(n1), 102, 146. *See also*
　Biological weapons; Chemical
　weapons; Nuclear weapons;
　Toxin weapons
World politics, 2, 3; absence of
　great power rivalry, 31–33,
　37–38; minimalist theory, 25;
　nuclear condition and, 69;
　transition to second nuclear
　age, 12

About the Book

Colin Gray returns nuclear weapons to the center stage of international politics.

Taking issue with the complacent belief that a happy mixture of deterrence, arms control, and luck will enable humanity to cope adequately with weapons of mass destruction (WMD), Gray argues that the risk posed by WMD is ever more serious. Policy that ignores the present nuclear age, he cautions, is policy that ignores reality.

Gray's iconoclastic analysis, which includes a rigorous examination of the major policy and conceptual issues associated with WMD, criticizes traditional approaches to nonproliferation and assaults as fallacious both the aspiration to "abolish" or "marginalize" nuclear weapons and the idea that there is a "nuclear taboo" in universal operation. *The Second Nuclear Age* dares to specify the policy merit in nuclear weapons today.

Colin S. Gray is professor of international politics and director of the Center for Security Studies, University of Hull (U.K.). He has been an adviser on nuclear policy to four U.S. administrations and served recently on the Panel of Experts for the British Labour Government's Strategic Defence Review.